THE VIKINGS IN ENGLAND
AND IN THEIR DANISH HOMELAND

The Danish National Museum,
Brede-Copenhagen   April 11 – August 16 1981

The Prehistoric Museum,
Moesgård, Århus   September 5 – December 31 1981

The Yorkshire Museum,
York   April 3 – September 30 1982

The exhibition is sponsored by The British Council, the Danish Ministry of Culture, the Egmont H. Petersen Foundation, *The Times* and the *Sunday Times*; with the support of the North Yorkshire C.C., DFDS A/S, Copenhagen, and British Airways.

NORWAY

SWEDEN

Aarhus ●

Copenhagen ●

DENMARK

● Ribe

BALTIC SEA

THE VIKINGS IN ENGLAND

Working committee
Peter Addyman
Patricia Connor
Birte Friis
James Graham-Campbell
Kenneth Pearson
Else Roesdahl
with the assistance of Dominic Tweddle

Exhibition designer: Ivor Heal

ISBN 0 9507432 0 8

Published by
The Anglo-Danish Viking Project,
13 New Quebec Street,
London W1H 7DD

Catalogue editors: Else Roesdahl. James Graham-Campbell, Patricia Connor and Kenneth Pearson

Designer: Bridget Heal

Photography: David Cripps
Illustrations; David Mallott
Translators: Kirsten Williams (chapters);
            Eva Wilson (catalogue entries)

Phototypeset by Southern Positives and Negatives
(SPAN), Lingfield, Surrey
Printed in Great Britain by
Penshurst Press Ltd., Tunbridge Wells, Kent

FRONT COVER *Viking warrior cross fragment,
Weston Church, N. Yorkshire.*
BACK COVER *Reverse side of same fragment (F16).*

CONTENTS

LIST OF LENDERS

(initials follow for identification in catalogue)

From England
Ashmolean Museum, Oxford **AM**
British Library **BL**
British Museum **BM**
A. Brooks Esq.
Canterbury Archaeological Trust **CAT**
Lt. Col. H. V. Dawson
Department of the Environment, London **DoE**
Derby Museums **DM**
Duke of Northumberland
M. Fitzherbert Brockholes Esq.
Goldsborough Rectory, Yorkshire
Grosvenor Museum, Chester **GM**
Harris Museum, Preston **HMP**
Hunterian Museum **HM Glasgow**
Alan King Esq.
Leeds City Museum **LCM**
Leicestershire Museums **Leics. M**
Letchworth Museum **Letch. M**
Lincoln Archaeological Trust **LAT**
Lincolnshire Museums **Lincs. M**
Lord Middleton
Merseyside County Museums **MCM**
Museum of London **Mus. of Lon.**
Museum of Wiltshire Archaeology, Devizes **MWA**
National Museum of Antiquities of Scotland,
   Edinburgh **NMA Edin.**
Newcastle University Museum
Norfolk Museum Services **NMS**
         Castle Museum, Norwich
         The Lynn Museum, King's Lynn
Pitt Rivers Museum, Oxford **PRM**
Reading Museum **RM**
Royal Museum, Canterbury **RMC**
Saffron Walden Museum **SWM**
Sheffield City Museum **SCM**
Society of Antiquaries, London **S of A Lon.**
South Lincolnshire Archaeological Unit,
   Stamford **SLAU**
Southampton Archaeological Research
   Committee **SARC**
University Museum of Archaeology and
   Anthropology, Cambridge **UMAA**
University Museum, Nottingham
Winchester City Museum **WCM**

Winchester Research Unit **WRU**
   (on behalf of the Dean and Chapter,
   Winchester Cathedral)
York City Council **YCC**
   (through the Yorkshire Museum)
Yorshire Museum **YM**
and the private lender

Sculpture loans from English churches
St Andrew's, Dacre, Cumbria
St Andrew's, Middleton, N. Yorks
Bishop of Durham and the Misses Gatheral of
   Sockburn Hall
Dean and Chapter, Durham Cathedral
Dean and Chapter, Norwich Cathedral
St John's, Cross Canonby, Cumbria
St John's, Kirkby Stephen, Cumbria
St John's Baptist, Levisham, N. Yorks
St Luke's, Great Clifton, Cumbria
St Martin's, Kirklevington, N. Yorks
St Mary and St Cuthbert's, Chester-le-Street,
   Co. Durham
St Michael's, Workington, Cumbria
St Wilfrid's, Burnsall, N. Yorks

And from Denmark
The National Museum, Copenhagen:
            First Department **NM I**
            Second Department **NM II**
            Sixth Department **NM VI**
Institute of Maritime Archaeology, Roskilde
   NM SL
Prehistoric Museum, Moesgård **FHM**

Aalborg Historiske Museum **AHM**
Antikvarisk Samling, Ribe **ASR**
Bangsbomuseet, Frederikshavn **BMF**
Kulturen (Cultural History Museum), Lund,
   Sweden **KM**
Langelands Museum, Rudkøbing **LMR**
Lolland-Falsters Stiftmuseum, Maribo **LFSM**
Lund University Historical Museum,
   Sweden **LUHM**
National Antiquities Museum, Stockholm **SHM**
Royal Library, Stockholm
Schleswig-Holstein Landesmuseum, Schleswig,
   West Germany **SHL**

BIRTH OF THE EXHIBITION

From **Professor P. V. Glob,** *Director-General of Museums and Antiquities in Denmark*

Each summer for the past fifteen years, the National Museum has been able to welcome the public to a large special exhibition at Brede, north of Copenhagen. These exhibitions have covered a variety of subjects, often very wide-ranging, and have thus been the result of co-operation, not only between the museum's departments, but also with other Danish institutions.

It was therefore with pleasure and excitement, that the National Museum accepted the offer from Dame Anne Warburton to have "The Vikings in England" as the subject of the Brede exhibition in 1981. Co-operation could hereby be extended to include our English colleagues, to have the inspiration of both parties.

The opportunity of showing the Anglo-Danish exhibition to an audience in Jutland, at Moesgård, added yet another inspiring collaborator, and fulfilled a wish also to show the exhibition outside Copenhagen.

The exhibition covers both English and Danish evidence of a part of our mutual past: how the Vikings and the Anglo-Saxons met, influenced one another, and left their mark on the cultural patterns on both sides of the North Sea.

We welcome with pride and pleasure "The Vikings in England" to Brede and Moesgård. And at the same time we look forward to showing their descendants in York the Danish contributions to their history.

From **Dame Anne Warburton:** *HE the British Ambassador to Denmark*

It all began with Peter Addyman's fitted attaché case full of finds from Coppergate in York. He arrived to show them to our Danish Patron, HM Queen Margrethe, in February 1977. Others of us then had the chance to see these objects made by Danish Vikings in Jorvik, and to hear evidence of the peaceful trade and craftsmanship they carried on there 1,000 years ago – evidence of our shared past, which goes a long way to explain the close relationship still existing between us.

Danish support flowed strongly to Coppergate: without it, it would simply not have been possible to complete the dig before the site had to be redeveloped. So the idea of an exhibition, to open in Denmark before it was even seen in England, grew into an expression of gratitude for the indispensable Danish help.

More and more people became involved. Strong support from David Wilson, director of the British Museum and himself a leading Vikingologist. Financial support from the British Council. Curators from many museums in east England enlisted. A proposition prepared and put to the Danes. Received enthusiastically by the Ministry of Culture who promised a matching financial contribution, Professor Glob and the Danish National Museum who gave their backing.

The late Professor Ole Klindt-Jensen offered Moesgård so that the people of Jutland could see the exhibition easily. Working committees were established in Britain and Denmark: among many names that of Kenneth Pearson, of *The Sunday Times*, stands out as the prime mover of planning. HM Queen Margrethe and HRH the Prince of Wales agree to be Patrons. The Committee of Honour takes shape, led by the two Ministers of Culture. A generous Danish sponsor, the Egmont H. Petersen Foundation comes forward. British sponsors respond.

The British and Danish committees, working in notable harmony, agree the story-line and the objects to be exhibited. Hereafter, it is for you, the public, to judge the success of this combined venture in unravelling a fascinating period of our common history, for in the end "The Vikings in England" exhibition is for you.

THE VIKINGS IN ENGLAND AND IN THEIR DANISH HOMELAND

Patrons   Her Majesty Queen Margrethe II
His Royal Highness The Prince of Wales

Committee of Honour   Professor Lise Østergaard *Minister of Culture, Denmark*
Mr Paul Channon *Minster for the Arts, United Kingdom*
Mr John Burgh *Director-General, British Council*
Mr Tyge Dahlgaard *Danish Ambassador in London*
Mr Esben Dragsted *Chairman of the Board of Trustees,*
Egmont H. Petersen Foundation
Professor P. V. Glob *Director-General of Museums and Antiquities in Denmark*
Sir Denis Hamilton *Chairman of Times Newspapers Holdings*
Colonel Lawrence Jackson *Chairman of the North Yorkshire County Council*
Mr Magnus Magnusson *Chairman of Committee of Stewards,*
York Archaeological Trust
Mr Niels Møllmann *Chairman of the Board, Moesgård Museum*
Mr A. W. Nielsen *lately Chief Executive of United Breweries*
Mr O. Perch Nielsen *Permanent Secretary, Ministry of Culture, Denmark*
Dame Anne Warburton *British Ambassador in Copenhagen*
Dr David Wilson *Director, British Museum*

The English national committee:

Kenneth Pearson (chairman), *The Sunday Times*
Peter Addyman *director, York Archaeological Trust*
T. Michael Clegg *curator, the Yorkshire Museum*
Patricia Connor *archaeological correspondent,*
The Sunday Times
James Graham-Campbell *lecturer,*
University College, London
Basil Greenhill *director, National Maritime Museum*
Ivor Heal *exhibition designer*
Michael Jones *director, Lincolnshire Archaeological Trust*
Christine Mahany *director, South Lincolnshire*
Archaeological Trust
Christopher Morris *lecturer, Durham University*
Andrew White *keeper of Archaeology,*
Lincolnshire Museums
Dr David Wilson *director, the British Museum*

The Danish working committee:

Birte Friis (chairman), *keeper,*
the National Museum, 10th Dept.
Kirsten Bendixen *assistant keeper,*
the National Museum, 6th Dept.
T. G. Bibby *assistant keeper, Moesgård*
Ole Crumlin-Pedersen *keeper,*
the National Museum, 20th Dept.
Dr Gillian Fellows Jensen *Copenhagen University*
Poul Kjærum *keeper, Moesgård*
Niels-Knud Liebgott *assistant keeper,*
the National Museum, 2nd Dept.
David Liversage, Ph.D. *assistant keeper,*
the National Museum, 1st Dept.
H. J. Madsen *assistant keeper, Moesgård*
Jørgen Nordqvist *keeper,*
the National Museum, 14th Dept.
Else Roesdahl *lecturer, Århus University*
Dr Mogens Ørsnes *keeper,*
the National Museum, 1st Dept.

FOREWORD

If exhibitions and their catalogues are good, they appear to the casual observer to have just fallen into place. In the cool, classic lay-outs of both, there is no hint of the struggle for loans and finance, of the long nights of discussion, of the even longer nights of checking facts, nor of the torturous paths by which the simple design is reached. That is why our expression of gratitude here is an important element in this book.

For her outstanding contributions to the exhibition and the catalogue, Else Roesdahl of Århus University must be thanked first. Her scholarship and application have been a remarkable inspiration. The same is true of James Graham-Campbell of University College, London, whose eagle eye for error endowed the project with an added sense of security. And though the book has a popular approach, the academic strength of its catalogue owes much to Dominic Tweddle of the York Archaeological Trust who wrote all the English entries and who in turn was sustained by Patricia Connor, with a wealth of ideas and practical assistance and an expertise she was also able to apply to the exhibition.

Since, however, we embarked on the hazardous journey of producing the book in two languages, we owe much to our leading translator Kirsten Williams, whose own name sums up the dual nature of this project. Other help, for which we are most grateful, came from Eva Wilson, Ingrid Nielsen, Helle Reinholdt and Bi Skaarup. And none of it, of course, would have meant much without the considerable design skills of Bridget Heal, whose translation of words and images into a flow of easy communication has pulled everything into a sharp focus.

As for the exhibition, half of it has been excavated from the Viking Coppergate site in York. This tremendous task was brilliantly led and executed by its director Peter Addyman, Richard Hall (excavation director), James Spriggs (conservation), with the assistance of Christopher Clarke (administration) and Sheena Howarth (drawings); much of this was helped by Danish financial assistance for which we are most grateful.

In putting the exhibition together, key contributions were made by Richard Bailey, who selected the sculpture; Gillian Fellows Jensen for her research work on place-names; Janet Backhaus of the British Library, who wrote the commentaries on the very important manuscripts; and for the work on the coins we are indebted to Elizabeth Pirie of Leeds City Museum, Christopher Blunt, and Kirsten Bendixen of the Danish National Museum.

For administration on the Danish side, I am warmly appreciative of the work and effort put into the project by Jørgen Nordqvist, Poul Kjaerum, and the indefatigable Birte Friis; and in York, of the deep sense of commitment of the Yorkshire Museum's keeper of archaeology, Elizabeth Hartley, and its curator Michael Clegg, to both of whom I owe a great debt.

If there is a triumvirate led by scholarship which underpins an exhibition, the other two elements are design and finance. First, then, my deep-felt thanks to Ivor Heal, whose cool approach to the most complex problems disguises, temporarily, the vast creative skills which are operating. And I am deeply grateful to Peter Saabor, of Carlton Cleeve Ltd., on whose administrative talents I have leant so heavily and could not have done without.

In the larger fields of finance we owe much to the British Council, ever sympathetic partners, the Danish Ministry of Culture, Mr Esben Dragsted and Mr Ole Dahl of the Egmont H. Petersen Foundation, to Mr A. W. Nielsen for his generous backing, and to the Danske Bank, to the North Yorkshire County Council, and the Museum and Art Gallery Service for Yorkshire and Humberside. And for transporting the exhibition to and fro across the North Sea, I am most grateful for the help of Ian Pearson of Wingate and Johnston (South) Ltd. and of Jean Rankine of the British Museum.

There remains for me to thank Dame Anne Warburton, the British Ambassador in Copenhagen, for her great support and encouragement, as I would thank Ole Perch Nielsen, Dr David M. Wilson and Sir Denis Hamilton.

And a final word of gratitude to Martin Biddle, Birthe Kjolbye-Biddle and those other scholars, whose generous permission to publish the results of their research in this book before they themselves had published, has made this a unique event.

KENNETH PEARSON *chairman, the Anglo-Danish Viking Project*

(For other acknowledgements see page 186)

THE ANGLO-SAXON CHRONICLE

The most important narrative source concerning the Vikings in England is the ANGLO-SAXON CHRONICLE. The first version of this was compiled in Wessex in the late ninth century, and in the following three centuries it was continued in various places by several authors. The following excerpts illustrate characteristic features of Viking activity as well as some of the most important events of the period: the conquests and settlements made by the so-called "Great Army" in the ninth century, and the conquest of England by Svein Forkbeard in the early eleventh. – Niels Lund.

Though the Anglo-Saxon Chronicle was never illustrated, those designs shown here are taken from contemporary manuscripts.

789   In this year King Beorhtric married Offa's daughter Eadburh. And in his days [786–802] there came for the first time three ships of Northmen and then the reeve rode to them and wished to force them to the king's residence, for he did not know what they were; and they slew him. Those were the first ships of Danish men which came to the land of the English.

850   In this year Ealdorman Ceorl with the contingent of the men of Devon fought against the heathen army at *Wicganbeorg*, and the English made a great slaughter there and had the victory. And for the first time, heathen men stayed through the winter on Thanet. And the same year [851] 350 ships came into the mouth of the Thames and stormed Canterbury and London and put to flight Brihtwulf, king of the Mercians, with his army, and went south across the Thames into Surrey. And King Æthelwulf and his son Æthelbald fought against them at *Aclea* with the army of the West Saxons, and there inflicted the greatest slaughter [on a heathen army] that we ever heard of until this present day, and had the victory there . . .

866   In this year Æthelbert's brother Æthelred succeeded to the kingdom of the West Saxons. And the same year a great heathen army came into England and took up winter quarters in East Anglia; and there they were supplied with horses, and the East Angles made peace with them.

870   In this year the army came into Wessex to Reading, and three days later two Danish earls rode farther inland. Then Ealdorman Æthelwulf encountered them at Englefield, and fought against them there and had the victory, and one of them, whose name was Sidroc, was killed there. Then four days later [871] King Æthelred and his brother Alfred led a great army to Reading and fought against the army; and

a great slaughter was made on both sides and Ealdorman Æthelwulf was killed ...

And four days later King Æthelred and his brother Alfred fought against the whole army at Ashdown; and the Danes were in two divisions: in the one were the heathen kings Bagsecg and Halfdan, and in the other were the earls. And then King Æthelred fought against the kings' troop, and King Bagsecg was slain there; and Æthelred's brother Alfred fought against the earls' troop, and there were slain Earl Sidroc the Old, and Earl Sidroc the Younger and Earl Osbearn, Earl Fræna, and Earl Harold; and both enemy armies were put to flight and many thousands were killed, and they continued fighting until night ...

Then [Æthelred's] brother Alfred, the son of Æthelwulf, succeeded to the kingdom of the West Saxons. And a month later King Alfred fought with a small force against the whole army at Wilton and put it to flight far on into the day; and the Danes had possession of the battle-field. And during that year nine general engagements were fought against the Danish army in the kingdom south of the Thames ... And that year nine [Danish] earls were killed and one king ...

878   In this year in midwinter after twelfth night the enemy army came stealthily to Chippenham and occupied the land of the West Saxons and settled there, and drove a great part of the people across the sea, and conquered most of the others; and the people submitted to them, except King Alfred. He journeyed in difficulties through the woods and fen-fastnesses with a small force.

And the same winter the brother of Ivar and Halfdan was in the kingdom of the West Saxons [in Devon], with 23 ships. And he was killed there and 840 men of his army with him. And there was captured the banner which they called "Raven".

And afterwards at Easter, King Alfred with a small force made a stronghold at Athelney, and he and the section of the people of Somerset which was nearest to it proceeded to fight from that stronghold against the enemy. Then in the seventh week after Easter he rode to "Egbert's stone" east of Selwood, and there came to meet him all the people of Somerset and of Wiltshire and of that part of Hampshire which was on this side of the sea, and they rejoiced to see him. And then after one night he went from the encampment to Iley, and after another night to Edington, and there fought against the whole army and put it to flight, and pursued it as far as the fortress, and stayed there a fortnight. And then the enemy gave him preliminary hostages and great oaths that they would leave his kingdom, and promised also that their king should receive baptism, and they kept their promise. Three weeks later King Guthrum with 30 of the men who were the most important in the army came [to him] at Aller, which is near Athelney, and the king stood sponsor to him at his baptism there; and the unbinding of the chrism took place at Wedmore. And he was twelve days with the king, and he honoured him and his companions ...

994   In this year Olaf and Svein came to London on the Nativity of St Mary with 94 ships, and they proceeded to attack the city stoutly and wished also to set it on fire; but there they suffered more harm and injury than they ever thought any citizens would do to them. But the holy Mother of God showed her mercy to the citizens on that day and saved them from their enemies. And these went away from there, and did the greatest damage that ever any army could do, by burning, ravaging, and slaying, everywhere along the coast, and in Essex, Kent, Sussex, and Hampshire; and finally they seized horses and rode as widely as they wished, and continued to do indescribable damage. Then the king and his councillors determined to send to them and promise them tribute and provisions, on condition that they should cease that harrying. And they then accepted that, and the whole army came then to Southampton and took winter quarters there; and they were provisioned through-out all the West Saxon kingdom, and they were paid 16,000 pounds in money ...

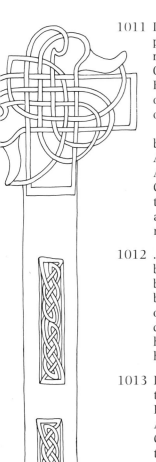

1011 In this year the king and his councillors sent to the army and asked for peace, and promised them tribute and provisions on conditions that they should cease their ravaging. They had then overrun: (i) East Anglia, (ii) Essex, (iii) Middlesex, (iv) Oxfordshire, (v) Cambridgeshire, (vi) Hertfordshire, (vii) Buckinghamshire, (viii) Bedfordshire, (ix) half Huntingdonshire, (x) much of Northamptonshire; and south of the Thames all Kent, Sussex, Hastings, Surrey, Berkshire, Hampshire, and much of Wiltshire . . .

And then in this year, between the Nativity of St Mary and Michaelmas, they besieged Canterbury, and they got inside by treachery, for Ælfmær, whose life Archbishop Ælfheah had saved, betrayed it. Then they captured there Archbishop Ælfheah . . . He was then a captive who had been head of the English people and of Christendom. There could misery be seen where happiness was often seen before, in that wretched city from which first came [to us] Christianity and happiness in divine and secular things. And they kept the archbishop with them till the time when they martyred him.

1012 . . . Then on the Saturday the army became greatly incensed against the bishop because he would not promise them any money, but forbade that anything should be paid for him. They were also very drunk, for wine from the south had been brought there. They seized the bishop, and brought him to their assembly on the eve of the Sunday of the octave of Easter, which was 19 April, and shamefully put him to death there: they pelted him with bones and with ox-heads, and one of them struck him on the head with the back of an axe, that he sank down with the blow, and his holy blood fell on the ground.

1013 In the year after the archbishop was martyred, the king appointed Bishop Lyfing to the archbishopric of Canterbury. And in this same year, before the month of August, King Svein came with his fleet to Sandwich, and then went very quickly round East Anglia into the mouth of the Humber, and so up along the Trent until he reached Gainsborough. And then at once Earl Uhtred and all the Northumbrians submitted to him, as did all the people of Lindsey, and then all the people belonging to the district of the Five Boroughs, and quickly afterwards all the Danish settlers north of Watling Street, and hostages were given to him from every shire. When he perceived that all the people had submitted to him, he gave orders that his army should be provisioned and provided with horses, and then he afterwards turned southward with his full forces and left the ships and the hostages in charge of his son Cnut . . . He then turned eastward to London, and many of his host were drowned in the Thames because they did not trouble to find a bridge. When he came to the borough the citizens would not yield, but resisted with full battle, because King Æthelred was inside and Thorkel with him.

Then King Svein turned from there to Wallingford, and so west across the Thames to Bath, where he stayed with his army. Then Ealdorman Æthelmær came there, and with him the western thegns, and all submitted to Svein, and they gave him hostages. When he had fared thus, he then turned northward to his ships, and all the nation regarded him as full king. And after that the citizens of London submitted and gave hostages, for they were afraid that he would destroy them. Then Svein demanded full payment and provisions for his army that winter, and Thorkel demanded the same for the army which lay at Greenwich, and in spite of it all they ravaged as often as they pleased. Nothing therefore was of benefit to this nation, neither from the south nor from the north . . .

1014 In this year Svein ended his days at Candlemass, on 2 February, and then all the fleet elected Cnut king . . .

A1   The Lindisfarne Stone, showing seven warriors often interpreted as Vikings
Lindisfarne, Holy Island, Northumberland
Department of Environment site museum

Fragmentary round-headed upright slab; sand-stone. First recorded in 1924 and probably found during restoration work at the monastery after 1915. Decoration: Side A shows two figures bowing before a cross flanked by *Sol* and *Luna*. Side B has a procession of warriors dressed in short kirtles and waving swords and axes. Late ninth or tenth century. H.28.0cm.

Side A shows a Doomsday scene, an event which would be preceded by the appearance of the cross in the sky. Side B presumably represents "the wars and rumours of wars" (Matthew XXIV, 6) which were among the other signs of the end of the world.

The catalogue entry (left) and those that follow each chapter are compiled to a set design. The name of the object is followed by its provenance and its location. There next comes a scientific description of it. The rest recounts the significance of the object and helps to unfold the Viking story.

THE VIKINGS STRIKE

A N EXCITABLE ENTRY in the *Anglo-Saxon Chronicle* under the year 793 not only signals the start of the Viking Age but expresses something of the attitude of the Anglo-Saxons towards the incursions across the North Sea from Denmark and Norway to England:

> In this year dire portents appeared over Northumbria and sorely frightened the people. They consisted of immense whirlwinds and flashes of lightning, and fiery dragons were seen flying in the air. A great famine immediately followed these signs and a little after in the same year, on June 8th, the ravages of the heathen men miserably destroyed God's church on Lindisfarne with plunder and slaughter.

This event, the first recorded Viking attack on Europe, ushered in the Viking Age, an era which was to leave few areas in Europe untouched and was to spread Scandinavian influence from Byzantium to Greenland and from Finland to Spain. But the Viking Age was not a simple entity, it enshrined a number of distinct phenomena; raids, settlements, and a growing political sophistication in the North, together with a spirit of adventure almost unique in early medieval Europe. In the 250 years from the beginning of the Viking Age to its end, Scandinavia changed from a pagan region, little known and poorly organised under a series of petty chieftains or dim kings, into three great nation kingdoms, members of the full Christian community of Europe. The Danish adventures in England were crucial to this development.

It is perhaps simplistic to see the Viking experience as triggered and sustained by a search for wealth: but in one form or another personal or institutional gain was the trigger of the Viking Age. As far as England is concerned, although there is some indication that the first Scandinavian approaches were of a peaceful mercantile character, raids appear sufficiently often in the historical record to show that the Scandinavians had understood that there were other more adventurous ways of achieving affluence. The raid on Lindisfarne was the first of a series recorded round the coasts of the North Sea. Many must have gone unrecorded. The raids took place almost every year, first in England and then in the Low Countries and France. For England this was not a period of continuous raiding, in fact the first thirty years of the ninth century were comparatively peaceful. But the raids grew in number and with them the number of raiders.

Gradually it became clear that the Danes were set on the colonisation of England. From 835 onwards barely a year passes without a record of raids, and a crescendo of attacks climaxed in 866 when, having wintered in East Anglia, a Danish army broke into York and took over the city, putting their own puppet (an Englishman) on the throne. The Scandinavians were in England to stay; they made war on the powerful kingdom of Wessex and nearly defeated its greatest king, Alfred. In 876 they settled in Northumbria and in the years that followed gradually took over the kingdoms of Mercia and East Anglia. North and east of a line drawn from London to Chester they held sway in a series of loose petty kingdoms and misty political groupings, in an area which became known as the Danelaw. Alfred, with his son-in-law Æthelred and his formidable daughter Æthelflæd (later known as the Lady of the Mercians) began to rebuild the English kingdom, and although Alfred had many setbacks by his death in 899 the English were ready to start the painful re-conquest of the Danelaw.

What did this region consist of under the Danes? The settlement was mainly agricultural; the Danes occupied newly-developed land, as well as well-tried farmland and, with the aid of the cheap labour their conquest afforded them, were able to farm perhaps more intensively than before. The great ecclesiastical estates, like that of the Lindisfarne community itself, were taken into private ownership and a new agrarian economy must have supervened. We know little of the details of this side of the colonists' life, all that remains physically are a handful of graves, two or three excavated farms, and some stone sculpture. We know more of their town life, for the Scandinavians had learnt the value of fortification and of the idea of a strong administrative and mercantile centre from their adventures abroad (at this time it should be remembered the only towns in Denmark were Hedeby and Ribe and they were certainly not fortified at the time of the English settlement). They fortified many towns – Thetford, Cambridge, Northampton, Huntingdon, for example – they took over the fortifications of the old Romano-British city of York, and established a chain of forts – the Five Boroughs – in the English Midlands at Stamford, Lincoln, Nottingham, Leicester and Derby. These centres served primarily as refuges for the inhabitants of the countryside, but became centres of local administration and soon developed as markets.

The most important centre was York. The value of this internationally famous market to the Danes must have been immense. For the first time the Danes had a major outlet of trade in the North Sea. Here they struck coins and established a major market. For many years, long after the final demolition of the Danelaw as a formal entity, Danish merchants added to, and drew wealth from, this important royal city. Around the merchants and administrators gathered the craftsmen who catered to their needs and to the needs of the local people buying and selling in the thriving town.

As Danish merchants established themselves and became part of the fabric of life in York and other centres, so the incoming farmers and military settlers of England became anglicised. They had accepted Christianity, formally at first but more fervently later on. They abandoned their old language and started to speak English. They defended themselves from attack by other Scandinavians from Ireland and the Isles, and from raids by Norwegian/Irish settlers in north-west England. Soon they found themselves accepting the gradual re-conquest of the Danelaw by the Anglo-Saxon kings Edward the Elder, Athelstan and their successors. In 954 Erik Bloodaxe was expelled from York and the reforming King Edgar ruled in some magnificence over the whole of a largely peaceful England.

During Edgar's reign the attention of the Danes in Denmark was concentrated elsewhere. Harald Bluetooth had consolidated his kingdom, probably benefiting financially from the trading connections in the west. He was, however, more involved with wars in the south, with his conquest of Norway, with trade in the Baltic and with the organisation of his own kingdom. There was little to interest him in a strong, centralised kingdom overseas. Towards the end of his long reign he over-reached himself at home – perhaps financially – and died in exile in the late 980s. His son Svein was left to repair the kingdom of Denmark and look for money to finance necessary reforms. Svein took a leaf out of the book of a man who was nominally his vassal, a rather wild Norwegian chieftain Olaf Tryggvason who had built up a fortune by raids in England, and who had returned to Norway and consolidated a rather shaky throne which he was to enjoy for very few years. Svein likewise turned his attention westwards to gain wealth.

The raids on England had started again. From small beginnings in 980, they grew in intensity until in 991 Olaf took the first of a regular series of payments – the so-called Danegeld – from the English: a colossal sum of £10,000 of silver. When Svein joined Olaf in 994 they shared £16,000 and, as Olaf returned to Norway in that year, the sorry story of the Danes in England (together with their Norwegian and Swedish mercenaries) is told in the pages of the *Anglo-Saxon Chronicle*. Under Svein the Danegeld rose in size from £24,000 in 1002, to £36,000 in 1007 and £48,000 in 1011. Political conquest was now in the air and Svein, joined by his son Cnut (Canute), set about the task with a will. In 1014 Svein died in the Lincolnshire town of Gainsborough, but his son fought on and was proclaimed king of England in 1017, taking in the following year an immense *geld* of £82,500 of which £10,500 alone came from London.

This was a different type of conquest from that of the ninth century. There was no major settlement of farmers or merchants, Cnut held England by force of his own personality with the aid of a few trusted chieftains and their relatives. England was glad to be at peace and Cnut had quite enough to do controlling his various other kingdoms, for he was king in Denmark and claimed the overlordship of Norway and part at least of Sweden. He was a Christian king, generous to the church and apparently liked by the English. He died in 1035 and was buried in Winchester.

With his death the story of the Danes in England effectively ends. For another seven years Cnut's sons struggled to retain the kingdom, but in 1042 Edward the Confessor succeeded to the throne when Harthacnut died after a wedding feast and, apart from the occasional flurry of military activity in the succeeding fifty years, the English never had to worry about a Danish threat again.

The Danish legacy is still to be seen in England. It is part of the fabric of our lives. England's place-names, language and certain administrative curiosities remain to remind us of a period when much of the North Sea could more truly be named the Danish Sea.

DAVID M. WILSON

FROM A DANISH HOMELAND

D ENMARK AND THE REST OF Scandinavia achieved a degree of importance in the Viking Age unsurpassed either before or since. Trading contacts reached far to east and west, north and south, but many men also sought wealth and fame by force of arms, while others settled abroad as farmers, townsmen and soldiers. To these ends the Danish Vikings set their sights on England, conquering the greater part by the end of the ninth century, and the entire country at the beginning of the eleventh century, thus establishing a period of Anglo-Danish unity under one king, first Cnut, then his son Harthacnut. This ranks as one of the greatest achievements of the Viking era, and must have sprung from an immense surplus of energy in Denmark itself.

The picture of Viking Denmark is a jigsaw, pieced together with the help of diverse disciplines: archaeology, history, philology, zoology, botany etc. For contemporary descriptions of Denmark are extremely rare; they are also brief, random and nearly always written by foreigners. The sources for the early Viking Age are particularly scarce, yet a picture is emerging of a country in a state of rapid development, experiencing economic, military, technical, social and cultural innovations, and with a fast-growing population. The well-spring of this was large-scale expansion of agricultural land and production.

The explosion out of Denmark at this time was most probably due to social instability caused by this dynamic community being situated at a vital crossroads in northern Europe. In days of expanding markets, the Vikings, already accustomed to widely varying cultural standards and social patterns, were quick to seize new opportunities wherever they arose, adapting themselves readily to new environments in new countries. The practical tools were available – good weapons, excellent ships, organisational ability and the knowledge of foreign political circumstances. The Vikings knew when and where there were openings and exploited them thoroughly.

Denmark has always been the key to the Baltic. It consists of mainland Jutland – which in the Viking Age bordered on the lands of the Saxons, Slavs and Frisians – and some five hundred islands forming a land bridge from

Jutland to the Scandinavian mainland. The sea could be reached in one day from all parts of the country, and fjords and rivers penetrated far into many areas. Ships could run onto the flat shores almost everywhere, or they could berth in estuaries and by river-banks. Suitable ships were essential to internal communications and also a vital precondition for the formation of the realm.

In the ninth century Denmark comprised, in addition to its present area, the now Swedish provinces of Skåne and Halland (later also Blekinge) and present-day German Schleswig, where there were continuing border disputes with the Frankish Empire. Godfred, King of the Danes, however, was a worthy opponent of Charlemagne, the Frankish Emperor. Around 800 he theatened to destroy Aachen, Charlemagne's royal seat, and he ordered the construction of an immense rampart to secure his southern boundary. This is the first we hear of the Danevirke, which, with its many sections and building phases, is one of the greatest building works of north European antiquity. The ramparts stretched for nearly 19 miles (30 km.) and until 1864 they marked Denmark's southern border. The earliest parts of the Danevirke, however, are dated by dendrochronology to about 737 and although we do not know by which king or against whom it was built, it is clear that even before the Viking Age the Danes were able to organise huge projects.

Denmark is a country well suited to agriculture, and in the Viking period, as indeed until recent times, it was the main occupation. Farms and villages have been excavated in central and west Jutland – in Vorbasse and Sædding for example, revealing that animal husbandry was here more important than crops. But it was not necessarily the same all across the country; soil conditions differ greatly. Animal-bone finds indicate that cattle, pigs, horses and sheep were kept, as well as some goats. There were also hens and geese, cats and dogs. The Viking-Age diet included barley, rye, oats and wheat alongside vegetables, and was supplemented by wild fruit, berries and nuts. Hunting played only a small role, but fish constituted an important dietary element in settlements close to fishing waters.

The expansion of agriculture led to the establishment of many new rural settlements; many of the place-names with the suffixes -toft, -torp and -by derive from this period. It also encouraged a new type of settlement – towns – in which trade, industry and specialised craftsmen flourished. These centres became administrative focal points for various activities including those of the Church.

The earliest Danish towns were Ribe and Hedeby. In Ribe excavations have revealed evidence of highly specialised industries, such as bead-making, bronze-casting and comb-making. The town had close contacts with both the rest of Denmark and the Rhineland, as attested by many finds including thirty-two Frisian silver coins – sceattas. The craftsmen of Ribe apparently lived by selling their wares to farmers who had come to town to

Vorbasse: a Viking farm in Denmark
The farm appeared to support more cows than were wanted for its own needs – which suggests trade in the animals. That the farm could raise a large number of cattle is cleary evident from the lush nature of the terrain around this Vorbasse site, seen on page 36.

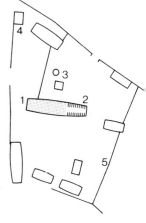

1 Living quarters
  of main building
2 Cattlestalls
3 Sunken-featured
  buildings
4 Smithy
5 Fence

20

have their produce shipped to the south.

Hedeby, the precursor of the town of Schleswig, became Scandinavia's largest town. The semi-circular rampart, although not built until the later tenth century, encloses an area of nearly 60 acres (24 hectares). Like Ribe, Hedeby dates back to the eighth century, but it was probably re-founded on an organised plan by King Godfred around 800. The first Scandinavian coins were struck in Hedeby, and widespread contacts, mentioned in written sources and substantiated by finds from the town, were established. Many imported goods found throughout Denmark probably arrived via Hedeby; these were not just luxury items, but everyday wares such as Norwegian whetstones and Rhenish querns.

Society was highly stratified. The king was at the head, elected from one or two leading families unless he had seized the throne by force of arms. He surrounded himself with a retinue and had representatives throughout the country and in the towns. He was both military and religious leader, and ensured the peace and stability required by the merchants. In return, he received taxes and fines to augment his income from land-property. When the opportunity arose he could add more from plunder and extortion abroad.

The king was supported by local lords, their power based on large estates, their allegiance owed primarily to their own kin. Most farmers probably lived in villages with the status of freemen. At the bottom of society were the slaves who undoubtedly provided much of the work force for land-clearance and grandiose construction schemes. Women were highly respected. They were responsible for hearth and home, and usually managed property during their husbands' absence. They were buried with as much ceremony as the men and – as some foreigners remarked with surprise – they could obtain a divorce if they wished.

The paganism of the Vikings caused them to be regarded with more fear in Europe than other robbers and conquerors, but Christian Vikings were accepted on an equal footing by Europeans. Until the official conversion of Denmark in about 960, people worshipped a pantheon with Odin and Thor as its principals. Odin, god of war, wisdom and poetry, presided over Valhalla, home of dead heroes, and was mainly worshipped by the chieftain classes. Thor was the most popular god, ruler of the sky and weather, and probably also the crops. Pagan Vikings were buried with a range of their property – unlike Christians – and their sacrificial feasts were a source of terror and perplexity to Christendom.

Christianity was, however, known in Denmark long before 960. Several missionaries had worked there, among them Ansgar who in about 850 was granted permission by the Danish king to build a church in Hedeby and, a little later, one in Ribe. Those Vikings who went abroad had also encountered Christianity and its buildings; some had even been baptized.

The Vikings had their own unique culture in many other fields. It found expression in, for example, the women's dress – a pinafore with shoulder

OVERLEAF *In this view from a Jutland coastline small boats shelter in a simple harbour. Fish constituted an important element in the diet of those Viking settlements in coastal areas. And if life proved hard, over the horizon there was always England.*

straps held in place by a pair of oval brooches. Writing was not in the Latin script, but in runes, which were specifically suited to carving in wood. Among their poetic accomplishments were the splendid, highly complicated Scaldic poems. Decorative art, which had its roots in the fourth and fifth centuries, reached new heights in the Viking Age. Proud, imaginative and assured, and based on the use of animal forms, it developed steadily through internal evolution and outside influences (Style E, Style F, Borre style, Jellinge, Mammen, Ringerike and Urnes styles). In these fields the Vikings made independent and original contributions to European art. When they colonised England at the end of the ninth century, Scandinavian culture was in full flower. Through the colonists it made its mark on England.

ELSE ROESDAHL

RIGHT *In Viking times, Denmark spread beyond its five hundred islands to embrace neighbouring parts of Norway and Sweden. The map shows the early towns of Ribe and Hedeby, and the later settlements of Odense and Aarhus. In addition, there are the village sites of Vorbasse and Sædding. And from Hedeby, stretching across the peninsular to the west, the great Danish earthwork – the Danevirke – formed a defensive wall against the enemy to the south.*

NORWAY

Limfjord

Limfjord

SWEDEN

HALLAND

JUTLAND

Aarhus•

SKANE

•Vorbasse

•Saedding

•Ribe

FUNEN

ZEALAND

BORNHOLM

BALTIC SEA

Danevirke ⎯•Hedeby

Elder

Hamburg•

FRISIA

Elbe

Weser

B1   Amber playing-piece; male figure with long beard
Roholte, Zealand; single-find. NM1 [C24292]

H.4.7cm.

B2   Bronze penannular brooch with three bearded heads
Høm, Zealand; single-find. NM1 [C6605]

The surface is covered with a white metal, except for the heads and the interlace on the pin which are gilt. L. (pin) 12.0cm. D. (ring) 7.1cm.
    Penannular brooches were used by men to fasten the cloak on the right shoulder. Their form was inspired from Ireland or Scotland.

B3   Gilt bronze oval brooch with four knobs shaped like human heads
Ågerup, Zealand; single-find, probably from a grave. NM1 [11869]

L.9.9cm.
    Double-shelled oval brooches were used in matched pairs to fasten the shoulder loops of the Scandinavian woman's dress.

B4   Amber bearded man's head
No provenance. NM1 [5307]

The back is flat with a crudely engraved ornament. L.4.5cm.

B5   A perforated piece of human skull inscribed with runes
Ribe settlement. ASR [D13764]

L.8.6cm.
    The inscription is difficult to interpret. It includes the name of the god Odin and was probably an evocation to him and to other gods against sickness. The object was perhaps an amulet and could have been suspended on a cord.

B6   Amber Thor's hammer
Lindholm Høje, north Jutland; grave find. AHM [129 × 1466]

L.2.4cm.
    Thor was the most popular of the gods; he was symbolized by his weapon – the hammer Mjollnir. Produced in many different materials, such a hammer was widely carried as an ornamental amulet.

B7   Bronze equal-armed brooch with animals and a central design in the round. Possibly a symbol of Thor
Vornedgård, Bornholm; possible grave find. NM1 [C3466]

L. now 7.2cm; one end missing.
    On the basis of the two goat-like animals and the central design, which resembles a fossil sea urchin (a 'thunder-stone' according to popular belief), the brooch may be identified as a symbol of Thor. In mythology Thor's chariot was pulled by goats, and as he drove across the skies there was thunder and lightning. The name Thor means 'the Thunderer'. Equal-armed brooches were used by women to fasten shawls, cloaks or jackets at the breast.

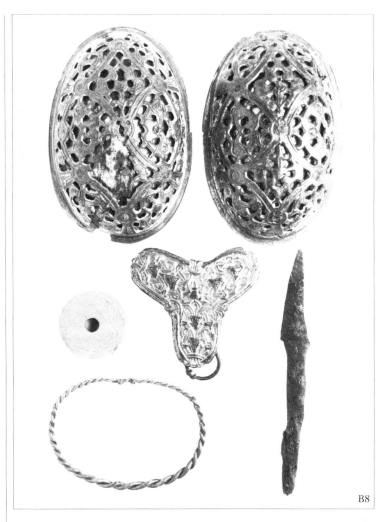

B8

B8   A woman's grave-goods: two oval brooches, a trefoil brooch, bead, arm-ring, spindle-whorl and knife
Lejre, Zealand. NM1 [C30078-84]

1 Two oval brooches of gilt bronze with gripping-beast ornament. Double-shelled. L.11.3cm.
2 Trefoil brooch of gilt and silvered bronze with symmetrical interlace ornament in the Borre style. On the back at the lower edge there is a loop with a ring from which something could have been suspended. W. (upper arms) 6.7cm.
3 Whitish, fluted glass bead (two fragments of beads from the grave are not shown).
4 Arm-ring made of two twisted bronze rods. W.8.2cm.
5 Cylindrical spindle-whorl of sandstone, the top decorated with concentric lines. D.3.6cm. H.1.1cm.
6 Iron knife with traces of a wooden handle. L.12.9cm.
    The brooches demonstrate that the woman was buried fully dressed (cf. no. B3). The trefoil brooch

was used to fasten a shawl, cloak or jacket at the breast. The spindle-whorl and knife, like the clothes and jewellery, were presumably thought to be of use in the land of the dead.

B9 Wooden spade
Jelling, central Jutland; from the soil-filling of the mound. NMI [20010]

L.95.0cm.

Both shovels and spades, sometimes shod with iron, are known from the Viking Age. They have been found mostly in the make-up of large earthworks, such as banks and mounds.

B10 Iron ard blade
Trelleborg, Zealand; from the civil settlement or the fortress. NMI [Q1375b]

L.11.4cm.

Although the mould-board plough was known in the Viking Age, the well-established ard was still used. The plough was much heavier than the ard and needed more power to pull it. Among the advantages of the plough was that it turned the sod; while the ard loosened the soil.

B11 Iron blade of pick or hoe
Aggersborg, north Jutland; from the settlement. NMI [A3-440]

L.15.1cm.

B12 Iron scythe blade with slightly curved point
Trelleborg, Zealand; from the civil settlement or the fortress. NMI [Q1232]

L.46.0cm.

Scythes vary greatly in length; this is one of the longer examples. They were used in particular to harvest hay, an important element of the winter fodder of domestic animals.

B13 Two iron harvesting knives
Aggersborg, north Jutland; from the settlement. NMI [A3-69-E, A3-322-B]

L. (largest) 12.9cm.

The tip is missing.

B14 Iron leaf-knife blade
Trelleborg, Zealand; from the civil settlement or the fortress. NMI [Q280]

L14.0cm.

B15 Fish-hook of iron
Aggersborg, north Jutland; from the civil settlement or the fortress. NMI [A3-3336-A]

L.9.1cm.

Fish provided an important additional source of food in settlements near good fishing-grounds. Cod, flat-fish and herring were common, but other species like horn-fish, eel, sturgeon, salmon and sea trout were also known. It is probable that there was also a trade in fish.

B16 Three iron leister prongs
Aggersborg, north Jutland; from the civil settlement or the fortress. NMI [A3-299-H, A3-707-F, A3-424a-E]

L. (longest) 19.0cm.

Leister prongs were mounted on a long shaft and were used to spear fish in shallow water.

B17 Artefacts of deer antler: semi-finished articles, completed products (playing-piece and comb) and debris
The comb is from the settlement at Aggersborg, north Jutland. NMI [A3-331-D]. The rest from the settlement at Ribe. ASR [D3076, D3132, D3399, D6660, D6937]

In towns and trading centres deer antler were primarily used to manufacture combs; but other articles such as playing-pieces, knife handles and needles were also made from this material.

B18 Amber-working: raw material and debris, rough-outs (three unfinished beads) and finished articles (pendant and spindle-whorl)
The settlement at Ribe. ASR [D13542, D9645]

Quadrilateral pendant. L.2.2cm.
Cylindrical spindle-whorl. H.2.2cm. D.3.4cm.

Amber was turned into beads and other ornamental objects. In Denmark it is most commonly found along the west coast of Jutland.

B19 Glass beads and bead-making: a string of 59 beads, raw material, half-finished and completed products and debris
The settlement at Ribe. ASR

The beads on the string were found scattered throughout the excavated area. The rest are from bead-maker's workshops. The raw material consists of mosaic tesserae, raw glass and sherds of broken glass vessels, imported from (or by way of) western Europe. The beads manufactured at Ribe included plain beads, plain beads with applied decoration, beads made from multi-coloured twisted rods (reticella beads), mosaic beads and perhaps some other types. The beads on this string were, however, probably not all produced at Ribe.

B20 Bronze casting: three, mosaic beads moulds and an oval brooch
Moulds from Ribe. Workshop find. ASR [D10474 etc., D10447, D10448]
The bronze brooch from Fourfeld Bæk, west Jutland. Single-find. NMI [3199/80].

The clay moulds are all incomplete: one is for an oval brooch, another for an equal-armed brooch, while the third is for a horse-shaped brooch and an unidentified object. L. (brooch) 8.7cm.

The first mould corresponds so closely to the finished brooch that this must have been produced by the Ribe bronze-smith.

B20a English sceatta: two faces/bird-whirl. *c.*725
Wt.0.55gm.
BMC-type no. 37. Register of Finds (RF) 3224, *Dankirke no. 42.* Photo.

B20b English sceatta: face/bird on cross. *c.*725
Wt.0.48gm.
BMC-type no. 27. RF 3224, *Dankirke no. 43.* Photo. *1 and 2, Bendixen 1974.*

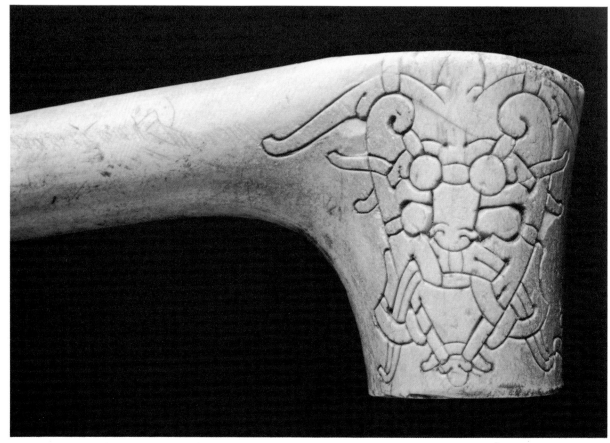

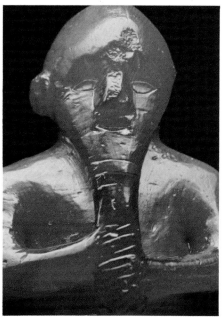

ABOVE *The handle of a walking stick or crutch made from deer antler and decorated in the Mammen style (B41).*
FAR LEFT *An amber playing piece from Zealand (B1); near left, this detail of a bronze brooch shows a Viking head (B3).*
RIGHT *A brooch (B2) for pinning a cloak is decorated with three heads.*

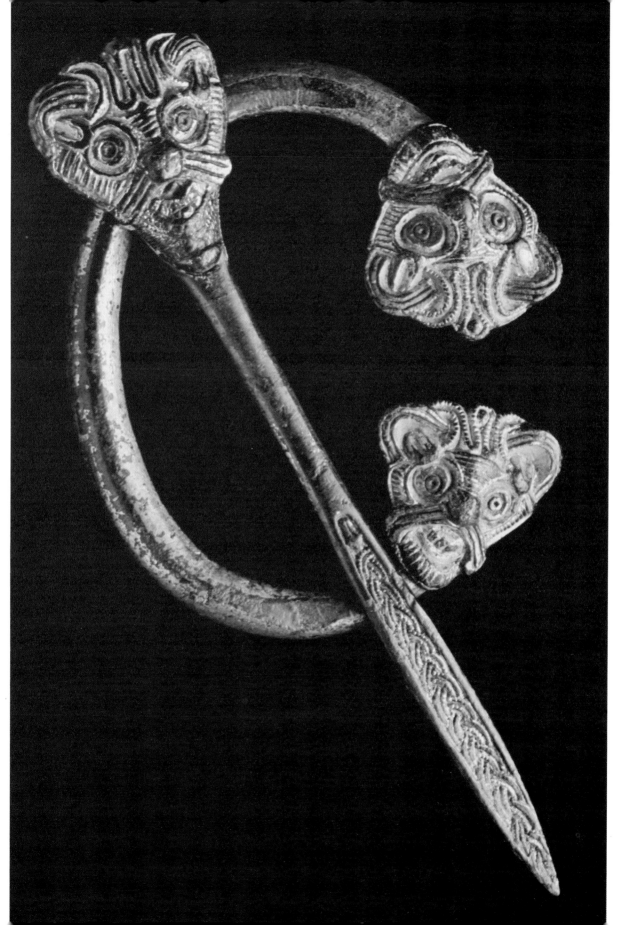

B21 Two Frisian coins, silver sceattas, type Wodan/monster
The settlement at Ribe. NM VI [FP Ribe no. 8 and 17]

Weight 0.71g and 0.39g respectively.
The coins are dated to c.720–750. Such coins were apparently in general use in Ribe at that time.

B22 Scandinavian coin, type – man's head/stag (copy)
Terslev, Zealand. From a hoard. NM VI [FP 1233]

The coin is dated to c.800. It represents one of the earliest Scandinavian coin types. The coin is thought to have been struck in Hedeby, perhaps for the powerful king Godfred.

B23 Soapstone pot with rounded bottom from Norway or south-west Sweden
Hals Barre, eastern mouth of the Limfjord. Found in the sea. NM I [C12529]

D. (rim) 31.0cm.
The pot is dated to the Viking Age. Large quantities of vessels made from fireproof soapstone were imported from Norway and south-west Sweden where there are outcrops of this rock. Pots and bowls were carved straight from the rock face.

B24 Six slate whetstones from Norway
Aggersborg, north Jutland; from the civil settlement or the fortress. NM I [A3-6A, A3-263-A, A3-277-A, A3-502B-C, A3-700-B, A3-1431]

L. (longest) 22.5cm.
The whetstones are dated to the Viking Age. It is probable that they came from the Eidsborg area in Telemark, Norway, where there was massive production of whetstones for export. Eidsborg whetstones occur in almost all Danish Viking-Age settlements.

B25 East European silver arm-ring
Erritsø, east Jutland. From a hoard. NM I [D5330]

The arm-ring is in the form of a spiral with facetted terminals, commonly known as a 'Permian' ring. Weight 200.7g.
Dated to the second half of the ninth or early tenth century, the ring was originally a neck-ring which, like many Permian rings found in Scandinavia, was re-modelled as an arm-ring. Permian rings conformed to a standard of weight, based on a standard unit of 100g, and were used as a means of payment – 'ring money'.

B26 One hundred and sixty-nine Arabic silver coins in a broken clay pot
Over Randlev, east Jutland. NM VI [FP 1798]

Part of a hoard of 237 silver coins. The latest was struck in 910.
The hoard was laid down in the beginning of the tenth century. Between about 900 and 970 very large quantities of Arabic coins poured into Scandinavia. In present-day Denmark about 3,500 such coins have been found. The coins were acquired mainly through trade and plunder in Russia, where the large rivers were used as transport routes.

B27 Slav clay pot
The settlement at Ribe. ASR [D12658]

Only about a third of the pot is preserved. It is flat-bottomed and decorated with horizontal grooves and a wave pattern below the rim; known as the Menkendorf type. H.17.0cm.
The pot is dated to the eighth century. It is one of many finds which testify to Denmark's contacts with the Slav tribes to the south of the Baltic.

B28 Frankish silver cup with plant ornament
Ribe. Part of a hoard. NM I [Df. $\frac{15}{68}$]

Silver with niello and gilt ornamental detail, the inside is also gilt. There are small breaks in the bottom and side. H.8.0cm. D. (rim) 9.0cm. Weight 438g.
The cup is dated to about 800. It is not known how this cup reached Denmark. From 820 and for at least a hundred years thereafter, the Frankish Empire was subjected to extensive plunder by the Danes. There were, however, also trade connections between the Danes and the Franks and occasional periods of peaceful political relations which resulted in the lavish exchange of gifts.

B29 Frankish silver strap-end with plant ornament and Latin inscription and adapted as a brooch
Als. Single-find. NM I [14201]

Silver with niello. The front face is gilt. The strap-end is tongue-shaped with some pieces missing. The inscription on the back reads: EGO IN D. NOMINE + ERMAD(US) ME FECIT. It is pierced by four secondary holes. L.12.7cm. W.3.9cm. Weight 134.8g.
The strap-end is dated to about 800 or a little later. The inscription tells us that the name of the maker was Ermadus.

B30 Two Rhineland pot sherds
The settlement at Ribe. ASR [D4229 + D3449, D11286]

Pale rim-sherd with stamped ornament of Badorf type, probably from a pot. L. (maximum) 10cm. Dark wall-sherd with a decoration of applied tin foil of Tating type, probably from a jug. L. (maximum) 9.2cm.
The sherds date from the eighth century. The pots were presumably trade goods.

B31 Silver mount, with animal and circle ornament, from the Rhineland or south Germany, and adapted as a brooch
Råbylille, Zealand; single-find. NM I [4632]

The mount is parcel-gilt and set in fields divided by arcs of circles. Cut to a roughly rectangular shape and provided with a pin, of which traces remain. L.10.3cm. W.4.9cm.
The mount is dated to c.750–800. It is a good example of the so-called Anglo-Carolingian art which was produced on the Continent under strong influence from England. The influence of Anglo-Carolingian art on Danish ornament resulted in Style F (see no. B37).

B32 Decorated stud made in Ireland or possibly Scotland
Aggersborg, north Jutland; from the settlement. NM I [A3-430-C]

Bronze with red and yellow enamel. The stud is

circular with a broken loop on the back. D. 3.9cm.

The stud is dated to the ninth century. Although the Baltic, the Frankish Empire and England were the Danish Vikings' preferred areas of activity, some also operated in Ireland and Scotland.

B33 Gilt-bronze mount, with ornament of human figures, snakes and interlace, made in Ireland or possibly Scotland. Probably adapted as a brooch

No provenance. NM I [20830]

The mount is circular and domed with an empty setting at the top. Two secondary holes perforate the edge. H. 2.7cm. D. 5.9cm.

The mount is dated to about 800. The secondary holes probably served to secure a pin.

B34 Copper-alloy bowl made in north England or Scotland

Nr. Longelse, Langeland; grave find. LMR [491]

The applied rim mounts are decorated with red enamel. Originally there may have been other colours as well. An animal-shaped mount in high relief as well as some small, transverse, half-cylindrical mounts are also applied to the rim. Only part of the rim and upper portion of the bowl survive. It is shown mounted in a modern reconstruction. D. about 33.5cm. W. (rim mounts) 2–2.5cm.

The bowl is dated to the eighth or ninth century, but it was not deposited in the grave of a high-ranking nobleman until the middle of the tenth century. It is one of many examples of the Viking's admiration both for the exotic and for sumptuous table-ware.

B35 Two arm rings, one silver and one gold, and two ingots

Arm-rings from Tostrup and Råbylille, Zealand; ingots from Erritsø, east Jutland. The ring from Råbylille is a single-find; the other objects are from hoards. NM I [8430, MMCLV, C5334]

The arm-rings are band-shaped with an expanded central portion. The silver ring has a simple stamped decoration. The gold ring is decorated with raised bosses and a stamped and punched ornament with motifs such as the 'Tree of Life' and small animal heads in heart-shaped frames. Weight of silver ring 24.2g. Weight of gold ring 53g. The ingots are 13.2cm and 15.9cm long respectively. Weight 100.7g and 100.6g.

They date from the ninth or early tenth centuries. All precious metal had to be brought in from abroad; jewellery produced in Scandinavia, such as these rings, must therefore contain the metal from plundered and traded goods.

THE VIKING ART STYLES

B36 Style E: the ornament on a bronze oval brooch

Lillevang, Bornholm; grave find. NM I [C2904]

L. 10.7cm.

The main motifs in the art of the Viking Age are stylised animals. Style E animals have rounded (sometimes bird-like) bodies, often drawn with a double contour. The heads are small and round with raised eyes; there is often a lappet on the top of the head or small pointed ears or horns. Date *c.* 750–850. (Style E is so called because it follows on the heels of pre-Viking art forms known as Styles A-D.)

B37 Style F: the ornament on a bronze oval brooch

Lillevang-Melsted, Bornholm; grave find. NM I [C6593]

L. 9.4cm.

Style F animals are as a rule small, compact and organically coherent, with hatched bodies in a resting, crawling or standing posture. The motifs are used in designs which cover the surfaces of delimited fields. The style is much influenced by the so-called Anglo-Carolingian art (see no. B31). Date *c.* 750–800.

B36

LEFT *A collection of beads, half-finished products and raw material (B19) from Ribe, a prolific bead-making centre on Jutland.*
ABOVE *A gold arm-ring (B35) with 'Tree-of-Life' decoration; and right, a bronze oval brooch (B38) with the 'gripping-beast' design from east Jutland.*

B38 'Gripping beasts': the ornament on a bronze oval brooch
Lisbjerg, east Jutland: single-find, probably from a grave (a matching brooch from Lisbjerg is in the Danish National Museum) FHM [6284]

L.9.4cm.

'Gripping beasts' are so called because their paws grip any feature of the design which surrounds them, whether a frame, a neighbouring creature or indeed their own body. The animals usually appear as well-nourished creatures with happy, cat-like faces. 'Gripping beasts' were a favoured motif in Viking art, particularly from the beginning of the ninth century until the second half of the tenth century.

B39 Borre-style gilt bronze pendant
Bornholm: probably a grave find. NM I [C20249]

L. (including loop) 4.1cm.

The typical Borre style animal is a 'gripping beast' with a ribbon-like body which forms a loop between chest and hip. The motifs also include the ring-chain and other symmetrical interlace patterns. The style takes its name from some decorated mounts in a richly furnished grave from Borre, south Norway. The Borre style, like the succeeding art styles, was brought to England by the Vikings. Date *c.*850–1000.

B40 The Jellinge style: the ornament on a bronze oval brooch
Hedeby, from the settlement. NM I [MXCIX]

Double-shelled; part of the rim is missing. L.10.5cm.

Jellinge-style animals have double-contoured, ribbon-shaped, scaly or hatched bodies. The head is seen in profile with a curled upper lip and often a lappet. The hip is usually represented as a spiral. The Style takes its name from the characteristic animal on the Jelling cup (see H3). Date *c.*875–975.

B41 The Mammen style: the ornament on the handle of a walking stick or crutch made from deer antler
Køge Strand, Zealand: single-find NM I [C18000]

The handle is a natural antler point; the socket is decorated with the bearded mask of a man on one side and with an animal on the other. The point is shaped like an animal head. L.30.0cm.

In the Mammen style plant-ornament has for the first time become an important element in Viking art. The animals are more substantial than those of the Jellinge style and, like other motifs such as the human mask, terminate in solid tendrils. This innovation was due to influences from English or German art. The style takes its name from the characteristic animal on the Mammen axe (see H15). The animal on the large Jelling stone probably represents one of the earliest examples of this style. Date *c.*950–1025.

B42 The Ringerike style: the ornament on a maple-wood walking stick
Lund, Sweden; from the settlement. KM [59126:795]

The upper part is shaped like an animal head with a mane of curved tendrils. The name 'Ulvkil' is inscribed in runes 29cm below the ornament. L.98.5cm.

Ringerike-style animals are well built and their anatomy is instantly recognizable. They are however characterised, and almost dominated, by attenuated curving tendrils, a feature which was the result of influences from abroad – from the contemporary Winchester style in England, for example (see K16). The style takes its name from Ringerike, a region in Norway where it is strongly represented. Date *c.*975–1050.

B43 An Urnes-style bronze brooch
No provenance. NM II [D11058]

D.4.3cm.

Urnes-style animals are slim and elegant attenuated quadrupeds or snake-like creatures involved in what appears to be a confusion of strands and ribbons. Brooches of differing quality decorated in the Urnes style became very popular. (See also L1.) The style takes its name from the wood-carvings on Urnes church, west Norway. Date *c.*1025–1150.

B39

B40

OVERLEAF *The lush meadows of Vorbasse where a Viking farm had once been established. Fields like these supported many heads of cattle on Jutland. (See page 20.)*

B42

THE LOOK OF THE ENGLISH

THE VIKINGS WHO FELL upon England attacked a land that was rich and comparatively peaceful, consisting of several kingdoms unprepared for such an onslaught. Anglo-Saxon England was a Christian country, renowned for its learning and its arts, with prosperous merchant, monastic and agricultural communities that would provide rich pickings.

By the seventh century the original Anglo-Saxon settlers, who had arrived from the Danish peninsula and the southern coastlands of the North Sea two hundred years previously, had already so expanded their settlement areas and organised their communities that powerful kings, a prospering aristocracy and a newly-established Church existed. The two centuries before the first wintering of the Danes in England saw a further process of expansion and consolidation. In the eighth century the Midlands kingdom of Mercia extended westwards to Offa's Dyke – the great earthwork constructed along its border with Wales. In the north there was a moving frontier within what is now southern Scotland; whilst in the south-west first Devon and later Cornwall were absorbed by the Anglo-Saxons.

Political developments among the kingdoms during these two centuries were characterised by the consolidation of Northumbria, Mercia and Wessex. The smaller realms of the east and south-east – East Anglia, Essex, Kent and Sussex – were demoted to sub-kingdoms. King Offa of Mercia, who died in 796, enjoyed extensive authority in the last years of his long reign – his court was attended by bishops from all England south of the Humber. His successors were unable to consolidate his achievements and Wessex grew in power. By 879, following the success of the Danish attacks, it was Wessex alone that survived intact to stem the advances of the Scandinavian invaders.

This gradual process of consolidation amongst the Anglo-Saxon kingdoms is reflected in their material culture, for the considerable regional variations in dress and jewellery fashions that existed in the fifth and sixth centuries gave way to a greater uniformity during the seventh and eighth. The ninth-century Anglo-Saxon art-style, known as the Trewhiddle style – named after the site in Cornwall where a hoard of finely ornamented silver objects was

LEFT *The Anglo-Saxon Irton Cross still standing in its Cumbrian graveyard where it was first raised more than a thousand years ago.*

FAR LEFT *A gold finger ring from York with a human face (C11); left, a gold ring (C2) from Hampshire which carries the inscription 'In Christ my name has been made Culla', testimony to the Christian society the Vikings found on arrival.* BELOW *The Lilla Howe hoard (D19) discovered in a mound at Goathland, Yorkshire. The four strap-ends are Anglo-Saxon, but the gold disc may be either English or Scandinavian.*

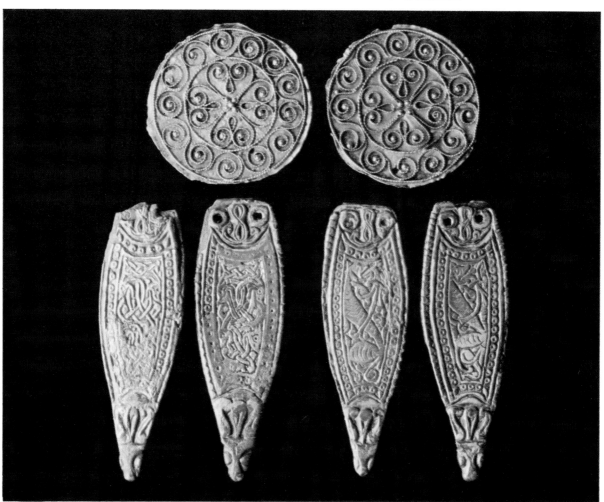

ABOVE and RIGHT The
Ormside Bowl, an Anglo-
Saxon masterpiece (C8). It
resembles bronze hanging
bowls known from pagan
Anglo-Saxon graves, but its
ornament is quite different. It
dates from the latter part of
the eighth century and may
have been made in York.

found – appears to have been universal throughout England.

Anglo-Saxon art of the eighth and ninth centuries continued the tradition of earlier Germanic art in using stylised animals as the basis for their patterns. Motifs of classical origin from the Mediterranean world were introduced following the coming of Christianity, in particular plaited band and vine-scroll ornament. But although these were at first faithfully reproduced, Anglo-Saxon taste exerted its influence and the motifs became less naturalistic so that an animal might degenerate into a tendril.

Then, about 900, the art of those areas of England settled by the Scandinavians was influenced by the taste of the newcomers (particularly in the sculpture of the north; see page 83ff.), whilst in the south the last major Anglo-Saxon style was developing. This, known as the Winchester style, developed from the lush acanthus-leaf patterns beloved on the Continent and from Byzantine figural art. Anglo-Saxon artists had looked across the Channel for inspiration, but this was then followed by a further and more general influx of Scandinavian taste in the eleventh century (see page 171ff.).

The contrast between Anglo-Saxon art of the eighth and ninth centuries may be seen in part between the birds and beasts that inhabit and feed on recognisable vines on the silver bowl from Ormside, Lancashire (no. C10), and the later animals, leaves and scrolls that form the patterns on such disc-shaped brooches as those from Beeston Tor, Derbyshire (no. C19), and ornamental strap-ends like those from Lilla Howe, Yorkshire (no. D19). Such ninth-century Trewhiddle-style patterns were those being practised on bone by York craftsmen when the Danes seized the town (no. C7).

The Beeston Tor disc-brooches form part of one of several coin-hoards buried about 875 when the Scandinavians were most active in their settlement of England. Such brooches illustrate the Anglo-Saxon love of silver for personal ornaments at this period (so much the more desirable as Viking booty which would for the most part have been melted down by the raiders and so have not been found in Denmark). To provide contrast for the patterns the incised surfaces were often inlaid with niello, the black sulphide of silver. This type of round brooch, usually worn singly, represents the main fashion for dress ornaments in the ninth to eleventh centuries (other than for such minor accessories as pins and strap-ends) and replaced an earlier fashion of the eighth century for wearing disc-headed linked pins.

Trewhiddle-style ornament in silver and niello can also be seen on the hilts of ninth-century swords, the most prestigious form of weapon and thus often lavishly embellished by their owners: such a sword is that from the river Witham with curved guards and a pommel in the form of a cocked hat (no. D2). Another important weapon, sometimes also ornamented, was the *scramasax*, a large single-edged knife. The less wealthy were armed with spears, but axes and bows were also used as offensive weapons. We know little or nothing at this period of Anglo-Saxon shields and body-armour.

A consequence of the coming of Christianity was the introduction to the Anglo-Saxons of two new artistic media – manuscript illumination and stone sculpture – both of which remained for some time as essentially the preserve of the Church. Some manuscripts – gospel-books intended for display on the altar – were elaborately painted and even embellished with gold and silver, according to the current stylistic fashion (no. D1). The technique of sculpture was introduced by masons imported from the Continent to build the first stone churches for the Anglo-Saxons. Theirs was a tradition of architectural embellishment and, although it was to continue, the crosses that the Anglo-Saxons themselves developed were greatly to impress the Scandinavian settlers (see page 83ff.).

To the Vikings who sailed westwards, stone buildings were as much a novelty as stone sculpture; for, by then, churches dotted the English landscape, and monasteries attacked by the Vikings, such as Monkwearmouth and Jarrow, had extensive ranges of masonry buildings – some with stained-glass windows. Secular stone buildings, however, were virtually unknown until the late Anglo-Saxon period and then remained rare. But the Scandinavians must also have wondered at the massive remains of Roman public architecture, for some of these major buildings, in York for example, were then still standing.

On the other hand, the buildings of Anglo-Saxon villages, such as Maxey, Northamptonshire, or Wharram Percy in Yorkshire (and even aristocratic sites like Goltho in Lincolnshire) presented the Scandinavians with timber buildings that would not have seemed strange to them. The mixed agricultural economy of the Anglo-Saxons would have been familiar too, although to them sheep appear to have been of greater importance than cattle. Domestic crafts and household goods, except perhaps for the superior quality of much of Anglo-Saxon pottery, also had a familiar look. According to the wealth and locality of the settlements, this pottery might include a few imports from the Rhineland or France. But for evidence of Anglo-Saxon trade and foreign contacts, we can naturally obtain a fuller picture from recent excavations in the towns and ports which had by 800 developed far more extensively than any such settlements in Scandinavia.

During the seventh and eighth centuries Anglo-Saxon England moved towards the re-emergence of an urban life that had earlier been extinguished with the economic collapse of Roman Britain. The greatest Roman centres, London and York, may never have been entirely deserted, but only then did they begin to develop again as towns, acting as centres of royal and ecclesiastical administration and then of trade and industry. Canterbury is another example of such an early town in Anglo-Saxon England; and others such as Winchester had just begun to develop again.

London and York acted as their own ports, but Canterbury and Winchester were served by coastal trading towns – the latter by Anglo-Saxon Southampton, known as Hamwih. Ipswich may have fulfilled a

OVERLEAF *The confrontation of Anglo-Saxon and Viking swords.*
LEFT *The Gilling Sword (D3) found by a small boy in a West Yorkshire river. It is decorated in silver with Anglo-Saxon Trewhiddle designs (see pp 20, 54).*
RIGHT *The Søndersø Sword (D12ii) from north Jutland. Its hilt is decorated with silver and brass in geometric patterns.*

similar role for East Anglia, but Hamwih remains to date the most fully excavated of these trading centres which appear to have been founded anew, not on the older nearby Roman sites.

Anglo-Saxon Southampton was an undefended settlement, unlike its medieval successor on the other side of the same promontory. Its buildings were arranged along regularly laid-out roads, housing merchants and craftsmen who worked in metal (including a mint), in wood, bone and antler, and who produced textiles and pottery. Glass, pottery and lava millstones were imported from the Rhineland, but the main trade seems to have been directly across the Channel with France. Much of the pottery, particularly tableware, seems to have been imported by foreign merchants for use in their own establishments in town, rather than for general sale. A great deal of their import trade was no doubt in French wine, whilst wool and cloth were the chief exports of Anglo-Saxon England.

Very little is known of the nature of Anglo-Saxon London or York at this period, but current excavations in advance of development hold out hope of enlightenment and thus for establishing the nature of the Scandinavian impact upon them. Like other Roman towns in use by the Anglo-Saxons, they had the benefit of the ruined Roman defences, and those at York appear to have been refurbished. Documentary evidence and excavation indicate that defences were being constructed in Mercia from the eighth century, but it was only the danger of the Vikings overrunning Wessex that initiated King Alfred's great programme of fortifications in the south.

JAMES GRAHAM-CAMPBELL

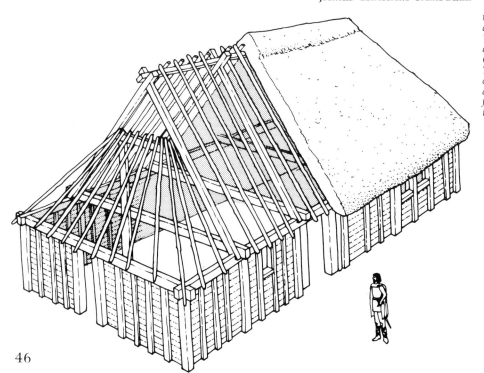

LEFT *A reconstruction drawing (after R. Warmington) of a seventh-century Anglo-Saxon house at Chalton in Hampshire. Though England's stone churches would have been alien to them, the Vikings found timber houses like these technically familiar.*

C1 The Bishophill Stone showing two Anglo-Saxon figures
St Mary Bishophill Junior Church, York
YM[1979.53]

This fragmentary gritstone cross-shaft was found in the wall of the church before 1861. Decoration: Side A shows two well-modelled figures in secular dress set over (?) scroll ornament. Side B depicts a ribbon animal in dense knotwork. Side C is destroyed. Side D has a medallion scroll. Ninth century. H.69.8cm.

The scroll is a typical element of pre-Viking carving while the ribbon beast is probably derived from a manuscript source. The well-modelled figures show the kind of art which lies behind some of the plastic figure sculpture produced in the city during the Viking period (see nos. YS1–3).

C2 Gold finger ring with Christian inscription
Bossington, Hants. AM, Oxford [1970.1067]

The ring's broad flat hoop is composed of a series of twisted wires soldered together. At the bezel these wires divide to encircle a disc struck with a crowned head looking left around which is the inscription "IN xpo NomEN ChLLA FIc [?]". The triangular fields either side of the bezel, created by the division of the hoop, are filled with granulation supported on a backing plate. H. (bezel) 3.8cm.

The inscription can be translated "In Christ (my) name has been made Culla" or "The name Culla is fixed in Christ". The ring is similar to one from Garrick Street, London, and although both rings have been dated to the seventh century, an eighth- or ninth-century date would be equally applicable.

C3 Fragmentary gilt-bronze mount
Whitby Abbey, Yorks. BM [W.27]

This octofoil mount is decorated with interlace. The pattern is composed of two equal-armed crosses having expanding arms with rounded ends set at forty-five degrees to each other. The fields between the arms of the crosses are pierced. D.10.4cm.

Two other similar mounts, one of which is probably from the same mould as this, are known from Whitby. All have been identified as book mounts. The form of the ornament and use of gilt bronze are consistent with an eighth-century date.

C3

C4 Bronze stylus
Whitby Abbey, Yorks. BM [W334]

The stylus has a sub-triangular head decorated with an applied repoussé sheet having a beaded border enclosing interlace ornament. The shank is divided into unequal lengths by five triple-reeded mouldings around the circumference. L.13.9cm.

Such a stylus would be used with a waxed writing tablet. The writing was done with the point and could be erased with the triangular head.

C5 The Hartlepool name-stone
Close Field cemetery, Hartlepool Moor, Cleveland
BM[80, 3-13, 4]

This limestone piece, found in 1833, carries a cruciform motif in low relief with the name EÐIL UINI (Æthelwine) cut in capitals across the lower quadrants. Late seventh or eighth century. H.19.1cm.

Small inscribed cruciform slabs are known from a series of early monastic sites in north-east England and the designs are clearly linked to the carpet pages of manuscripts like the Lindisfarne Gospels.

C6 Overchurch fragmentary shrine (?)
Upton Church, re-used from Overchurch Church, Cheshire
GM, Chester

Decoration shows an incised arch on the end; knotwork with zoomorphic terminal on the top; runic inscription in two lines on the side reading: "folcæararær donbec (un) (ge) /. bidda pfoteæ pelmun (de)" meaning "the people/army erected a monument, pray for Æthelmund". Ninth century. L.54cm.

Upton Church was built in 1813 from the re-used materials of Overchurch Church. This fragment was found during the demolition of Upton Church in 1887. The zoomorphic head is typical of ninth-century Mercian art. Æthelmund cannot be identified but was clearly a man of some status: his monument is unique in being dedicated by a community. The inscription, which contains at least one error ('t' for 'r' in line 2), is written in Anglo-Saxon runes and not in the shorter Scandinavian alphabet employed on the St Paul's stone (see no. I19).

C7 Bone trial piece
Railway Station, York YM [581.48]

This piece is decorated towards the upper edge with a frieze of five quadrupeds in different attitudes. Below the frieze are three half-worked plant motifs; from one of them a pair of quadrupeds develops. The ornament is in the ninth- early tenth-century Trewhiddle style. L.c.10.0cm.

C8 The Ormside Bowl
Ormside, Cumbria YM [un-numbered]

This shallow bowl is composed of a plain gilt-bronze inner shell, and a gilt-silver outer shell whose repoussé decoration is divided into four equal fields by plain mouldings. Each field contains an inhabited bush scroll. On each of the plain mouldings is a metal boss surrounded by filigree which conceals the head of a rivet holding the two shells together. A similar boss covers the head of the rivet on the interior. A circular field in the centre of the base is recessed and decorated in repoussé with an equal-armed cross having a metal boss mounted in false filigree in the centre and in each of the angles of the arms. On the interior a corresponding raised field is edged with twisted wire, and was originally decorated with a central blue glass stud surrounded by a zone of smaller glass studs. The glass is now lost. The rest of the field is ornamented with four areas of repoussé interlace separated by blue glass studs mounted in false filigree, all but one of the glass studs being lost. D.13.8cm. H.4.6cm.

The form of the bowl closely resembles that of

C7

Lindisfarne

Jarrow
Tyne
Wear

Simy Folds

Tees
Whitby

NORTHUMBRIA

Ribblehead
Wharram Percy
Settle
York

Ouse

Dublin

Chester

Torksey
Fossedyke
Lincoln
Goltho

Trent
Witham

Northworthy (Derby)
Nottingham

Repton

Leicester
Stamford
Welland
EAST ANGLIA
Nor

Nene
Ouse
Thetford

Severn
Huntingdon

Avon
Cambridge
Ipswic

Northampton
Bedford

Wye
MERCIA

Lea
ESSEX

Ashdown ✕
London

Avon
Englefield
Reading
Thames

Wedmore
Edington ✕
Rochester
Sheppey
Thane

✕ ✕
Basing
KENT
Canterbury

Athelney ✕
WESSEX
Wilton ✕

Winchester
SUSSEX

Hamwih (Southampton)

DANELAW

LEFT *The map shows the Danelaw area of England settled from the ninth century by the invading Vikings; the Anglo-Saxon kingdoms; the Five Boroughs of Derby, Leicester, Lincoln, Nottingham and Stamford; and the battles fought in Wessex between Alfred the Great and the Danes in the 870s.*
RIGHT *The most powerful weapon of the Vikings – their ships. Top left, a ship's prow appears as an engraving on a piece of amber; top right, a full-scale replica under sail in Danish waters; right, a coastal trading vessel (see p. 68) and, far right, an ocean-going cargo ship such as might have sailed to England with Viking families and animals when they settled there.*

the bronze hanging bowls known from pagan Anglo-Saxon graves, but the ornament suggests a date for the bowl in the latter part of the eighth century. The animal heads on the rim are a ninth-century addition. The recent discovery at Coppergate of a blue glass stud mounted in false filigree of exactly the same form and size of those in the interior of the bowl suggests that it may have been made in York. The layout of the ornament closely parallels that on the base of the Ormside bowl.

C9   Cast silver gilt pin
St Andrew's Street, Hitchin Letch. M

The pin has a shank of circular section and a flat disc-shaped head decorated with an interlace equal-armed cross. In the centre, and in each of the angles of the arms, is a glass setting mounted in beaded wire. L.7.5cm.

It was probably one of a set of linked pins, like those from the River Wiltham, Lincs. Similar pins are known from Kegworth, Leics.; Ross, Yorks.; and Birdoswald, Cumberland – probably all of eighth-century date.

C10   The Beeston Tor hoard
Beeston Tor Cave, Staffordshire BM [1925, 1-14, 1, 2 and 3, 1925, 2-17, 1, 2 and 3]

1 Silver disc brooch. In the centre is a circular field containing an openwork equal-armed cross having a bossed centre and expanding arms. Touching the centre field and the outer beaded frame of the brooch are four equally spaced outer fields each decorated in openwork with an inward-facing *fleur-de-lys*. The fields which separate them are filled with animal and plant ornament having the background filled with niello. Towards the outer edge of each field is a boss. The pin and its attachment project beyond the edge of the brooch. D.4.9cm.
2 Silver disc brooch. This is decorated with nine equally-spaced dome-headed rivets, one of which is lost, linked by lentoid fields each having a three-element frame, the median one of which is beaded. The lentoid fields and those which they delineate are filled with interlace, foliate or geometrical ornament having a background inlaid with niello. D.7.3cm.

C10

3 Copper-alloy binding made of a narrow sheet which tapers at each end and terminates in a lobed extension. The strip is bent over and linked on the open end with a rivet through these extensions. There are two subsidiary rivet holes, and the side has a beaded edge. L.2.7cm.
4 Gold ring of lozenge-shaped section. D.3.0cm.
5 Two plain copper-alloy wire rings. D.1.8cm.
6 Group of Anglo-Saxon silver pennies.
The hoard was contained in a leather bag or purse which no longer survives, and which also contained a quantity of gold wire. Some of this adheres to the back of the second disc brooch. Only a selection of the original *c.* 50 coins are exhibited. Such hoards were hidden for safe-keeping during time of trouble. This one is of Anglo-Saxon character, and its deposition is dated on coin evidence to *c.*873–5, a period when the Viking attacks on England were at their height.

C11   Gold finger ring with human face mask
Fishergate, York YM [1951.53]

The ring has a small bezel in the form of a human face between a pair of confronted bipeds viewed from above. The rear quarters of the animals develop into plant ornament. D.2.8cm.

The use of bipeds developing into plant ornament is a typically ninth-century feature, and the ring may have been made before the Vikings took York in 866. It is clear, however, that objects decorated in Anglo-Saxon style, such as this, continued to be made into the Viking Age.

C12   Silver pin
Cathedral Green, Winchester WRU [SF 1387]

It has a large spherical head an grooved shank. The pin was found in a grave in the cemetery north of the Old Minster, and dates to the eighth or ninth century. L.4.0 × W. (head) 0.7cm.

C13   Pair of silver garment hooks
Cathedral Green, Winchester WRU [SF 323 and 325]

Each hook has a triangular plate developing at the apex into an underturned hook. There are three perforated lobed extensions at the broad end. The plates are decorated with foliate ornament, the background being inlaid with niello. L.3.9 × W.2.0cm.

The hooks were found by the legs of a burial inside the Old Minster, and have been identified as hooks for fastening cross-gartering. But they are best regarded as all-purpose garment fastenings. These are decorated in the Trewhiddle style current in the ninth and early tenth centuries and are particularly splendid examples of the type. The burial in which they were found also had gold braids around the neck and head, and was evidently of very high status.

C14   Gold finger ring
Dorchester, Oxon. AM, Oxford [1930.638]

The ring has an openwork bezel formed by the heads and bodies of a pair of snakes interlacing with each other and with a thin gold wire. The ends of the animals' bodies are extended to form the pentagonal hoop which tapers towards the back. D.2.4cm.

Similar filigree is used on a sword pommel from

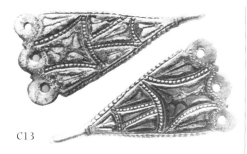

C13

Windsor and an unprovenanced ring in the Ashmolean Museum. These three pieces have been used as evidence for the existence of a southern English school of free-standing gold filigree in the late eighth and early ninth centuries.

C15 Silver strap-end with an animal-head terminal
St Paul-in-the-Bail, Lincoln LAT [SP78 Ag2]

The strap originally fitted into a split at the upper end and was held in place by two rivets. The main field is decorated with two outward-facing bipeds whose tails develop into interlacing plant ornament. The background is inlaid with niello. L.4.1 × W.1.1cm.
  This is a ninth-century Anglo-Saxon strap-end decorated in the Trewhiddle style, see no. D19.

C16 Copper-alloy pin
St Paul-in-the-Bail, Lincoln LAT [SP75 Ae120]

It has a polyhedral head decorated with ring-and-dot. L.6.0cm.
  Similar pins are known from other Anglo-Saxon and Anglo-Scandinavian sites including Whitby Abbey, Southampton (no. C23) and York.

C17 Composite two-sided bone comb
Southampton, Hants. SARC [XI CW18]

There are two connecting plates, one decorated with incised ornament, and ten tooth plates held together by eight iron rivets. The comb tapers towards the ends and the final tooth plates project beyond the ends of the connecting plates. L.19.5 × W.3.0cm.

C18 Two-sided composite bone comb
Southampton, Hants. SARC [XXIV CW16]

The comb has two undecorated connecting plates and eleven tooth plates held together by seven iron rivets. The final tooth plates project beyond the ends of the connecting plate. L.18.4 × W.4.4cm.

C19 Unfinished, damaged, antler tooth plate
Southampton, Hants. SARC [XXIV CW2]

The plate has cut teeth and a single rivet hole, now partially broken away. L.3.5 × W.1.8cm.
  The presence of unfinished tooth plates and comb backs suggests that combs were being manufactured in Saxon Southampton.

C20 Two undecorated antler connecting plates
Southampton, Hants. SARC [XXIV CW12]

Each plate has a perforation at both ends. L.12.4 × W.1.8cm.
  Such connecting plates were used for the backs of single-sided composite combs, no. J8. Alternatively they could have been used for comb cases like no. J9. Similar unfinished connecting plates are known from York.

C21 Fragmentary connecting plate for a comb decorated with vertical grooves and an incised latin cross
Southampton, Hants. SARC [XXIV CW75]

L.4.3 × W.1.7cm.

C22 Bone pin made from a pig's fibula. The naturally expanding head is perforated
Southampton, Hants. SARC [IV CW19]

L.12.1 × W.1.9cm.
  Debris from the manufacture of such pins is known from Saxon Southampton, but they also occur widely elsewhere in England and in Scandinavia.

C23 Bronze pin
Southampton, Hants. SARC [XV B22]

It has a shank of circular section separated by a collar from the polyhedral ring-and-dot decorated head. L.6.3cm.
  Similar pins are known from other middle Anglo-Saxon sites including Whitby.

C24 Locally-made pottery vessel, reconstructed
Southampton, Hants. SARC [XV F1]

H.12.5 × D. (rim) 12.7cm.
  This pot is typical of the locally-made domestic wares used in Saxon Southampton in contrast to the more highly finished and technically competent imported wares.

C25 Rim and body sherds from a Tating-ware pitcher, with applied tinfoil decoration
Southampton, Hants. SARC [v P96]

Rim: H.4.5 × W.10cm. Body H.6.5 × W.9cm.
  The wide-ranging trading connections of Saxon Southampton are demonstrated by the discovery there of large quantities of imported pottery, including Tating and Beauvais wares (no. C26) and imported glass. The pottery reveals that the town's trading links were with North France and the Rhineland.

C26 Rim sherd of Beauvais ware with red-painted decoration
Southampton, Hants. SARC [I F30]

H.3.0 × W.9.7cm.
  The sherd is from a pitcher made in the Beauvais region of North France.

C27 Silver sceatta
Southampton, Hants. SARC [26.526]

Obv: small head facing, around, circle of annulets enclosing pellets. Rev: fantastic bird surrounded by pellets. Five pellets below the bird's head form a cross shape. BMC type 49. Wt.0.525gm.
  The sceatta was the normal coin in circulation

LEFT *The hill at Athelney, protected in the Viking Age by the Somerset marshes, where King Alfred took refuge during his campaign against the Vikings, restored his army, and emerged finally to inflict defeat on the heathen forces.*
RIGHT *The Alfred Jewel. Made of cloisonné enamel, rock crystal and gold (D18), it may have been the head of a pointer used to pick out the text in holy manuscripts. An inscription reads: 'Alfred ordered me to be made'.*

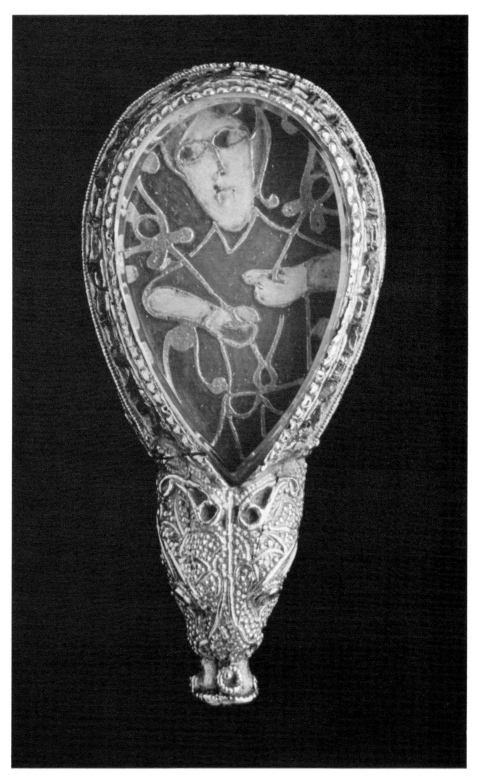

in southern England in the late seventh and eighth centuries, before pennies were introduced towards the end of the eighth century. The large numbers of this type found in Saxon Southampton suggests that it was minted there.

C28 Bone pin beater
Marlowe Theatre Car Park, Canterbury CAT [79.M3.278]

The pin is of circular section and pointed at each end. Towards the middle is a zone of hatched decoration confined between two groups of incised parallel lines. L.9.3cm.

C29 Copper-alloy drop-shaped mount
Canterbury, Kent CAT[CB/R.2.78.70.456]

The mount is decorated with a pair of confronted quadrupeds whose bodies, limbs and jaws interlace. L.2.5 × W.1.8cm.

This is an Anglo-Saxon product of eighth-century date and illustrates the production of high-quality metalwork in Canterbury.

C30 Bun-shaped fired clay loom weight
Cakebread Robey site, Canterbury CAT [CB/R.78]

D.12.0 × T.2.42cm.

C31 Discoid fired clay spindle whorl
Marlowe Theatre Car Park, Canterbury CAT [80.M4.1398]

The spindle whorl is decorated with a row of incised circles around the perforation, and a second row around the edge. Between the two rows is a zone of incised diagonal lines. D.3.0cm.

C32 Silver sceatta
Canterbury excavations. Cakebread R site. RMC [Marlowe 2.79.B77.1211]

Wt.1.03gm (16gr).
Obv: Standing figure holding a cross-staff in a 'boat'. Rev: Celtic cross design with central boss and pellets on cross arms, pearl circles between.

C33 Silver sceatta
Canterbury excavations. Cakebread R site. RMC [CB/R2.78.29.49]

Wt.1.03gm (16gr).
Obv: Hound with long tongue. Rev: Branch spiral, annulet at end.

C34 Offa, 757–796. Silver penny. Late issue, c.792–796
BM [BMC 38]

Wt.1.28gm (19.7gr).
Obv: OFFA REX M in three lines. Rev: BEAGHEARD (runic 'G') in two lines.

C34

LEFT *The drawing shows decoration from drinking horn mounts found in a silver hoard at Trewhiddle in Cornwall in 1774. Their characteristic of the art of the ninth century in England and gives it the identity 'the Trewhiddle style'.*

THE ATTACKERS RETURN

T HE EARLIEST VIKING RAIDS hit hard at a prosperous and peaceful Northumbria. News of the first attack, on Lindisfarne in June 793, reached Alcuin, the greatest Northumbrian scholar of his age, at the court of Charlemagne. His letters of commiseration to friends at home express eloquently the shock felt by the English that such attacks could take place at all; the horror that of all places the Church should be a target; and the guilty feeling that this must be retribution for sin. He wrote to King Æthelred of Northumbria:

> Lo, it is nearly 350 years that we and our fathers have inhabited this most lovely land, and never before has such terror appeared in Britain as we have now suffered from a pagan race, nor was it thought that such an inroad from the sea could be made.

and to the survivors at Lindisfarne itself:

> ... the pagans desecrated the sanctuaries of God, and poured out the blood of saints around the altar, laid waste the house of our hope, trampled on the bodies of saints in the temple of God, like dung in the street. ... Truly it has not happened by chance, but is a sign that it was well merited by someone.

The English chroniclers who recorded first the raids, then the Viking invasions, thought of the intruders quite unspecifically as the *heathen*, or the *host* or, without any particular attempt at differentiation, as the *Danes*. Initially Ireland bore the brunt of the Viking attacks, but in the 830s and 840s raids, sackings and battles in England became ever more frequent. Places as large as London and Hamwih, the predecessor of Southampton, were attacked, sometimes repeatedly.

The number of attackers also increased. At Southampton in 840 the English beat off thirty-three ships. By 850–51, the first year the Scandinavians wintered in England, there was a fleet in the Thames estimated by the *Anglo-Saxon Chronicle* as 350 ships-strong. From it a great host stormed Canterbury, put Beorhtwulf, King of Mercia, and his army to flight, and

OVERLEAF The Codex Aureus, an eighth-century manuscript (D1) from Canterbury which was first stolen by the Vikings invading Kent, and later ransomed back by Earl Alfred. The earl then had his act of charity recorded in Anglo-Saxon around the margins of the most splendid pages in the book. There could be no more graphic reminder of the immediate results of the Viking attacks. See p. 63.

55

Ond for ðon ðefðu noldan dǣt dæʒ halʒan bóc lóieʒ Inʒhie hǣðburȝre punaðoi, ⁊ nupillað hǣ ʒþellan Inirō
ʒyrtʒ cyrcan ʒode toloþe ⁊topuldre ⁊topundraʒa þhip ðnoþunʒa toðoncunʒa, ⁊Sōn ʒodeamdan ʒ̄ʒhi peiþe toþrucōi
de Incyrtʒ cyrcan dǣ þhonlice ʒod ʒ̄ lof ⁊ʒiad, teðonʒ̄hiade dǣt hēomon apede ʒ̄hpelce monade þor Ælfred
⁊þor þhibuntʒ ⁊þor alhðryðe hēopa þaulum to ēcum lǣt dome, ða þile dēʒō ʒ̄hteon hæbbe dǣt þulpiht ʒ̄
doþþe þope bēon mote., ⁊þþelce ic Ælfred dux ⁊þhibuntʒ biddað ⁊halʒiad onʒodʒ almæhtiʒeʒ noman ⁊on allpa
hiʒ halʒpa dǣt nænzmon þēo toðonʒedrypʒ, ðǣte dæʒ halʒan bloc aʒelle oððe aðēode þromcyrtʒ cyrcan dahþile

entered Surrey, before being temporarily driven off by the tougher forces of Wessex. From 850 onwards the Vikings were no longer raiders bent on plunder alone. They were now attacking as armies, and bent on conquest.

When campaigns of conquest began in earnest in the years after 865 the Scandinavian army, now under the leadership of Ivar the Boneless, Halfdan and Ubba, said to be sons of the legendary Ragnar Lothbrok, turned first to the least strong Anglo-Saxon kingdoms. East Anglia and Mercia were politically weak; Northumbria was torn by civil war. Thus a great Scandinavian army was able to land in East Anglia in 865 and to make its base at Thetford, already as recent excavations have shown a large and prosperous town. There the army was able to assemble supplies, especially horses, and it was ready late in 866 to seize the opportunity provided by civil war in Northumbria.

There King Osberht was being challenged by Ælla, the popular choice as king. The Scandinavians moved rapidly to Yorkshire by land and sea, arrived unannounced at York, the undefended capital, and took it with ease. The Northumbrians, reunited in the face of threat, attempted a recapture early in 867. They failed; both king and would-be usurper were killed and the Scandinavians were able to set up their own puppet king to administer the city and the kingdom for their benefit while attention was turned elsewhere. Mercia was ravaged next, but its King Burgred bought an uneasy short respite and the army turned its attention to the destruction of East Anglia (869–70). The last East Anglian king Edmund, killed in 870 while a captive of the Scandinavians, was soon regarded by the English as a martyr and a saint.

In 870 the great army moved to a new base at Reading and began an onslaught on the strongest remaining Anglo-Saxon kingdom, Wessex. The year 871 is remembered as the year of battles. The Scandinavians won some – at Basing and *Meretun*. Wessex won others – at Englefield and Ashdown. During the campaign King Æthelred died. His brother Alfred came to the Wessex throne and was forced to end the year, following English defeats at Reading and Wilton, with a treaty which left London and the mouth of the Thames in Scandinavian hands. The move at least bought respite for Wessex. The Danes – by now they were probably the predominant element in the armies active in England – returned to complete the conquest of Mercia. Initially King Burgred bought them off, and the bishop of Worcester in 871–2 found himself raising money for the "immense tribute for the barbarians" who were then in London. Soon, however, the Vikings were back in Mercian heartland.

The winter of 872–3 was spent at the strategically placed borough of Torksey in Lincolnshire, then and later, an important trading and manufacturing centre. The next year the army was at Repton in Derbyshire, where the great burial church of Mercian kings seems to have been incorporated in the defences of a Scandinavian stronghold. Mercia crumbled. Burgred fled, and a puppet king Ceolwulf II was put in his place to administer the kingdom at the disposal of the Scandinavians.

The army then split. One half returned under Halfdan to Northumbria to consolidate the conquest and turn it into settlement. Northumbria – the southern part of the kingdom at least – became a landscape of villages with new Scandinavian lords, new names, new cultural, administrative and artistic traditions; and it owed allegiance to the army dependent upon York and to its Danish kings.

The second part of the army under its three leaders Guthrum, Oscetel and Anwend moved from Repton to Cambridge, and the next year began what was doubtless intended to be the last onslaught on Wessex. In 878 they almost succeeded, driving King Alfred and the rump of his Wessex army into the marshes of Somerset, from which he emerged after recouping his forces in the now almost legendary space of six weeks to defeat Guthrum and his army at Edington. The resultant Treaty of Wedmore established the partition of England between a Danelaw in the north and east and Anglo-Saxon Wessex to the south and west (page 48). It left Guthrum free to proceed with the settlement of East Anglia. The Danish leader was then baptised under the English name Æthelstan, with Alfred standing as his godfather.

The course of ninth-century Scandinavian attacks and settlement is known almost entirely from English accounts, themselves often biased towards a Wessex point of view. The reality of the events, however, is not in doubt. The attack on Northumbria in 866–7, for instance, is verified by the numerous coin hoards – always a sign of troubled conditions – buried in or near York at that time. Excavations have shown that the Northumbrian monastery of Whitby was so thoroughly sacked in 867 that it was abandoned for centuries. The attacks on Mercia and Wessex in the 870s are confirmed by large numbers of coin hoards: and the twenty years of relative peace which followed by the absence of them.

After 878 Wessex consolidated its defences by completing the great string of fortified towns known, after the document which recorded them, as the Burghal Hidage system. Each area looked to its heavily defended burh for refuge in time of trouble – and was responsible for its maintenance in good repair. In the Danelaw the army also based its strength on a number of boroughs, to which people owed allegiance and looked for defence.

The partition of England was confirmed by a second great Scandinavian attack in Wessex in the 890s. The Burghal Hidage system worked, so the would-be settlers, now frustrated in their attempts to invade Kent and Wessex, joined, for the most part, the settlers of an earlier generation to confirm the Scandinavian character of the Danelaw. In the north-west of England, too, there were new Scandinavian settlers. The place-names of the Wirral and Chester area, and those of north Lancashire and Cumbria indicate that the newcomers were chiefly Hiberno-Norse, from the Viking Kingdom of Dublin. The art of their stone sculpture confirms their origin.

The Anglo-Saxon reconquest of England

902-6 A.D.

York
YORK KINGDOM
Lincoln
Derby ● Nottingham
Leicester ● Stamford
MERCIA DANELAW
EAST ANGLIA
London ●
WESSEX

916 A.D.

York
YORK KINGDOM
Lincoln
Derby ● Nottingham
Leicester ● Stamford
MERCIA DANELAW
EAST ANGLIA
London ●
WESSEX

918 A.D.

York
YORK KINGDOM
DANELAW
Lincoln
Derby ● Nottingham
Leicester ● Stamford
MERCIA
London ●
WESSEX

Anglo Saxon Settlements

Danish Settlements

Norwegian Settlements

920 A.D.

York
YORK KINGDOM
Lincoln
Derby ● Nottingham
Leicester ● Stamford
WESSEX
London ●

LEFT *The series of maps (based on the work of David Hill) show the gradual reconquest of English territory from 902 to 920, by when the Danelaw had almost disappeared.*
ABOVE *A cross fragment (F16) from Weston Church, North Yorkshire, depicts a Viking warrior with his sword and battle axe. And, above right, can be seen the other side of the stone showing the warrior with sword and woman. No single object in the exhibition could epitomise the story more clearly, for the Viking monument was re-carved on an earlier Anglian cross.*
RIGHT *The silver side-plate and roof-plate of a house-shaped shrine (E7). The ornament is a combination of Anglo-Saxon Trewhiddle and Scandinavian Jellinge designs.*

Contacts between Dublin and the Kingdom of York, already real enough by 903 as the huge treasure hoard from Cuerdale in Lancashire shows (it includes York Viking coins and Hiberno-Viking metalwork), soon became a political reality. Edward, son of Alfred the Great, and his sister Æthelflæd, progressively returned Mercia and the southern part of the Danelaw to English control by judicious warfare and by extending the system of fortified burhs. Æthelflæd's death, however, gave Ragnall, a Norwegian from Dublin, the opportunity of making himself king at York in 919. Edward's son Athelstan, however, captured York in 927, and by the battle of *Brunanburh* in 937 – famous both in Viking saga and Anglo-Saxon history – seemed on the point of returning the whole of England to English rule. But his death in 939 brought a Norwegian king back to York – Olaf Guthfrithsson – and a succession of Norwegians ruled the city until Erik Bloodaxe was expelled for the second time in 954 and killed.

Although political control of York and the Danelaw then returned to the kings of England, the influence of the Scandinavian settlement continued. Excavations have shown that York and Lincoln, and no doubt other towns of the Danelaw, had been transformed in the early tenth century into centres of industry, trade, administration and defence. Industries, the pottery industry being the best documented example, grew up both in town and country to serve the swelling population.

A generation of peace, and particularly the reign of the reformer king Edgar (959–75), enabled England to benefit from these prodigious capital investments – just in time, it must have seemed to contemporaries, to attract the attentions of a second series of Viking invaders towards the end of the century.

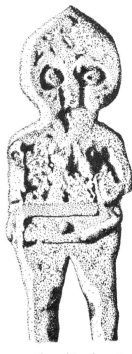

ABOVE *The sculptured warrior shows how the scramasax (see D4 opposite) was worn – in a sheath slung from a belt horizontally across the waist.*

PETER ADDYMAN

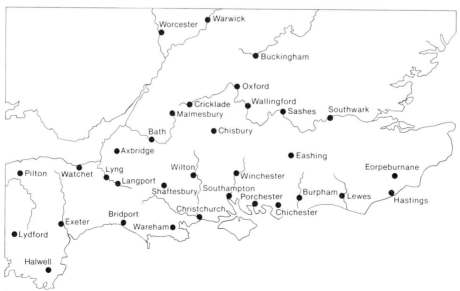

LEFT *The burghs, forts and fortified towns of southern England, established by Alfred the Great and his children, gave the Anglo-Saxons greater security against possible Viking threats from the Danelaw.*
OVERLEAF *Above are seen the remains of a Viking-Age farmhouse at Ribblehead in the Pennines of North Yorkshire. The paved entrance at bottom centre can be seen more clearly in the reconstruction on p 70. See also E2.*
BELOW *The map shows the disposition of villages with Anglo-Saxon and Scandinavian names in the Howardian Hills in Yorkshire. See 'Signposts to settling' p 80.*

D6

D4

D1 THE STOCKHOLM CODEX AUREUS
Stockholm, The Royal Library [MS A.135]
Vellum; 193 folios, 39.5 × 31.5cm. Latin. Written
and illuminated in Canterbury in the mid-eighth
century.

This double opening comes from a sumptuous
copy of the Four Gospels. The manuscript includes
miniatures of St Matthew and St John (similar
miniatures of St Mark and St Luke have been lost),
four major decorated initial pages out of an
original total of five, a number of lesser decorated
initials and eight pages from a set of ornamental
canon tables. The text is written on alternate
purple and white leaves, that on the purple pages
being either in white or in gold.

In the margins on folio 11, a richly decorated
page marking the beginning of the story of the
Incarnation in St Matthew's Gospel, are a number
of notes in Anglo-Saxon, added probably in the
second quarter of the ninth century. These record
how the Ealdorman Ælfred and his wife, Werburg,
bought the book back from the heathen army,
paying for it with gold. They then presented it to
Christ Church, Canterbury, which may well have
been the original owner. This they did for "the love
of God and for the good of their souls". There could
be no more graphic reminder of the immediate
results of the invasion of England by a pagan force.

The full translation of the Anglo-Saxon in the
margin reads: *"In nomine domini nostri Jesu Christi.*
I, Earl Alfred, and Werberg my wife, have acquired
this book from a heathen army with our true
money, that is, with pure gold, and this we have
done for the love of God and for the good of our
souls, and because we are not willing that this holy
book should remain any longer in heathen hands.
And we now desire to give it to Christ Church
(Canterbury) for the praise and glory and worship
of God and as a thank-offering for His Passion and
for the use of the religious community which daily
celebrates God's praise in Christ Church."

By the sixteenth century the manuscript had
arrived in Spain, in the library of the scholar
Jerónimo Zurita. It afterwards passed through the
hands of the Carthusians of Aula Dei, Saragossa,
and of Gaspar de Guzmán, Conde-Duque de
Olivares (d. 1645), from whose son it was
purchased in 1690 by Johan Gabriel Sparwenfeldt,
acting for the Swedish Royal Library.

D2 The Witham Sword
River Witham, Fiskerton, Lincs. SCM [J.1954.3]

This iron sword has a two-edged fullered blade.
The undecorated guard and upper guard curve
away from the grip. The trilobate pommel is
embellished with narrow silver strips decorated
with animal and foliate ornament, and three
narrow silver rings with foliate or geometrical
ornament encircle the grip. L.90.2cm.

This is an Anglo-Saxon sword of the ninth- or
early tenth-century having Trewhiddle-style decoration. The Gilling Sword (no. D3) and the sword
pommel (no. YD42) are of the same type.

D3 Two-edged iron sword with a fullered blade
Gilling West, Yorks YM [1959.51]

The guard and upper guard curve away from the
grip, and there is a trilobate pommel decorated
with applied silver strips, and fields with conventionalised plant ornament. Five similarly-
decorated silver strips encircle the grip.
L.83.8 × W.8.6cm.

This is an Anglo-Saxon sword decorated in the
Trewhiddle style, and is of the same basic form as
the River Witham sword (no. D2).

D4 Iron scramasax
River Cam, Pike and Eal, Chesterton UMAA, Cam.
[1931.448]

This weapon has a tang of rectangular section. The
cutting edge is slightly curved, and towards the
back the blade is inlaid on both faces with
horizontal copper-alloy wires. L.30.0cm.

At least six other scramasaxes with such simple
inlay are known, including one from the River
Ouse, Cambridgeshire. More elaborately inlaid
scramasaxes are also known from Dover, Kent
and Battersea. This example probably dates from
the ninth- or tenth-century.

D5 Iron spearhead
River Thames, Vauxhall
Museum of London [A1978]

The spear has a pattern-welded blade separated
from the open socket by a band of beading. There
are two grooves around the lower end of the
socket. L.39.5cm.

D6 Socketed iron spearhead
River Ouse, Braham's Farm, Cambs. UMAA, Cam.
[1929.283]

The spearhead has a pointed leaf-shaped blade.
The socket is winged and encrusted with copper-
alloy, silver and gold.

This is either a Carolingian import, like D16, or
an Anglo-Saxon copy.

D7 Two-edged iron sword
River Thames, Temple, London BM [56, 7-1, 1404]

It has a fullered blade. The guard and upper guard
are flat and curve away from the trilobate pommel.
L.84.0cm.

D8 The Play Hatch iron sword
Sonning Eye, Berks. RM [112.66]

The sword has a two-edged fullered blade, now
broken. It is inlaid just below the guard with a
trellis pattern. The guards are straight and the
pommel is lost. L.95.0cm.

Found during quarrying at Play Hatch, Sonning
Eye, together with a bronze ringed pin and iron
knife, six iron arrowheads, an iron strip, and
human bones. These finds almost certainly represent a Viking male burial and represent the wide-
ranging nature of Viking activity. The sword
originally had a triangular pommel and is a
Scandinavian type in use from the early Viking
period to the tenth century. The knife, however, is
an Anglo-Saxon type, while the ringed pin is Irish.

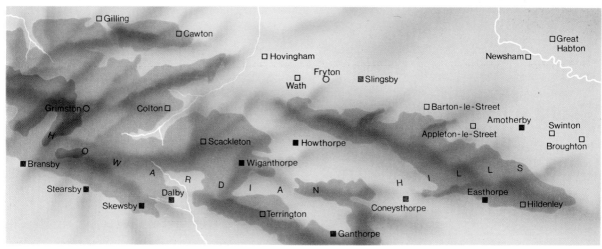

■ Scandinavian named villages □ English named villages ○ Grimston hybrids

D12

D9   Four iron arrow-heads
Sørup, Zealand; single-find NMI [C24551]

Leaf-shaped blades with offset tangs. L. (maximum) 12.4cm.

D10   Three iron axe-heads
1 Bearded axe. No provenance. NMI [C7335]

L.21.5cm. Edge 12.2cm.

2 Bjerup Mose, Zealand; single-find. NMI [C13780]

L.13.2cm. Edge c.7.0cm.

3 Hoby, Lolland, probably from a grave. NMI [C7332]

L.13.7cm. Edge c.6.5cm.

D11   Two iron spear-heads
1 Riis Fattiggård, north Jutland; grave find. NMI [C11776]
2 No provenance. FHM [6221]

1 A slim leaf-shaped blade. L.36.5cm.
2 A leaf-shaped blade. The socket has two wings: the end is missing. L.37.3cm.

D12   One single-edged and two double-edged swords
1 Sørup, Zealand; single-find. NMI [C24550]
2 Søndersø, north Jutland; single-find. NMI [C1572]
3 Osted, Zealand; single-find. NMI [C5818]

1 Single-edged sword. The upper and lower guards are straight and the pommel triangular. The covering of the grip is missing. The rest of the hilt is decorated with a yellow metal (? brass) which originally covered the surface but now has a striped effect. Total length 89.5cm: length of blade (incomplete) 74.0cm; grip 9.5cm.
2 Double-edged sword. The blade is pattern-welded, the upper and lower guards are straight and the pommel tripartite. The whole hilt is decorated with silver and brass mainly in geometrical patterns. Total length 89.5cm, length of blade (incomplete) 73.0cm; grip 9.3cm.
3 Double-edged sword. The blade is pattern-welded, the upper and lower guards are straight and the pommel tripartite. The covering of the grip is missing. The rest of the hilt was decorated with silver of which only small traces of fine zig-zag patterns of inlaid wire and plain encrusted areas remain. Total length 79.0cm; length of blade (incomplete) 64.5cm; grip 8.7cm.

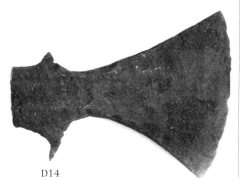

D16   D15   D14

D13   Iron stirrup
York YM [644.47]

The stirrup is made from a rod of circular section hammered flat to provide the foot rest. The ends are then bent up to form a D-shape and twisted together to provide the loop for the stirrup leather. L.10.0 × W. (loop) 4.92cm.

This type of stirrup is thought to date from the early or middle Viking period and is transitional towards the more normal type of Viking-Age stirrup in the West. This has a rectangular foot-plate often with triangular side plates (see no. I5).

D14   Iron axe with expanding blade
Coppergate, York YM [551.45.48]

The axe has a slightly asymmetrically expanding blade with a convex cutting edge. There are spurs projecting from either side of the socket. L.14.5 × W.10.8cm.

D15   Iron sword
York YM [643.1.48]

It has a two-edged fullered blade, a straight guard, and a semi-circular pommel. L.47.8 × W.12.0cm.

A second sword of this type is known from York, and an example is known also from Nottingham. In Scandinavia this sword-type was current in the tenth century.

D16   Iron socketed spearhead with a pointed leaf-shaped blade
River Ouse, York YM

The socket is vertically grooved, and has a pair of wings. L.43.4 × W.5.2cm.

Such winged spear-heads are thought to be ninth-century imports from the Carolingian Empire. Similar spearheads are known in England from Nottingham and Braham's Farm, Cambs. (no. D6).

D17   Danish-form iron axe-head
Jubbergate, York SCM [J.93.1172]

The axe has an asymmetrically expanding blade, and a convex cutting edge. L.21.0 × W.16.4cm.

For comparable axes see nos. D14 and I6.

D18   The Alfred Jewel (replica)
N. Petherton, Somerset AM [original, 1836.371]

The jewel consists of a gold base-plate decorated with a cloisonné enamel human figure holding a pair of plant stems which are linked at the base. The plate is covered by a piece of rock crystal which tapers towards the flat top and is held in place by an openwork gold frame decorated with the inscription "AELFRED MEC HEHT GEWYRCAN" below which is a zone of gold filigree and granulation. At the apex of the jewel, the ends of the frame terminate at an animal's head covered in granulation, and with the features picked out in filigree. A plain cylindrical tube pierced by a single rivet issues from the animal's mouth. The flat underside of the jewel is decorated with an incised plant scroll having a hatched background. L.6.2cm × W.3.1cm.

It is known that King Alfred sent an *æstel* – thought to be a pointer for picking out the text in a manuscript – to each bishop in his kingdom together with a copy of Pope Gregory's Pastoral

Care. The Alfred Jewel and a closely comparable piece from Minster Lovell, Oxfordshire, are usually identified as such *æstels*, the inscription on the Alfred Jewel being taken to refer to King Alfred. This interpretation is supported by the suggestion that the figure on the jewel should be interpreted as a personification of Sight which would be appropriate to such a function.

This theory has been challenged on the grounds that since there is no royal title in the inscription it does not refer to King Alfred. Moreover the inscription which can be translated "Alfred ordered me to be made" appears to be in a Mercian not a West Saxon dialect. These criticisms must carry some weight, but no convincing alternative function for the jewels has been suggested.

D18a Silver penny of Alfred, King of Wessex, 871–899
Cuerdale hoard Lancs. BM [BMC 303]

Wt.1.33gm (20.5gr).
Obv: EL FR ED REX, cross in centre. Rev: ELDA ME FEC (Elda made me) in two lines.

D18b Silver penny of Guthrum, baptised with the name of Æthelstan (II) 878–890
Cuerdale hoard, Lancs. BM, [BMC 97]

Wt.1.36gm (21gr).
Obv: ED EL IA RE, small cross in centre. Rev: ELDA ME FEC (Elda made me) in two lines.

D19 The Lilla Howe hoard
Lilla Howe, Goathland, Yorks. MCM, L[12.6.79.14-19]

1 Four silver strap-ends each having an animal head terminal. In each case the strap fitted into a split in the upper end and was held in place by two rivets. Each strap-end has the long edges beaded and is decorated with a rectangular panel having a beaded frame. In two cases the panel is filled with a contorted ribbon-like animal involved in conventionalised foliage. Each of the remaining strap-ends is decorated with two pairs of outward-facing animal heads, one above the other, linked together by interlacing strands. L.c.6.3cm.
2 Two sheet-gold discs decorated in beaded filigree with four inward-facing *fleurs-de-lys* inside a circular field surrounded by a running scroll. D.3.6cm.

Found in a mound with other jewellery, now lost, and clearly forming part of a Viking-Age hoard. The strap ends are of the normal ninth-century Anglo-Saxon type, although a little broader and more pointed than usual, and appear to have been the work of a single craftsman. The filigree of the discs has been compared with similar Anglo-Saxon filigree work, but the technique was known also in Scandinavia, and the ornament of the central field corresponds closely with that of a disc brooch from York which has clear Scandinavian parallels.

D20 The Bolton Percy coin hoard
Bolton Percy, Yorks. YM[1967/6]

1 The pot: Small Badorf-type vessel with everted rim and flat base.
2 The coins: The complete hoard numbered 1,775 copper stycas, issued in the ninth century in the names of the kings of Northumbria and the archbishops of York. This coinage was subject to

D24

much contemporary forgery and imitation; it is not yet possible to say exactly when such irregular issues ceased. The hoard may have been deposited about the year 867 or a little later; found in 1967.

Bolton Percy, eight miles south-west of York, was the site of another such hoard, discovered in 1847. The composition of both hoards matches that of those found in York itself. The 1967 find was dispersed at auction in 1971, after all the coins had been recorded. About 250 coins, together with the pot, now belong to the Yorkshire Museum, York.

D21 The Croydon hoard
Old Palace, Croydon, Surrey AM [1909, 556, 558-61] and MCM, L[53.114.64 and 65]

The silver hoard consists of two ingots and several pieces of hack silver, most of which are fragments of armlets. When discovered the hoard contained a number of coins which serve to date its deposition to *c.*875. The hoard is, thus, of unusually early date. It is also unusual in that it is the only Viking-type silver hoard known south of the Thames.

D22 Lead-alloy pendant in the form of a ship
16-22 Coppergate, York YCC [YAT 1980.7.7606]

In the position of the mast is a long parallel-sided extension pierced at the top for suspension. Lightly incised on it is the mast, and similar lines indicate the planks of the hull. L.5.7 × W.3.4cm.

D23 Ship's prow and other motifs engraved on a piece of amber
Elsehoved, Fyn; single-find. NM1 [C28602]

L.5.6cm.
The Vikings were fascinated by ships; casually scratched images of them are found on many objects. The spiral prow sketched on this piece of amber is reminiscent of the prow of the Oseberg ship from Norway.

D24 Bronze brooch in the form of a ship
Lillevang, Bornholm; grave find. NM1 [C2894]

The brooch is in the form of a stylized Viking ship. It has strakes, animal-head posts at stem and stern, a face at the mast-head and shields along the gunwale. L.5.9cm.

The elegant lines of ships were used for many images. They appear on jewellery like this brooch and in the form of monuments (as in the ship-settings). They were also depicted on runestones and coins. Poets sang their praises and foreign writers spoke of them in fear and admiration.

D18a

D18b

D25

D25   Bronze horse-shaped mount from a ship's vane
Probably from Lolland; purchased. NM II [D12128]

Originally completely gilt. The figure is in the round, perforated through feet and ears. The head, mouth and legs are emphasized by engraved contours. The fullness of the body is indicated by three engraved lines. Spirals mark the hips and Ringerike-style tendrils form the mane. H.9.5cm.

The magnificent vanes of the Viking-Age ships were secured to the mast-head or the prow. Vanes from Norway and Sweden show that they consisted of a gilt and decorated bronze sheet, the lower edge convex, the upper edge straight – with an animal, like the Lolland horse, mounted on top. Small holes bored along the convex edge of the vane presumably held ribbons which would indicate the direction of the wind. Such objects hint at rich furnishings in these ships.

D26   T-shaped axe with original handle
Milk Street, London
Museum of London

The axe has an incomplete iron T-shaped head held in place on the expanding wooden haft by an iron wedge. The original haft is curved as if to keep the carpenter's hand from scraping the wood he is shaving. L.43.0cm.

This was the typical late Anglo-Saxon carpenters' axe; from an eleventh-century context.

D27   Iron T-shaped axe head
River Thames, Battersea
Museum of London [A17302]

17.5 × 26.5cm.
For similar axes, see nos. D26 and YW2.

D28   Keelson from a ship
Hasnæs, east Jutland; found on the beach NM SL

Oak. Only the central portion with the step for the mast remains, both ends are missing. The step measures 15 × 15cm at the bottom and 18 × 75cm at the upper edge; towards the stern the step forms a channel in the keelson with a rising, gently curving bottom. In the front of the step a vertical natural grown strut rises to a height of 42cm above the base of the hole in which the mast was stepped; the strut is the same width as the step. The total height at this point is 60cm. At both ends the keelson tapers to half the height and a third of the width of the central portion. Along the edges at the top are traces of a flat rabbet. The bottom of the keelson is rounded with notches to accommodate the ribs. Above the notches are traces of the iron nails which fastened the knees, securing the keelson to the ribs. L.255cm. W.28cm. H.60cm.

The keelson lay across the ribs on top of the keel and formed the lower support for the mast. The method of raising and lowering the mast depended on the design of the keelson and the mast-fish (see no. D29) and this design also determined the stability of the mast.

D29   Mast-fish from a ship
Mariager Fjord off Hadsund, north Jutland; found in the water. NM1 [C6010a]

Oak. A long split in the mast-fish is held together with a modern iron band. From a rectangular base, 56cm wide and 5.6cm in thickness, the timber rises to a 45cm-wide top; at one end is a flat channel with 6-10cm high edges, open at the end of the fish and finished with a low ridge against the straight edge of the mast step, where it is 32cm wide. The other side of the step is carved from the rounded, domed portion which rises in a curve from the forward end of the fish. The hole which forms the step for the mast is about 38cm long, indicating a mast thickness of about 25cm as the mast was presumably secured with wedges. The bottom of the hole is much enlarged (40 × 90cm), as the domed part is hollowed-out from below. This design allowed the mast to be lowered to a position some 30° above the horizontal, the low ridge acting as a pivot. L.380cm. W.56cm. H.35cm.

A mast-fish was fixed at deck level. It served to guide the mast when it was raised or lowered and, together with shrouds and stays, to hold it steady in an upright position. With a keelson and mast-fish like nos. D28 and D29, the mast was lowered forward in the ship. A characteristic of the Viking-Age warships – in contrast to trading vessels – is that the mast could be raised and lowered without much trouble.

D30   Ship's steering-oar
Found in Kattegat off Vorså, north Jutland. BM F

Made of oak, the oar has a painted fore-edge while the aft-edge is square cut. The section varies both in form and thickness. At the top of the oar are two oval perforations for the attachment of the rudder bar. Near the top of the blade is a circular hole for the suspension of the steering-oar. Total length 280cm. Length of blade 192cm. The thickness of the blade tapers gradually from 10cm at the suspension hole to 1.5cm at the bottom.

The steering-oar was on the right side of the ship as it sailed – the starboard side.

D31   Ship's anchor
Ribe, from the settlement. ASR [D7887]

Iron T-shaped anchor with curved arms. At the top a ring for a rope or chain. At the base traces of a ring for the attachment of a float. L.c.150cm. W.c.96cm.

D32   Ship's stem-piece (copy)
Skuldelev, Zealand; found in the water as part of Wreck 3. NM SL

The original was carved of a single piece of oak. It has a V-shaped cross-section with stepped after-edges for the attachment by clinkernails of a strake to each step. The outside is carved to give the impression that the strakes continue towards the tip of the stem. Below the point of the stem is a bored hole 4cm in diameter. The outer curve of the stem is 405cm long and follows the arc of a circle of about 350cm radius. L.370cm.

This wreck, together with four other vessels, was sunk in the Roskilde fjord off Skuldelev in order to create an obstruction for defensive purposes across an important sailing channel leading to Roskilde. Wreck 3 was a small trading or cargo vessel, about 13.8m long, 3.3m wide and about 1.6m from bottom to gunwale. It could have transported a load of about 5 tons and was a proper sailing ship with the mast firmly fixed in the keelson and few oar-holes.

D33 Cross-section of a Viking cargo ship; a reconstruction

The remains of the original, called the Skuldelev Wreck 3, are to be seen at the Viking Ship Museum, Roskilde, Denmark. The ship was 13.8 metres long, 3.4 metres wide across the beam, and 1.3 metres deep from the top of the gunwale to the lower edge of the keel. The structure was mainly of oak.

This coastal trading ship, excavated in 1962 in the Roskilde Fjord, Denmark, gives a unique presentation of Viking ships – the slenderness and grace of the structure, the high quality of the timber and the elegant and sound principles of construction. The cast of the stem-piece as well as the reconstructed cross-section amidships, seen here, serve to illustrate this.

This ship was built around the year 1000, probably in the Roskilde Fjord region, of selected high-quality oak. The oak trunks were split to give slender and durable planks as well as the keel and stringers, and the supporting internal structure of frames and knees was made of compass timber, i.e. wood grown to the required shape. The cross-section amidships shows the basic lay-out of the hull with eight overlapping planks each side, supported at the bottom by a transverse floor-timber nailed to the planking with wooden pegs, and in the sides by stringers acting as longitudinal frames. The mast-foot is seated in a hole in the keelson, and at the mast-frame a particular strong transverse beam is introduced to strengthen the hull amidships. In contrast to the warships, the cargo ship has no deck in the middle, and thus there was room for stowing cargo there while the crew worked the ship from the halfdecks fore and aft.

The cargo-hold took up 3.7m of the total length of the ship, providing about 350 cubic feet for the goods which, in this ship, would probably be a varied selection of trade items carried between trading centres and beach markets in the Baltic and North Sea areas. The skipper and crew, totalling five or six men, would most likely all work as sailors on the way and as merchants in the ports.

The worn-down bottom planks and keel of the original vessel show this ship as having had a long life when it was chosen to block the channel at Skuldelev and thereby protect the inner reaches of the Roskilde Fjord and the town of Roskilde itself from sea-borne attacks in the mid-eleventh century.

OLE CRUMLIN-PEDERSEN

Though the scene (left) from the Bayeux Tapestry is of a later date, it closely resembles the moment of disembarkation from a Viking ship: the mast is lowered and horses step easily from the shallow-draught boat.

FROM SWORD TO PLOUGH

And that year, Halfdan shared out the lands of the Northumbrians, and they proceeded to plough and to support themselves.

THIS TERSE CHARACTERISATION of the most significant events of 876 in the north, as the *Anglo-Saxon Chronicle* saw it, serves to underline the importance of the rural economy for the Scandinavians coming to England in the ninth century. Of course, there were the town-dwellers of York, Lincoln and elsewhere, but the relationship of town and country at this period was more intimate than that today, and the functioning of the urban economy would have been dependent to a considerable extent on the exploitation of the land.

Ironically, in view of the chronicler's statements, historians and archaeologists have far less evidence to hand for a picture of settlement in the country than for the towns. It is rare for individual rural settlements to be described in any great detail in literary sources, although recent work on land-charters and records of land-holdings have perhaps indicated the general nature of the exploitation of large parts of the landscape through estates held by great landowners or the Church. In some cases, there are records of Scandinavians taking over such land-holdings, and in others of Anglo-Saxons buying back land from Scandinavians after such seizures.

Archaeologically, the contrast between our knowledge of urban and rural settlements in the Viking period is stark. There are, on the one hand, the great deposits of Coppergate in York, and on the other, the relative sparseness of artefacts from Ribblehead on the Pennines. It is essentially the same contrast between Lincoln and Goltho on the Lincolnshire clay-lands. It is not simply that foreign objects are to be found in commercial centres and only infrequently on small farms, but also that the nature of the deposits in the towns is much more conducive to survival of a greater quantity and wider range of articles than elsewhere.

The relative absence of artefacts in terms of quantity makes cultural interpretation of rural sites that much more difficult. If the few artefacts likely to be found are the basic articles of everyday living, will they differ from one another on an Anglo-Saxon farm, a Danish village, or on a Danish Viking hamlet in England? And if farms or villages were established by incoming Scandinavians, they would surely have been as likely to use local materials

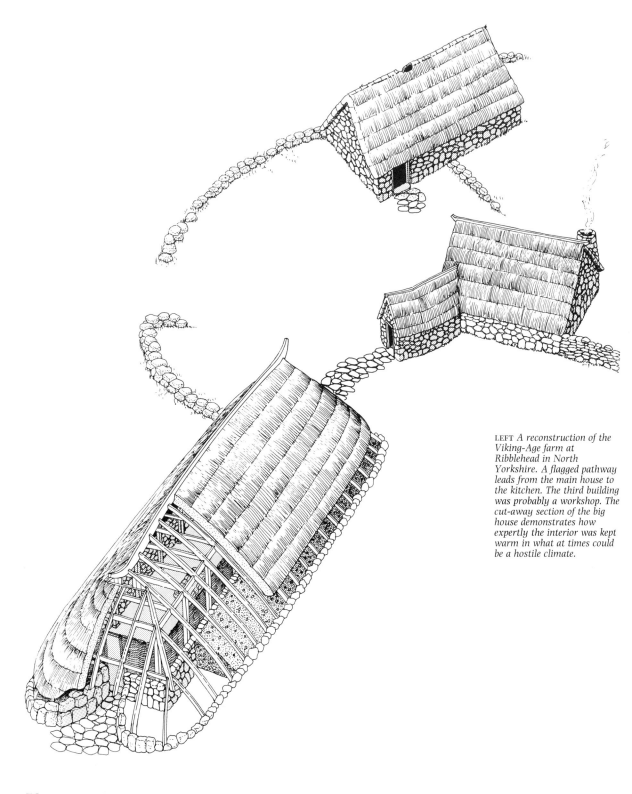

LEFT *A reconstruction of the Viking-Age farm at Ribblehead in North Yorkshire. A flagged pathway leads from the main house to the kitchen. The third building was probably a workshop. The cut-away section of the big house demonstrates how expertly the interior was kept warm in what at times could be a hostile climate.*

and local traditions for house-building as their own imported methods. When the earliest little timber buildings with, presumably, clay walls were found below the later deserted village of Goltho, it was difficult to assign a close dating to this phase, because of the sparseness of finds, and thus to decide who might have built the houses: Anglo-Saxons, Scandinavians, or perhaps even Normans.

The contrast between the situations in Denmark and in England is considerable. Recent years have seen the large-scale excavations of rural settlements such as Vorbasse and Sædding, revolutionising the Danish picture, previously dependent largely on the results from the excavation of a small part of one Jutland village – Lindholm Høje. No such major programme has taken place in England for this period.

How, then, do we try to look for Viking rural settlement in England? In the first place, the approach has to be based on a variety of evidence. Certain literary sources, place-names and pagan graves will help to give some understanding of the nature of Viking activity in an area in relation to the local people. In any particular area it will indicate whether settlement was a Scandinavian take-over, both economically and politically, or an infilling around existing settlements implying peaceful co-existence with the local inhabitants. More specifically, with a particular locality, records from charters or other historical sources and archaeological evidence should be searched for indications of links with the Viking incomers. Secondly, in archaeological terms, it is a question of looking at a specific localised project where Viking activity is suspected – as at Repton in Derbyshire; or at the multi-period survey of an area, preferably with a fossil landscape that has been preserved, which might cover a phase associated with the Viking period.

In recent years two survey projects of upland areas in the North of England have been undertaken by individuals who have come across rural settle-ments with some claim to be farms dating from the Viking period. In the area of the Upper Pennines in the Dent, Settle and Lune Valley area, there is considerable evidence to support the location of settlements in the Viking period. There are distinctive Scandinavian features of the dialect in this area; the place-names of the Sedbergh-Settle area are approximately sixty per cent Scandinavian in origin; and stray archaeological finds from the area include a huge silver brooch from Casterton and a hoard from Halton Moor with a very fine silver torc. In addition, stone sculpture from the region has distinctive features associated with Viking styles.

Excavations at Ribblehead, following detailed survey work, revealed a quasi-courtyard grouping of three buildings associated with a field system extending over three acres (1.21 hectares). A date in the second half of the ninth century is proposed for the farm on the basis of four coins, three of which were found in the wall-fill of the major building. Artefacts recovered reflect a mixture of craft and agricultural activities, most notable of which are a small clapper bell and a rotary quern for grinding corn (no. E2a).

These Ribblehead excavations have revealed a farmstead whose layout and relationship to adjacent field-systems seem to be reflected at four or five sites discovered in Upper Teesdale on a terrace above the river at Simy Folds. Here again, there appear to be buildings arranged around a courtyard and associated with a network of field boundaries, either contemporary or earlier than these settlements. Two of these have been partially excavated: one site showing domestic occupation; the other, considerable evidence of iron-working. The charcoal from one small building has been used for radio-carbon dating which may well place the farmstead between the years 710 and 850.

The direct dating from coins found at Ribblehead, together with the related evidence both archaeological and linguistic, seems to indicate that it must have been occupied in the Viking period, although it is much more difficult to assert conclusively that it was occupied by Scandinavians. The excavator's own conclusions are rightly cautious. It is equally impossible on the basis of one radiocarbon date and two limited excavation seasons to draw sweeping cultural or chronological conclusions about Simy Folds, although again there is some support from the linguistic evidence and other sources for Scandinavian influence if not settlement in this area. Nevertheless, the exciting possibility remains of examining a group of similar rural settle-ments. Total excavation of the group and some of the associated field-systems might well indicate whether they were contemporary land-holdings or successive settlements; whether all from one period, or spanning a range which includes the Viking period. At present the sites of Ribblehead and Simy Folds are the nearest we can get to seeing the likely nature of upland rural settlement in the Viking period.

For the lowland areas, the picture is more difficult to get into focus. Ploughing and later building on the sites of farms and villages will, in many cases, have destroyed the critical evidence. Even to establish the existence of settlement on a site in the Viking period is therefore difficult enough. In the absence of conclusive morphological or typological evidence, it is quite impossible to assert with any confidence that particular structures found are Scandinavian in origin.

A fine series of halls on the manor-site of Goltho in Lincolnshire and a hall at Waltham Abbey in Essex, dated to the Viking period, give an indication of the nature of high-status sites in eastern England, but were they Anglo-Saxon, Viking or Anglo-Scandinavian in character? Corroborative evidence is hard to find. In the past few years, a number of large-scale excavations of the early Anglo-Saxon period have taken place. An urgent need now is to find the English equivalents of the Danish farms at Vorbasse and Sædding.

CHRISTOPHER MORRIS

E1 Kirkby Stephen hogback
St John's Church, Kirkby Stephen, Cumbria

Sandstone; decorated with three rows of tegulation below the curved ridge-moulding. L.80.6cm.

Stones like this are thought to be based on the architecture of north European farm buildings. In England, during the Viking period, farmhouses with similarly shingled roofs would have dotted the landscape. Tenth century.

E2a Matching top and bottom stones from a rotary quern, both of millstone grit
Ribblehead, Yorks. Alan King Esq.

D.45.0 × T.22.0cm.

The quern is intact except for the original handle used for turning the top stone. Such querns were the normal implement for grinding corn.

E2b Group of lead flows
Ribblehead, Yorks. Alan King Esq.

L.*c.*5cm.

Similar lead flows are known from York where they are associated with metalworking debris. Their presence at Ribblehead suggests an Anglo-Scandinavian settlement in which lead or silver-working took place.

E2c Æthelred II. Copper styca. Second reign, *c.*867
Ribblehead, Yorks. Alan King Esq.

Obv: EDILDE (Æthelred). Rev: OICL (Odiler – the moneyer).

E3 Viking-period pot sherds
Wharram Percy, N. Yorks. Lord Middleton

Wharram sherds do not represent a great many pots, but it is important that they were found scattered over the whole site of this deserted medieval village. They match exactly the same sort of pot that was being used in contemporary York.

Wharram Percy – the first part of its name is said to be a Scandinavian word for 'valley' – first developed as an Anglo-Saxon settlement in this Yorkshire dale along a line of eight springs. The series of excavated mills by the mill-pond were used for grinding corn from middle Anglo-Saxon times through the Viking period. And it is more than likely, think the excavators, that Wharram Percy was then occupied, partially at least, by Scandinavian farmers.

E4a Part of an iron bridle bit
Goltho Manor, Lincs. L.M. [643]

It consists of a straight bar which swells slightly at one end before terminating in a circular loop. At the other end is a slightly larger ovoid loop. The surface is lightly grooved. L.8.5cm.

Found in the stone path leading to the bow-sided hall, and dated to *c.*875–940. The grooving suggests that it was originally plated or inlaid with a non-ferrous metal.

E4b Bun-shaped lead-alloy spindle whorl
Goltho Manor, Lincs. L.M. [629]

D.2.5cm.

Found in the clay floor of the bow-sided hall kitchen, dated to *c.*875–940. Similar whorls are known also from York.

E4c Iron knife with broken blade
Goltho Manor, Lincs. L.M. [613]

This is shouldered at the junction with the long tang, which is also broken. L.13.8cm.

Found in the ninth/tenth-century levels of soil south of the halls. Similar knives with the handles surviving are known from York.

E4d Iron knife having a slightly leaf-shaped blade and broken tang
Goltho Manor, Lincs. L.M. [637]

L.7.7cm.

Recovered from the old soil level in the yard north of the halls and dated to *c.*800–940.

E4e Iron knife with a pointed blade. The tang is broken away
Goltho Manor, Lincs. L.M. [618]

L.6.4cm.

Found north of the weaving shed in levels dated *c.*875–940.

E1

E4f Iron spud
Goltho Manor, Lincs. L.M. [638]

The spud consists of a flat trapezoid plate from the narrow end of which develops a short tang. L.13.2. W.6.7cm.

Recovered from the old soil level in the yard north of the halls, and dated *c*.800–940. Such tools were used for weeding.

E5 Copper-alloy disc
Oxshott Wood, Surrey BM [1955, 10-2, 1]

The disc has a plain frame with a median groove. Inside it is an equal-armed cross having ribbed arms whose ends are drawn out into loose interlace. D.2.9cm.

This is one of a group of such discs known from East Anglia, although loosely provenanced examples are known also from Kent and Leicester (no. G39). The south-eastern distribution of this group is underlined by the close comparison between the ornament on the discs and that of the pendants from the Saffron Walden grave (no. E27). The ornament is derived from the Scandinavian Borre-style ring chain. Objects decorated with a similar derived version of the Borre style were also made in York (see no. YMW13).

E6 Bone cylinder decorated in low relief in the Ringerike style
No known provenance. BM [1921, 7-14, 1]

The decoration consists of a collar around the circumference composed of three downward-facing plant sprays linked by curved bands. A human head emerges from the top of one of the sprays. Above the collar is a coiled animal with a ribbon-like body, and a lightly sketched plant spray. Below it are a series of lightly incised designs including a pendant cross and a ribbon-like animal with its body facing an interlace knot. L.10.5cm.

This is one of a number of objects from southern England decorated in the eleventh-century Scandinavian Ringerike style. The cylinder appears to have been a trial piece rather than a functional object.

E7 Rectangular silver side-plate and rhomboid roof-plate from a house-shaped shrine
Unknown provenance. BM [1954, 12-1, 1 and 2]

The side-plate is decorated with three wheel crosses, each with the angles of the arms filled with interlace triquetras. The interstices between the crosses and the edge of the plate are filled with further interlace triquetras. The roof-plate is divided by a saltire into triangular fields, three of which are filled with contorted animals having speckled, contoured bodies. The other contains interlace flanking a human mask. On both plates the engraving was filled with niello. L.12.6cm.

Although the technique of the plates, using a combination of silver and niello, is that of the Anglo-Saxon Trewhiddle style, the animal ornament seems to belong to the Scandinavian Jellinge tradition. The pieces, therefore, seem to be an attempt by an Anglo-Saxon craftsman to use a Scandinavian style which was foreign to him. The plates can be placed in the late ninth or early tenth century.

E6

E8 Iron knife with a swivelling blade and bone handle
77-9 Castle Street, Canterbury CAT [CB/R. 76-112.97]

The handle consists of two plates held by a pair of rivets at each end, on one pair of which the blade pivots. The projecting blade is short with a sloping back, the other end is longer and more rounded. The handle is decorated on one side with a panel of interlace, and on the other with a panel filled with a Borre-style ring chain. Both panels terminate in animal masks. L.10.3cm.

Similar swivelling blades are known from Winchester, Thetford, Northampton, and York, all in late Anglo-Saxon/Anglo-Scandinavian contexts. The decoration of the handle is best compared with that on Anglo-Scandinavian sculptures in northern England.

E10

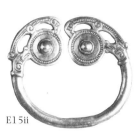

E15ii

E15i

E9 Cylindrical bone sleeve
Sawdon, Yorks. YM [632.48]

The sleeve is divided vertically by opposed pairs of perforations. One side of the sleeve is decorated with four rectangular interlace-filled fields; the other has a few lightly-incised lines, and another perforation towards the upper edge. L.6.8 × D.3.1cm.

The pelleted interlace in two of the panels is reminiscent of the tenth-century Scandinavian Mammen style.

E10 Cast copper-alloy disc brooch, decorated with a backward-looking quadruped within a billeted border
Ixworth, Suffolk. UMAA Cam. [1902.252]

D.3.0cm.

For discussion, see no. YD11.

E11 The Newbiggin brooch
Newbiggin Moor, Dacre, Cumbria BM [1909, 6-24, 2]

This silver "thistle" brooch has a ball-shaped pin head and terminals, each of which has the front brambled and the reverse decorated with an incised marigold pattern. The section of the pin ranges from circular at the top, to hexagonal before becoming lozenge-shaped. L.51.2 × D. (loop) 19.0cm.

The type originated in Ireland in the second half of the ninth century, but became much more widespread and elaborate during the first half of the tenth century. Such large brooches must have been made for the display of wealth rather than for everyday wear.

E12 Penannular silver brooch and ring
Orton Scar, Cumbria S of A, Lon.

1 The brooch has flat, expanding terminals, each decorated with five bosses, and a background filled with incised animal ornament. L.28.3cm.
2 A circular silver arm or neck ring made of a twisted bar tapering towards the ends, which are hooked together. D.14.1cm.

The objects were found in 1847 in a crevice in the limestone on the top of Orton Scar. This type of penannular brooch was made in Ireland in the late ninth and early tenth centuries. Fragments are known in England from the Cuerdale and Goldsborough hoards dated to *c*.903 and *c*.920 respectively (see no. E15). The arm or neck ring with its hooked ends is typical of the Viking Age.

E13 Copper-alloy ringed pin
Meols, Cheshire. GM [174.S.1976]

The pin has a looped head and penannular ring of circular section decorated with areas of transverse hatching alternating with undecorated areas. The top of the shank is flattened and decorated with incised ornament, and the shank is shouldered about half-way along its length. L.12.7 × D. (head) 3.6cm.

Ringed pins with a shouldered shank whose upper end is flattened were probably made in Scandinavia. Similar pins are known, for example, from Birka in Sweden and Aggersborg, Denmark.

E14 Copper-alloy ringed pin
1-11 Crook Street, Chester GM [CRS 73-4. SF 193]

It has a polyhedral head decorated with punched dots, and a stirrup ring. L.15.4cm.

Such pins were an Irish type much favoured by the Vikings.

E15 The Goldsborough hoard
Goldsborough Church, Knaresborough, Yorks. BM [59, 5-11, 1-11, and 59, 7-26, 1-10]

1 Thistle brooch with a brambled, ball-shaped pin head and terminals. D.6.8 × L.19.5cm.
2 Hoop of a bossed penannular brooch. D.8.5cm.
3 Part of a penannular brooch terminal. L.3.0cm.
4 Silver Thor's hammer (see no. F2).
5 Various pieces of hack-silver. L.6.0cm.
6 Anglo-Saxon and Kufic coins.

When discovered the hoard also contained two silver ingots. The coins serve to date its deposition to *c*.920. The burial of this hoard, and another from the Bossall/Flaxton area (see no. E24) dated to *c*.927, reflects the political instability in the reign of York as the Viking kings of Dublin and the Anglo-Saxon kings struggled for control of the city.

E16 Gold penannular arm ring
Wendover, Essex BM [49, 2-10, 1]

The arm ring is made of two rods twisted together, with additional twisted wires between the rods. The rods taper towards the ends where they are hammered together. D.8.7cm.

Such massive twisted arm and neck rings either in gold or silver are characteristic of the Viking Age, and this is one of the commonest types. Such rings were intended for wear, but were also a convenient way of storing bullion. When necessary they would be cut up and used as a medium of exchange. Some types were even produced to fairly standard weights for this purpose.

E17 Plaited gold finger ring
Soberton, Hants. BM [51, 3-13, 1]

The ring is composed of several rods plaited together. These rods taper towards the ends where they are hammered together. D.2.9cm.

Found with a second finger ring of circular section ornamented with punched dots, and coins from the reigns of Edward the Confessor to William the Conqueror. These coins place the deposition of the hoard in the late eleventh century, although the finger ring is typical of the Viking Age.

E18 The Castle Esplanade hoard
Castle Esplanade, Chester GM [44a, 5.1969]

Five ingot bars, ten pieces of hack silver, and a group of coins from the Castle Esplanade hoard, Chester; together with the pot in which they were found. The pot has a flat-topped rim, slightly concave neck, high rounded shoulder and sagging base. There is roller-stamped decoration at the shoulder. H. (pot) 14.5 × D.12.0cm.

The hoard contained forty-two pieces of hack silver, eighty-four ingots or fragments of ingots, sixteen small pellets or flattened bars and five hundred and twenty-two coins. Five ingots were recovered subsequently. Some fifty to a hundred coins were dispersed. The coins date the deposition of the hoard to *c*.970.

E19   Stone mould for casting ingots
24-46 Lower Bridge Street, Chester GM [LBS 74-6 SF 443]

The mould has a square section with a different-sized slot for casting ingots in each of the long faces. The mould was found in association with industrial waste and a smelting hearth. L.9.0 × W.3.0 × T.2.5cm.

E20   Gold finger ring
St Werburgh Street, Chester GM [80.R 1971]

It is composed of two rods twisted together. The rods taper towards the back where they are shaped into a straight bar linking the ends. D.c.3.0cm.

Like the ring from Hungate, York (no. YD28), this finger ring is a smaller version of the massive Viking-Age arm and neck rings.

E21   Gold finger ring
Middlewich, Cheshire GM [112.R 1976]

The ring has an octagonal section. The ends taper towards the back where they overlap and are twisted around each other. D.2.3cm.

Although similar in construction to other Viking-Age rings, it has recently been suggested that it is of earlier date.

E22   Penannular silver arm-ring
Long Wittenham, Berks. AM[1957.61]

This arm-ring is composed of rods twisted together and having globular terminals. D.6.5cm.

Similar arm-rings are known from the Douglas hoard, Isle of Man; and the hoard from Port Glasgow, Scotland, both deposited c.975. The use of globular terminals is not a Scandinavian feature, and it has been suggested that this type of armlet is of Anglo-Saxon manufacture.

E22

E24   Circular silver armlet
Flaxton, Yorks. YM [700.48]

This armlet has a convex section tapering abruptly towards the ends which are hooked together. It is decorated with a median beaded line on either side of which are two rows of punched trefoils. D.8.3 × H.2.3cm.

Found in a lead box with hacksilver and coins which date the deposition of the group to c.927. Fragments of similar armlets with punched ornament are known from the Cuerdale hoard, Lancs.

E25   The Cuerdale hoard
Cuerdale, Lancs. MCM, L[53.114] and AM[1909.519-522, 526-527, 539-541, 545]

Group of silver ingots, hack-silver, and coins. D.12.0cm.

The hoard was discovered in 1840 during repairs to the banks of the River Ribble, and originally consisted of some 40 kilos of silver contained in a lead chest. Its principal components were 7,000 English and Continental coins, together with a small number of Kufic coins and some from Hedeby; together with about 1,300 pieces of silver, mostly ingots and hack-silver. The coins date the deposition of the hoard to c.903.

E25

E29

E26   The Wensley grave group

Wensley Churchyard, Yorks. BM [1967, 7-3, 1-4]

1 Two-edged iron sword, the pattern-welded blade being broken and heavily corroded. The undecorated guard and upper guard curve away from the grip. The trilobate pommel is decorated with applied silver strips and panels carrying incised geometrical and formalised leaf ornament filled with niello. There is a similarly-decorated silver strip below the pommel. L.81.5cm.
2 Fragmentary iron spear-head with an unsplit socket pierced by four bronze rivets. L.56.0cm.
3 Fragment of a curved iron sickle blade. L.15.3cm.
4 Iron knife. L.15.5cm.

The objects were discovered during grave-digging and accompanied a male skeleton oriented East-West. The sword was on the man's right and the other objects were on the left with their points towards the skeleton's feet. The sword falls into the same group as the River Witham and Gilling swords nos. D2 and D3, and is Anglo-Saxon; but the burial from which it comes is clearly Viking. The discovery of a pagan burial in a Christian churchyard shows the incoming settlers using the local cemetery for burial. This may explain the relative scarcity of Viking burials in England, since most of their burial places have remained in use down to the present day.

E27   The Saffron Walden grave group

Saffron Walden, Essex SWM [1902]

1 Pair of worn silver gilt pendants each decorated with an equal-armed cross, with the ends of the arms developing into double loops which interlace with a square. The original barrel-shaped loops have been replaced. L.5.5 × D.4.0cm.
2 Circular silver pendant decorated with an incised cross and having a circular perforation in each of the angles of the arms. L.4.2 × D.3.5cm.
3 Two spherical silver beads together with two cornelian, two crystal and two glass beads. D.1.8, L.2.2, D.1.5, D.1.6cm.

The grave in which these objects were found formed part of a late Anglo-Saxon cemetery. The pendants and beads were presumably strung together as a necklace. The decoration of the pair of pendants is related to the Scandinavian Borre style, but the third pendant and a copper-alloy strap end from the same grave but not on display are straightforward Anglo-Saxon products.

E28   Pair of gilt-bronze, double-shelled oval brooches

Bedale, Yorks. NMA, Edin. and Duke of Northumberland

The outer shell is decorated with cast openwork animal ornament and covers the plain inner shell, the two originally being wired together. The separately-cast bosses are lost. L.10.8cm.

The oval (or tortoise) brooch was the commonest women's brooch-type in Viking-Age Scandinavia, although it went out of use in the late Viking period, i.e. from the second half of the tenth-century onwards. Its occurrence in graves in England is a sure indication of Viking settlement. Such brooches were worn in pairs high on the chest, often with a third brooch of a different type between them. Necklaces might be strung between the two oval brooches.

E29   Cast copper-alloy trefoil brooch

Lakenheath Warren, Suffolk UMAA, Cam [1902.35]

There is an animal mask at the junction of the arms. Each arm is decorated with a convention-alised plant scroll. W.7.0cm.

Trefoil brooches were widely used in Viking-Age Scandinavia as the woman's third brooch, to go with a pair of brooches of another type (see no. E28). The trefoil shape and use of plant decoration were both derived from imported western European trefoil mounts.

E30   Flat, rectangular whalebone plaque

Ely, Cambs, UMAA, Cam. [1922.895]

At the top are a pair of incised, confronted animal heads, the carving of which is incomplete. Between the heads is a projecting ovoid handle. L.31.5 × W.19.0cm.

Such plaques are well known from rich female graves in Norway, but they are rare elsewhere. They were probably used for smoothing linen.

E31   Cast copper-alloy double-shelled oval brooch

Santon, Norfolk BM [88, 1-3, 1]

L.11.6cm.

This is one of a pair of identical oval brooches found in a grave together with an iron two-edged sword. The finds suggest that this was a double burial of a man and a woman.

E30

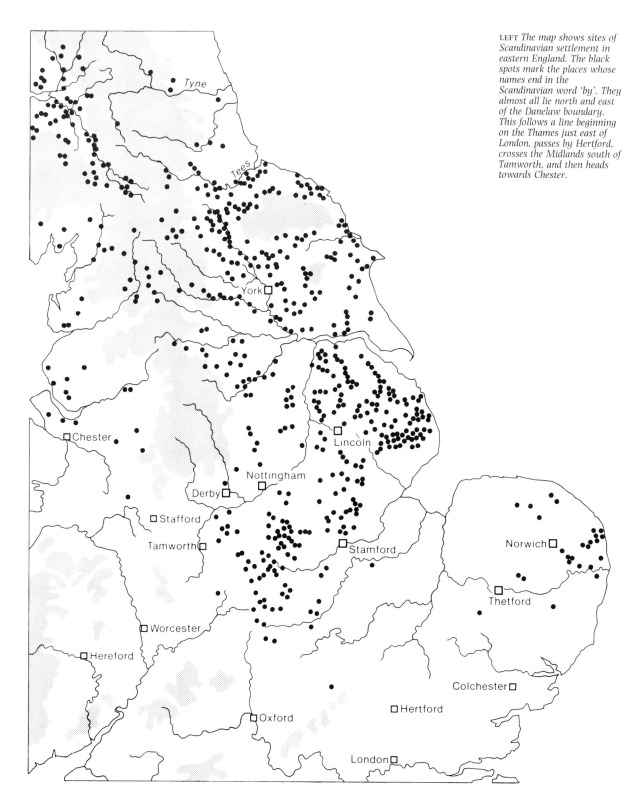

Tyne

Tees

York

Chester

Lincoln

Nottingham

Derby

Stafford

Tamworth

Stamford

Norwich

Thetford

Worcester

Hereford

Colchester

Oxford

Hertford

London

SIGNPOSTS TO SETTLING

T HE AREAS IN WHICH THE Vikings settled in England are best shown by a
distribution map of the place-names they coined. Any such map shows
the sites of the 854 place-names which end in *by*, a Scandinavian word
which was used in England to denote any kind of settlement from a
prosperous borough to a single farmstead. Although names ending in *by*
were still being coined after the Norman conquest, particularly in north-
west England, there is good reason to believe that most of the names were
adopted in the early years of the Viking settlement. Their distribution shows
that the Danes respected the boundary drawn in about 886 between their
territory and that of the English in the treaty between Alfred and Guthrum,
and it clearly reveals the areas of densest Scandinavian settlement. The
general pattern would remain largely unaltered, even if all the other
Scandinavian settlement names were to be plotted on the map, except that a
concentration of names in *thorp* – "dependent secondary settlement" –
would be observed on the Yorkshire Wolds.

Some caution must be shown when interpreting the evidence of place-
name distribution. Scandinavian settlement was not confined to places
which now have Scandinavian names. That the invaders occupied many
towns whose pre-Viking names survived is recorded in the historical sources
and emphasised by the numerous Danish street-names in *gata* (e.g.
Coppergate, Hungate, Skeldergate) surviving in towns such as York,
Lincoln, Nottingham and Norwich, while an abundance of field-names
composed of Scandinavian words betrays the presence of Scandinavian
settlers in areas where most villages have English names. The introduction
into the English language of a large number of Scandinavian terms
connected with farming (e.g. *deill* "share of land", *hlada* "barn" – in English
dialect "lathe" – *stakkr* "rick, stack") is, incidentally, a good indication that
there must once have been a substantial Danish-speaking farming population in England.

Sometimes archaeological finds reveal that Scandinavians settled in
villages with pre-Viking names. The pagan burial excavated in the
churchyard at Wensley in Yorkshire, for example, is that of a Scandinavian

farmer who was buried with his weapons and also a sickle (no. E26). Elsewhere there is linguistic evidence for the use of English place-names by the settlers. They altered the pronunciation of names such as Shipton and Cheswick to Skipton and Keswick in order to avoid sounds that were unfamiliar to them. Adaptations of this kind, however, only reveal that there were Scandinavians present in the neighbourhood of the villages. They do not prove that the Scandinavians actually settled in the villages bearing the names.

It must not be assumed that all the purely Scandinavian place-names in England are borne by settlements that were established by the Scandinavians on vacant land. Areas as extensive and as fertile as those marked by the concentrations of Scandinavian place-names cannot have lain desolate in the Anglo-Saxon period, when the agricultural resources of England are thought to have been fairly fully exploited. Some at least of the names must be borne by settlements established long before the arrival of the Vikings. The only recorded instance of a Scandinavian name replacing an English one is provided by the borough of Derby. This was known by the English as *Northworthy* "northern enclosure", but the Vikings renamed it Derby (*djúra-bý* "deer farm"), a name which they also gave to settlements in Lancashire (West Derby), Lincolnshire (Darby and possibly Dalderby), and the Isle of Man (Jurby).

It would perhaps, however, be more correct to say that the Scandinavian settlers in Derbyshire used the name Derby to refer to the fortified Roman site of Littlechester, now in Derby, on which they had probably established their military headquarters. The name Derby may, then, have been a re-modelling of the Romano-British name of this fort, *Derventio*. In later years the Danish name for the fort must have displaced the English name for the civil settlement. Elsewhere there is archaeological evidence to prove that a settlement on a site with a Scandinavian name must be older than its name. At Kirby Hill and Whitby in Yorkshire, for example, there is pre-Viking fabric in the church, showing that there must have been churches on the sites before the arrival of the Vikings.

When there is no documentary or historical evidence available, it can be very difficult to decide whether a Scandinavian place-name was given to a pre-existing settlement or to a newly established one. In recent years attempts have been made to solve the problem by examining the topographical and geological evidence for the suitability of individual sites for settlement. The settlement pattern in the Howardian Hills can serve as an illustration of this method. There is a string of English-named villages along the northern edge of the hills, where there is a mile-wide band of good arable land: Hovingham, Barton-le-Street, Appleton-le-Street, Swinton and Broughton. The Vikings may well have settled in these villages, even though they did not tamper with the names. In Hovingham church, for example, stands a carved stone cross that was decorated with a degenerate Scandinavian interlace pattern probably fairly late in the tenth century and this shows that by that time at least the lord of the manor was prepared to accept a work which reflected Scandinavian taste. He need not himself, of course, necessarily have been of Scandinavian origin or descent.

The chain of English names is broken by a hybrid name Fryton, presumably an English village with a name ending in *tun* (Old English for "settlement") that was taken over and partially renamed by a Dane called *Frithi*, and by two Scandinavian names ending in *by*, Amotherby and Slingsby – the settlements of men called *Eymundr* and *Slengr*. These two villages may be either new settlements squeezed in by Danish settlers on small patches of vacant land or else pre-existing English settlements taken over and renamed by them.

There are four *bys* on the southern slopes of the hills: Brandsby, Stearsby, Skewsby and Dalby – the settlements of *Brandr*, of *Styrr*, in the wood, and in the valley respectively. The land here was not well suited for agriculture and it was earlier considered unlikely that the sites would have been developed for settlement before the arrival of the Scandinavians created a demand for more land. A third wave of settlement was thought to be marked by the five *thorps* in the central band of woodland: Wiganthorpe, Howthorpe, Ganthorpe, Coneysthorpe and Easthorpe – the farms of *Vikingr* (or of the Vikings), in the hollow, of *Galmr*, of the king, and in the east respectively. These *thorps* must all originally have been secondary settlements dependent on the *bys* or the English-named villages.

The relative desirability of settlement sites only indicates the order in which they are likely to have been occupied and does not provide an absolute dating for their occupation. The *thorps* in the wooded belt, for example, are not necessarily young. They may, like their English-named neighbour Coulton – charcoal farm – have been founded as bases for charcoal-burning and this could have been at a very early date. In theory, every village whose site is marked on the map of the Howardian Hills may have been in existence before the first Viking ever set foot on English ground.

Even though the place-names do not allow us to date the foundation of settlements in the Danelaw, they do, however, reveal one very important fact about the role of Scandinavian settlers. Recent calculations suggest that between forty per cent and sixty per cent of the names ending in *by* in Yorkshire and the East Midlands contain a personal name as their first element, while only ten per cent of the names ending in *by* in Denmark contain personal names. The frequency of occurrence of personal names in the *by* names in the Danelaw would seem to reflect individual ownership of land. While some of the *bys* were probably newly founded by individual Vikings on marginal land or on or near deserted sites, it seems most likely that the majority of the names ending in *by* are borne by subsidiary units of large estates, such as that once centred on Hovingham, which were broken up by the Danes.

Before the arrival of the Vikings, land in England had not been bought or sold. It was either inherited or granted to a tenant by the king, the Church, an earl or some other powerful lord in exchange for life-long service, reverting to the donor on the death of the recipient. It seems probable that the habit of buying and selling land, which developed in England in the tenth century, was the result of the transfer of these small units of land into Danish hands. There is no surviving documentary evidence for the purchase of land by the Vikings from the English but there are some tenth-century charters which record the sale of land in Derbyshire, Bedfordshire and Lancashire to the English by the Scandinavians.

That the type of place-name most characteristic of the Danelaw is one in which a Scandinavian personal name is combined with a habitative element such as the English *tun* (Fryton), or the Scandinavian *by* (Slingsby) or *thorp* (Ganthorpe) is a reflection of that reorganisation of the pattern of land-holding which is one of the most significant results of the Viking settlement in England.

GILLIAN FELLOWS JENSEN

THE HAMMER AND THE CROSS

English had long been a Christian country when the Scandinavian settlers arrived, and sculpture in stone was one of its distinctive religious arts. The walls of Anglo-Saxon monasteries were decorated with stone friezes and panels; the relics of saints rested beneath stone shrines; free-standing crosses like those at Irton and Ruthwell stood as objects of contemplation at sacred sites; and crosses and slabs marked the graves of the Christian dead.

By contrast, the pagan settlers who came to Britain had no such tradition of carving in stone. We might therefore have expected that the art of sculpture would die with the new political and social order. Yet, para-doxically, the Viking settlement gave it renewed life. New kinds of decoration were introduced alongside traditional English motifs and new forms of ornament were developed. There was also a startling increase in the popularity of sculpture and this has left us with a huge quantity of Viking-Age carving scattered across the churches of northern England. In Yorkshire alone the remains of more than 500 monuments still survive.

The reasons for this unexpected flowering of sculpture are still not fully understood. It must, however, be linked to the spirit of compromise which seems to have governed relations between the Christian church and the settlers. The renaissance of stone carving is probably also connected to a change in patronage. Pre-Viking sculpture in England had, in the main, been a monastic art but by the tenth century few monasteries still survived. Whilst some ecclesiastical patronage may have persisted, the sculptors seem increasingly to have turned to a new (and potentially larger) lay market, and this stimulated the creation of new workshops to supplement long-established centres like Otley, Leeds and Halton.

Slowly we are beginning to identify the work of individual artists and workshops. We can, for example, recognise the distinctive style of one sculptor who worked exclusively for a powerful and learned patron at Gosforth in Cumbria. We can also now see how the concentration of population in York allowed the masons' yards to mass-produce standard grave-slabs for the churches of the city. Out in the country, by contrast, workshops had to serve a much wider area embracing several villages, a fact which is betrayed by the use of the same distinctive template to provide both the outline of a warrior's helmet on a cross at Sockburn (no. F18) and the curved breast of a bird on a shaft at Brompton some seven miles away.

The quantity of carving is impressive, but what makes it so useful for the historian and the archaeologist is that sculpture is a relatively immobile art. The styles and the geology of the stones show that they were usually carved in or near the church where they are now found. As a result the carvings give us valuable insights into the political groupings and cultural tastes, the economic links and religious beliefs of a wide range of communities in the north. Thanks to their wide distribution, the crosses and slabs give us access to the Viking-Age history of numerous small towns and villages which have otherwise left no record in any contemporary source.

Northern sculptors in the tenth and eleventh centuries remained faithful to traditional types of monument like crosses and slabs, but they added new varieties of ornament and form to their repertoire. One novelty was the introduction, from some source in the Celtic west, of a ring to connect the arms of the cross-head (no. F4). But a more dramatic innovation was the hogback. These impressive carvings were inspired by the building-shaped shrines of Anglo-Saxon England, but the concept was drastically re-modelled by Viking-Age sculptors so as to take on the form of a contemporary house, with shingled roof, curving ridge and boat-shaped ground plan. Several of these hogbacks have decorative zoomorphic terminals on the ridge (page 94). In the area around Brompton this feature was exaggerated to the point where the entire gable-end of the stone is dominated by the powerful shoulders of a muzzled beast (page 94).

Among the new forms of ornament were some which reflected the motifs and styles of contemporary Scandinavia. The ring-chain for example, which appears in differing forms at Burnsall and Gosforth (nos. F6, F24), is a common motif in Borre-style art. The numerous slabs and crosses from York are covered with animals treated in the tenth-century Jellinge style, their ribbon bodies decorated with contoured outlines and spiral hips, writhing in the tangled knotwork which issues from their tongues, tails and ears. Derivative and idiosyncratic versions of the same style were developed in regional workshops: the sagging animal from Middleton (no. F4) represents a distinctive Ryedale breed, whilst the Great Clifton sculptor has combined his variety of Jellinge beasts with a local Cumbrian theme of combat between men and monsters (no. F10).

Something of the spirit of the later tenth-century Mammen style was captured by carvers at Workington and Levisham, and one of the finest examples of eleventh-century Ringerike-style art is supplied by the sarcophagus from St Paul's in London (no. I19). The final phase of Viking art, the Urnes style, has also left its mark on the tympana and capitals of the new buildings of Norman England (no. L9) – the culmination of nearly two centuries in which Christian English sculpture had absorbed and trans-

RIGHT *A distribution map of northern England showing the sites of the Anglian and Anglo-Scandinavian sculpture on exhibition as originals, casts, or photographs.*

formed the native Viking-Age art of Scandinavia.

Carvings like these, which respond to Scandinavian styles, can be dated, though not with any great precision. But for most sculptures we still lack any firm chronology. One of the reasons for this uncertainty is that few carvings have been found in dated contexts. The unfinished slab from Coppergate in York (no. YS1), which emerged from a mid-tenth century level, was thus a very welcome find. Yet even excavated material is not without its problems: the slabs and headstones found beneath York Minster seem to belong to an early eleventh-century graveyard but many of the stones, for reasons of reverence or parsimony, were apparently re-used from an earlier cemetery.

What makes dating even more difficult is that the vast majority of Viking-Age sculptors paid scant heed to Scandinavian-derived fashions. Most ignored them completely. We find workshops seizing nostalgically on the motifs of an earlier Anglian monument in the area and developing their own eccentric versions of its decoration like the spiral scrolls of Cumbria or the multiple linked figures of the Tees valley. Other groups invented their own novel ornament like the masons who produced crosses from Sockburn,

Kirklevington and elsewhere with delightful portraits of individual birds and animals combined with well-modelled figure sculpture.

Whatever their decoration these stones were designed to stand in Christian graveyards. On many of them Christianity is only signalled by a cruciform shape or the symbol of a vine-scroll. On others it is more overt: the Newgate stone from York has a deeply-cut portrait of Christ alongside its panels of Jellinge-style animals (no. YS2), whilst a priest in full liturgical vestments appears at Brompton. There are even traces of more complex teaching on a shaft from Dacre (no. F14) where there are three scenes which together form a complete Christian statement about Man's Fall and his Redemption and imply, intriguingly, a knowledge of medieval liturgy and biblical commentaries.

Yet, despite these thoroughly Christian stones, it cannot be denied that the Scandinavian settlement introduced a secular element to English sculpture. Portraits of armed warriors, surrounded by their weaponry, are found over a wide area and reflect the ideals of the new patrons of sculpture. They also incidentally provide useful information on such issues as the shape of saddles or helmets – and even, at Middleton (no. F4), show how the scabbard of a knife was slung below the belt.

Another group of carvings which reflect the change in tastes following the Scandinavian settlement is that which shows the deeds of legendary heroes. These scenes have the additional interest of depicting the stories at a period centuries before they were recorded in our surviving literature. Prominent among the heroes is Sigurd the Volsung whose dragon-killing and mystic feast is fully portrayed on crosses at Halton, Kirby Hill, Ripon and York. His presence may represent some claim to a distinguished ancestry or it may be a conventional method of praising a dead man to compare him to a great hero of old. There might even be an implicit comparison between Sigurd's adventures and that struggle between St Michael and the Dragon which was a favourite theme of later tympana (see page 183).

Wayland, the great smith of Germanic legend, also makes his appearance on four carvings which show his miraculous escape from captivity (no. F15). The later literary accounts knew that he used a pair of wings: the sculptures show that a tenth-century audience envisaged him strapped to a flying machine complete with wings, bird's head and tail. He is surrounded by his tools and grasps the pigtail and skirt of the princess he has just raped. We should not, however, assume that the message of these scenes was totally secular or non-Christian for on the large shaft from Leeds parish church the winged Wayland is accompanied by panels showing evangelists with feathery cloaks and winged symbols. Was some contrast or parallel intended?

Such speculation is strengthened by other carvings where it is quite obvious that the sculptor is exploring the relationship between Christian teaching and pagan mythology. Gosforth in Cumbria provides the most convincing evidence for this type of radical theological speculation. Inside the church is part of a frieze depicting Thor's fishing expedition which led to his encounter with the World Serpent (no. F23). In the panel above is the Christian parallel of a hart trampling down a snake, a well-known symbol of Christ's victory over Evil. Significantly both scenes present Evil in a serpent form.

This commentary from one theological system on another is more fully worked out on the large cross in the churchyard at Gosforth. Here the Christian scene of the crucifixion (no. F24) is surrounded by carvings showing the day of Ragnarök when the world of the Scandinavian gods would be overthrown by monstrous forces of evil. The patterning of the scenes is clearly designed to bring out the parallels and contrasts between three climactic events: Ragnarök, the Crucifixion and the Last Judgement.

The great cross at Gosforth is the work of a skilled artist and was planned by a subtle mind. But the approach which it adopts may not have been so rare elsewhere. Perhaps there were uncompromisingly pagan stones – a large hogback from Lowther in Cumbria is a good candidate – but other scenes, now only surviving as fragments, could have been fitted to a Christian pattern. On some, dual interpretations must always have been possible. Is that Odin with his ravens at Kirklevington or a warrior saint inspired by Divine Wisdom (no. F21)? Are the naked men struggling with monsters at Great Clifton from some Scandinavian myth or are they the Damned in a Christian Hell? The puzzles remain, but no other documentary or archaeological material brings us so close to the meeting point of pagan and Christian belief.

Finally, however much is explained to the layman, he may still have difficulty in unravelling the decoration of these stones. His confusion stems from the fact that we now see the sculptures in a half-finished state; they were originally painted. The red lead which acted as a primer for other colours can still be seen on the shafts from Burnsall and Newgate in York. Elsewhere a gesso base was applied first and traces of this remain on the St Paul's stone (no. I 19) which also retains sufficient paint to show that its decoration was once picked out in blue-black and brown-yellow with speckles of white. It was this finish which covered the marking-out lines of the Newgate stone and which masked the miscuttings and geological anomalies of the Great Clifton shaft. Painting would have clarified the complexities of ornament and could have added details like facial features and identifying inscriptions. The present reticent appearance of all Anglo-Scandinavian carving belies its original garish appearance.

RICHARD N. BAILEY

F4

F1 The Claughton Hall hoard
Claughton Hall, near Garstang, Lancashire
HM, P on loan from M. Fitzherbert Brockholes, Esq.

1 Pair of gilt-bronze, double-shelled oval brooches similar to no. E28. L. 10.0cm.
2 Silver-gilt oval mount converted into a brooch and decorated with conventionalised acanthus ornament either side of the median stem. L. 3.5cm.
3 One red and one blue glass bead.

The objects were found in 1922 under a small mound, and were apparently contained in a wooden box interpreted as either a chamber grave or a coffin. Also found were a Bronze-Age axe, hammer and a pot containing a cremation, but since the latter is now lost it is difficult to know whether the mound covered a Bronze-Age cremation into which a Viking grave was inserted, or whether the pot belonged to the Viking burial.

An iron sword, spearhead, axe and hammer were also found but are now lost, although a watercolour of the sword and spearhead suggests that they were of Viking type. The silver brooch was imported from the Carolingian Empire.

F2 Undecorated silver pendant in the form of a hammer
Cuerdale, Lancashire. Private lender

The upper end of the stem is flattened and bent over to form the suspension loop. L. c. 5.0cm.

The pendant formed part of the Cuerdale hoard (no. E25). The hammer was the symbol of the Scandinavian god Thor, and such pieces were probably used as pagan amulets. Similar hammer-shaped pendants are well-known from Viking-Age Scandinavia.

F3 Undecorated silver pendant cross
Goldsborough, Yorks. Goldsborough Rectory

It is perforated for suspension near the end of the longest arm. L. 2.2cm.

The pendant formed part of the silver hoard from Goldsborough (no. E15). It has been suggested that the design of the pendant confuses the pagan Thor's hammer with the Christian cross, but the pendant cross from York (no. YD5) has the same form, and appears to be an Anglo-Saxon piece.

F8

F4 Complete monolithic ring-headed cross with huntsman and hunting scene
St Andrew's Church, Middleton, N. Yorks

The sandstone cross was extracted from the fabric of the late Saxon tower of St Andrew's church in 1948. Decoration: both main faces, the ring and the sides of the cross-head are decorated with knotwork and key pattern. Side A shows a hunt scene with stag, two dogs, and a huntsman with a spear. Side B: three-strand plait. Side C: ribbon animal with contoured body and single back leg bound in enmeshing strands. Side D: ring-twist. Tenth century. H.106.8cm.

The double ring of the head is a local Ryedale variant on the ring-head, and the beast represents a characteristic Ryedale presentation, in a long panel, of the crouching Jellinge-style animals of York. The hunt scene, by contrast, shows another widespread form of Viking-Age ornament in England – the free style – used for narrative scenes.

F5 Hogback, in two pieces, with end beasts
St Wilfrid's Church, Burnsall, N. Yorks, on loan to the Craven Valley Museum, Skipton, N. Yorks.

The hogback is made from yellow gritstone. It was found under the font in the tower of St Wilfrid's church between 1889 and 1914. The decoration shows end-beasts (bears?), their shoulders cut away, with well-marked muzzles, eyes and nostrils together with traces of clasping paw; *tegulæ* are found below the ridge moulding. Tenth century. L.134.6cm.

F6 Hogback with muzzled end-beasts
Arncliffe Hall garden, Ingleby Arncliffe, N. Yorks. Durham Cathedral Library [no. LXV]

This sandstone hogback was originally found in the 1860's in Arncliffe Hall garden. The decoration shows muzzled end-beasts clasping the roof with four-toed paws; above an arched niche are three panels of knotwork. Tenth century. L.132.1cm.

Large muzzled end-beasts were an eccentric fashion of hogback decoration in the Brompton area. The niche probably derives from apertures in pre-Viking Anglian shrines through which pilgrims could touch the saint's bones.

F7

F8

F10

F7 Cross-shaft with Borre-style ornament
St Wilfrid's Church, Burnsall, N. Yorks.

Carved from yellow gritstone, it was found in the chancel of St Wilfrid's church between 1876 and 1888. Decoration shows sides A and C with knotwork and ring-chain; sides B and D, ring-twist. Tenth century. H.104.0cm.

The ring-chain derives from a Borre-style motif and appears in a variety of forms in British sculpture (see no. F24); the one seen here is a type universal on Viking-Age carvings on the Isle of Man.

F8 Recumbent slab fragment with ribbon beast
St Mary's Church, Levisham, N. Yorks
St John Baptist's Church, Levisham

The sandstone slab was first recorded in St Mary's Church, Levisham, in 1907; and is now to be found in St John Baptist's Church, Levisham. Decoration: a single ribbon beast with contoured body and spiral hips bound in strands issuing from its tongue and ears; these strands, like the beast's back and tail, sprout twin scrolls and one fetter terminates in a small mask head. Tenth century. L.124.0cm.

The beast shows a typical Ryedale treatment of the more coherent crouching Jellinge beasts of York (see nos. YS1–3). The pierced jaws are a local feature whilst the scrolls can be paralleled both at Newgate, York, and on Odd's cross on the Isle of Man.

F9 Fragmentary cross-shaft with beasts and serpent
St Andrew's Church, Gainford, County Durham
Durham Cathedral Library [no. XXXII]

The yellow sandstone cross-shaft was found in the south wall of the nave of St Andrew's Church during the restoration of 1864. Decoration: Side A: two contoured backward-biting quadrupeds enmeshed in strands issuing from their tails and tongues. Sides B and D: knotwork. Side C: coiled and contoured serpent whose tail and (?) tongue run into basket plait below. Tenth century. H.124.5cm.

The coiled serpent has analogies in contemporary Viking metalwork but the substantial beasts on Side A, with their arched necks, are the offspring of an earlier Anglian menagerie (despite such Jellinge details as the spiral joints and contoured bodies).

F10 Cross-shaft fragment with ribbon animals and human figures
St Luke's Church, Great Clifton, Cumbria

This red and white sandstone cross-shaft was found re-used as the lintel of a Norman doorway during the restoration of St Luke's Church in 1900. Decoration: Side A: two parallel rows of ribbon animals, straddled by small human figures; the lower part of the composition is dominated by the coiled body and head of a beast set above a bound human figure. Side B: bifurcating knot-work. Side C: two parallel rows of ribbon animals with a small human figure. Side D: undulating frieze of ribbon animals. Tenth century. H.144cm.

Jellinge-style animals are here combined with local themes of men riding snakes, and bound figures, apparently to depict Hell where (as an

Anglo-Saxon poet wrote) "naked men struggle amongst the serpents". Such struggles were also a well-established theme in pagan Scandinavian literature and the carving might have been interpreted in non-Christian terms.

F11   Fragmentary cross-shaft with interlocked animals
St John's Church, Cross Canonby, Cumbria

The red sandstone shaft was found among walling rubble during restoration of St John's Church in 1880. Decoration: Side A: four beasts set in pairs back to back, each biting its own body and with front paw raised. Side B: ring-twist. Side C: six strand plait. Side D: interlocked ribbon animals. Tenth century. H.55.0cm.

The crouching, backward-turned animals of Side A with their raised paws, collars and ear lappets derive from pre-Viking English art though their contoured outline and twisted lips are probably Jellinge contributions. By contrast the swelling, bifurcating ribbon animals of Side D adhere more closely to Jellinge and earlier Scandinavian styles.

F12   Fragment of an unidentifiable monument with interlocked ribbon beasts
Tynemouth Priory, Tynemouth, Tyne and Wear
University Museum, Newcastle upon Tyne, Tyne and
Wear [1956 210A]

This sandstone fragment was found in a post-medieval wall at Tynemouth Priory in 1963. The decoration shows two interlocked ribbon beasts, with contoured bodies, bound in strands issuing from the heads and tails. Tenth century. L.41.0cm.

Near-identical compositions are known on crosses from St Oswald's, Durham, and Aycliffe. The balanced lay-out is probably dependent on revived interest in earlier manuscript motifs in the Cuthbert Community area, but details such as the animal's head show a response to Jellinge art in Yorkshire.

F13   Cross-shaft fragment with plaits and ribbon animals
St Michael's Church, Workington, Cumbria

This fragment of the shaft of circle-headed cross made in white sandstone was found in the tower wall of St Michael's Church in 1887. The decoration shows Sides A and C with a six-strand plait. Side B: knotwork set over a ribbon beast with contoured, pelleted, body and a foliate and tendril tail. Side D: triquetra ornament set over two crossing ribbon animals which have foliate tails and contoured bodies. Late tenth century. H.46.0cm.

The combination of pelleted bodies, semi-circular 'bites' in the outlines, and waving tendrils seem to represent a local response to Mammen art.

F14

F14   Shaft with backward-turning beast and Biblical scenes
St Andrew's Church, Dacre, Cumbria

The white sandstone shaft of a ring-headed cross was found among walling rubble during re-storation of St Andrew's Church in 1875. The decoration shows Side A with a backward-turning beast above Abraham and Isaac; a hound leaping on the back of a stag; a Fall scene. Sides B and D: three-strand plait. Side C: defaced. Tenth century. H.96.5cm.

Patristic commentaries suggest that both Isaac's sacrifice and the hart and hound motif refer to Christ's Redemptive death and thus balance the Fall scene below. Dacre was the site of a pre-Viking monastery and earlier models may have been

F11

available to the tenth-century sculptor who carved this rare example of thoughtful Christian iconography.

F15 Cross-shaft fragment with Wayland scene
St Peter's Church, Leeds LCM

Decoration: Side A: shows part of a scene with Wayland bound to a bird's wing and tail, surrounded by spade-shaped blanks and a pair of pincers. Side B: has knotwork with a zoomorphic terminal. Side C: circular knotwork. Tenth century. Sandstone. H.36.8cm.

The stone was most probably found during restoration of St Peter's in 1838. Both Scandinavian and English literary traditions embraced stories of the hero Wayland, famed as a metalworker and smith. In one of his adventures he was captured by a king, hamstrung, and forced to work in the royal employ. Wayland subsequently escaped by aerial flight; hence the bird image.

Other parts of the same Wayland flight scene are known on the large cross in Leeds parish church, and on sculpture at Sherburn and Bedale in Yorkshire. A more realistic version, with Wayland transformed into a bird, is found on a stone from Ardre on the Swedish island of Gotland.

F16 Viking warrior cross fragment
Weston Church, N. Yorks. Lt. Col. H. V. Dawson

A fragmentary round-headed upright slab carved from gritstone. It was probably discovered in Weston church during its nineteenth-century restoration, and is now in Weston Hall. Decoration: Side A: a man with a short kirtle holds a sword and thrusts back a female figure with his right hand; below is open flat knotwork. Side B: a man holding an axe and sword. Tenth century. H.44.0cm.

The warrior scenes typify the secular elements introduced into Viking-Age sculpture as a result of the change in patronage from the earlier Anglian period. The tenth-century carver has here re-used an earlier Anglian cross, preserving the knotwork from the original lower arm but re-cutting the upper part of the shaft for his arched figural scene.

Sockburn, *Co. Durham. A monastery is recorded as existing here in the late eighth century but no traces of it now survive. The twenty-six sculptures known from the site all belong to the Viking period when its burial-ground was taken over by the new aristocracy. New secular tastes are reflected in the numerous depictions of armed warriors and scenes from Scandinavian mythology. Evidence from the use of identical templates shows that Sockburn was served by the same workshop which supplied the neighbouring churches of Kirklevington, Brompton and Northallerton. Sculpture is recorded from the site as early as 1822, but most of the material was recovered during excavations in 1900.*

F17 Hogback fragment with two mounted warriors
Sockburn, Co. Durham

On the sandstone fragment tegulation remains on the roof on both sides. Decoration on side A shows two mounted warriors with spears, domed helmets and high-backed saddles. Side B has open knotwork. Tenth century. L.63.5cm.

The helmet type differs from those at Brompton, Middleton and Weston (nos. F4, F16). The saddle implies familiarity with cavalry whilst the knotted tail may not be mere ornamental whimsy; a horse carved at the Viking settlement of Jarlshof in the Shetlands is similarly treated.

F18 Cross-shaft fragment with warrior
Sockburn, Co. Durham

Decoration: below a panel of knotwork is a frame containing a warrior with shield, helmet and spear. Tenth century. Sandstone; H.70.5cm. Identical portraits, using the same templates, are known from Brompton and Kirklevington.

F19 Fragmentary cross-shaft with horseman carrying a bird
Sockburn, Co. Durham

Fragmentary cross-shaft. Decoration: Side A: knotwork with, below, a snake set over a horseman who carries a bird on his wrist; underneath, a cloaked figure proffers a horn to a

F18

F17

F20

F21

man with a shield. Side B: ornament derived from ring-chain. Side C: two warriors with shields set above knotwork. Side D: ribbon animals. Tenth century. Sandstone. H.81.3cm.

The horseman with bird and snake has been identified as Odin. The panel in which a woman proffers a horn is suggestively reminiscent of scenes on the Gotland stones showing the Valkyries welcoming dead heroes into Valhalla. Such depictions were presumably once widespread in the Viking world in perishable media like tapestries, shield paintings and wood carvings.

F20 Cast of cross-shaft fragment with armed warrior
Sockburn, Co. Durham

This cast of two panels from a fragmentary cross-shaft depicts an armed warrior with sword, spear and pointed helmet set over a stag. Original, tenth century. Sandstone. H.115.5cm.

Decorative schemes with panels showing individual beasts and well-modelled human beings are a feature of a workshop serving the churches at Sockburn, Brompton and Kirklevington in the Tees and Leven valleys (see nos. F17–21).

F21 Cross-shaft fragment with man and two birds
St Martin's Church, Kirklevington

This fragment of sandstone was found during restoration of St Martin's in 1882. Decoration: Side A: the cross-head, decorated with knotwork, was linked to the shaft by rings at the corners of the shaft. Between the panels of knotwork is a well-modelled figure of a man with pointed helmet or cap, dressed in a kirtle and with two birds on his shoulders. The other sides are defaced (apart from a small fragment of interlace). Tenth century. H.80.0cm.

Well-modelled figures, and linking rings in the upper corners of shafts, are characteristic of a school of sculpture in a small area around Brompton in Yorkshire. The figure has been interpreted as Odin with his ravens, but elsewhere Christian saints and Christ himself are depicted with bird symbols.

F22 Cross-shaft fragment with animal heads and horseman
St Mary and St Cuthbert's Church, Chester-le-Street, Co. Durham

The sandstone shaft was found in a wall of St Mary and St Cuthbert's Church during the restoration of 1883. Decoration: Side A: two pendant animal heads, inscribed "EADmUmD" in runes and capitals, set above a horseman with shield. Below are two ring-knots. Sides B, C, D: circular knotwork patterns, badly bungled on C. Tenth century. H.92.4cm.

Chester-le-Street was the home of the Community of St Cuthbert from *c*.883 to *c*.995. In the areas controlled by the Community, sculptors favoured motifs which were nostalgic revivals of earlier manuscript ornament. But even Chester-le-Street, whilst displaying monastic literacy in the inscription, was not immune to the impact of the Anglo-Scandinavian art of the Tees valley in its use of pendant animals and horsemen (see no. F19).

F23 Cast of a fragmentary slab or frieze showing a Thor fishing scene
St Mary's Church, Gosforth, Cumbria

The original red sandstone frieze was found in the graveyard of St Mary's Church in 1882. The decoration shows in the upper panel a (?) horned beast trampling on a serpent; the lower depicts

F22

Thor's fishing expedition. Thor, a Viking god, is equipped with his hammer and ox-head bait whilst his giant rival holds his axe aloft. The world serpent, which Thor eventually hooked, is shown at the top of the panel and, vestigially, in the lower right corner. Original, tenth century. This slab was apparently carved by the artist who produced the main cross standing in Gosforth churchyard (no. F24). Both carvings explore the relationship of Christian doctrine and pagan mythology. Here Thor's struggle with his enemy is deliberately patterned against a well-known symbol of Christ's triumph over the Devil, with both evils portrayed in serpent-like form.

F24 Cast of the Gosforth Cross
St Mary's churchyard, Gosforth, Cumbria

This cast of the complete ring-headed cross in St Mary's churchyard, Gosforth, shows, among many images, a crucifixion scene with Christ set in a separate frame, blood pouring from His side; below is a spearman (Longinus) partnered by a female with a horn (? Mary Magdelene). At the bottom is a double-headed snake. Original, tenth century. Red sandstone. H.442.0cm.

This is the only explicitly Christian scene on the cross. The rest of the decoration shows episodes from the story of Ragnarok which describes the end of the world of the Scandinavian gods. In the patterning of his scenes the sculptor draws attention to the links and contrasts between Ragnarok, the Crucifixion and Doomsday. Even in this Christian scene there are elements derived from Scandinavia: the female with trailing dress, pigtail and drinking horn closely resembles the valkyries depicted on Gotland stones and on bronze pendants from Sweden.

BELOW *The hog-back grave-stones of Brompton church in Yorkshire. The large animals at each gable-end appear to be muzzled bears. Two of the house-shaped stones have roofs carved as if shingled.*

MARKETS OF THE DANELAW

ENGLISH RECORDS TELL FAR more about the impetus the Viking invasion gave to the development of towns in 'English' England than about urban settlement in the Danelaw; nevertheless the scattered references are important, for it would be difficult to prove from the archaeological evidence alone that Viking armies or settlers ever visited some of the Danelaw towns.

After the Danish conquest the writers of the *Anglo-Saxon Chronicle* described their enemies as armies from various centres in the Danelaw, including Northampton, Leicester, Bedford, Huntingdon, Derby and Cambridge. These places, and others including Stamford, Nottingham and Lincoln, were presumably chosen as bases and rallying points by Scandinavians living in their hinterland because they were situated on good natural communications networks.

It might be expected that the Scandinavian occupation of the towns would have resulted in their receiving Old Norse names, but normally the existing Old English names remained current. Only at Derby was the English name – *Northworthy* – replaced by one of Scandinavian formation; and only in Lincoln and York do street names suggest strong Scandinavian influence.

In York other names may indicate the positions of important buildings in the Anglo-Scandinavian city. *Earlesburgh*, by the church of St Olave (Olaf) which Earl Siward founded *c.*1030–55, was presumably where the earls had their residence; and King's Square *(Kuningesgard)* where the palace of the Viking kings stood. Neither has yet been excavated.

The names of some people who walked these streets and saw these buildings are known because after a reform of the coinage about 973 the officials responsible for striking coins in the towns were required to have their names recorded on each one. The surviving pennies show that Old Norse names were then very common among the moneyers of York and Lincoln, where seventy per cent and fifty per cent respectively of their names have an Old Norse derivation, but elsewhere in the Danelaw such names were in a very small minority. An Old Norse name does not necessarily imply Scandinavian parentage; but like the street names they do suggest that in Lincoln and York, the northernmost of the Danelaw towns, Scandinavian influences were still strong several generations after the English re-conquest.

The graves of Viking warriors or settlers are as elusive in the towns as in the countryside: only at Nottingham and York have skeletons been found accompanied by Scandinavian style grave-goods, and in each case only two bodies are certainly involved. Those from Nottingham, buried with weapons, were found during road-works in the nineteenth century and are imperfectly recorded, but those from York were excavated within the churchyard of St Mary Bishophill Junior. This suggests that the absence of large pagan Viking cemeteries may be because the Scandinavian settlers soon followed the English custom of churchyard burial, and also soon adopted the Christian tradition of going to the next world without the trappings of this.

How much this change owed to true religious convictions cannot be known, but an eleventh-century dedication stone from the site of St Mary Castlegate in York testifies that two of the church's patrons at that date had Old Norse names, and indeed it is a small number of churches, constructed of stone, which are now the only buildings of the Anglo-Scandinavian period surviving above ground in the Danelaw towns.

Until recently this archaeological evidence was limited almost entirely to objects discovered by chance during building works. Most of the towns had yielded only a very small number of finds which could be dated to this period, and even these usually had English rather than Scandinavian affinities. The exceptions were York and, to a lesser extent, Lincoln, where the quantity and range of chance finds combined with the great number of coins, which survive from their mints, to suggest that they were more prosperous and important than the other Danelaw towns. Now controlled archaeological excavations on sites about to be destroyed during redevelopment in these two cities have revealed for the first time complete houses and workshops spanning the entire era from just after the Scandinavian settlements in the 870s up to the Norman conquest, and have also provided a spectacular collection of well-dated associated objects.

The building remains from Coppergate in York are more recognisable because the archaeological layers were waterlogged and have therefore preserved organic objects, including the timber buildings, in good condition. Two totally different methods of construction have been found, with the change apparently occuring in the decade 950–60. On each of the four tenements which have been excavated the later buildings, averaging seven by three metres in size, were constructed with floors sunk nearly 2 metres below the surrounding ground surface, and had walls consisting of horizontal oak timbers, supported by closely and regularly-spaced squared uprights, resting on substantial foundation beams.

These buildings were in two ranks, houses on the street frontage and workshops behind, and replaced earlier tenth-century structures whose walls, surviving up to about 50 centimetres in height, were made from posts and stakes with twigs woven between and then probably daubed with clay

RIGHT *A group of amber products (YAJG 1–5, p 137) which includes wedge-shaped pendants, beads, rough-outs and pieces broken during manufacture; all were excavated in York.*

LEFT A York street scene as it might have appeared in the late ninth century: boats on the Fosse, a wagon passes a Coppergate house, two traders bargain for a bundle of furs weighing the cost in a pair of scales.

for weatherproofing. In both phases the buildings were separated by fences whose lines were perpetuated, despite the rising ground level, into the nineteenth century, and it seems that York owes not only part of its street system but also the layout of many individual properties to its settlers.

In Lincoln dry soil conditions at the Flaxengate site meant that only a few charred timbers survived, but nonetheless buildings of two types could be recognised, with post-built structures first erected in the late ninth century being superseded by buildings with foundation beams – a sequence similar to that seen at Coppergate. Thanks to a recent slight realignment of Flaxengate itself the original street surface lay within the excavated area, and was proved to be contemporary with the later ninth-century buildings, thus underlining once again the influence which Viking-Age settlers have had on the layout of modern towns.

Finds from both sites have highlighted the long-distance contacts which the Danelaw enjoyed: pottery from North Syria, amber from the Baltic, and ivory are among the foreign goods found at Flaxengate, while Coppergate has yielded East Mediterranean silks, jewellery from the Low Countries and Scandinavia, whetstones from Norway, and lava quern-stones and pottery from the Rhineland. Other foreign goods including hides, fats and oils from the Arctic, spices from the Orient, and slaves from many lands must also have passed through York, Lincoln and other Danelaw towns, although they are not identifiable in the archaeological record. From nearer home, there is evidence for contact with Ireland and northern Scotland, and from documentary sources we know that York merchants were active in Thanet, Kent, in 969, and in Cambridge about 975.

Not only goods but ideas were introduced from abroad, and are attested in some Danelaw products, notably in the innovation of glazed pottery whose manufacture started at Stamford just after the Scandinavian settlement, and

RIGHT *A plan of York showing streets with Scandinavian names, early churches, and excavation sites with the rich Coppergate dig at the centre.*

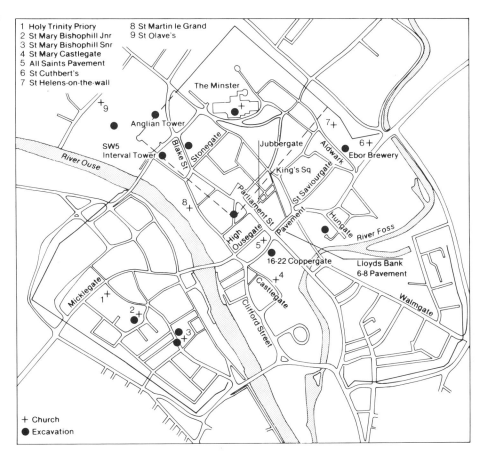

1 Holy Trinity Priory
2 St Mary Bishophill Jnr
3 St Mary Bishophill Snr
4 St Mary Castlegate
5 All Saints Pavement
6 St Cuthbert's
7 St Helens-on-the-wall
8 St Martin le Grand
9 St Olave's

+ Church
● Excavation

which was also made briefly at Lincoln. The Danelaw towns were regional production centres for a variety of essential and luxury items, and once again Lincoln and York show most clearly the range of trades and crafts which were practised. From one or other has come direct evidence for the turning of wooden vessels, shoe-making and repairing, and the manufacture of needles, combs, etc. from bone and antler. The production of jewellery in copper alloy, lead alloy, silver, glass, amber and jet testifies to the surplus wealth available for such minor luxuries; and highly decorated leather scabbards, inlaid and silver-studded wood carving and sculptured grave-markers further indicate the high standard of living – and dying – which some at least attained.

In spite of the lack of evidence, it can be assumed that the trade and industry now recognised at York and Lincoln were echoed, if in a minor key, in the other Danelaw towns, and by the Norman conquest they were considerable centres of population, enjoying varying but generally high degrees of prosperity.

RICHARD HALL

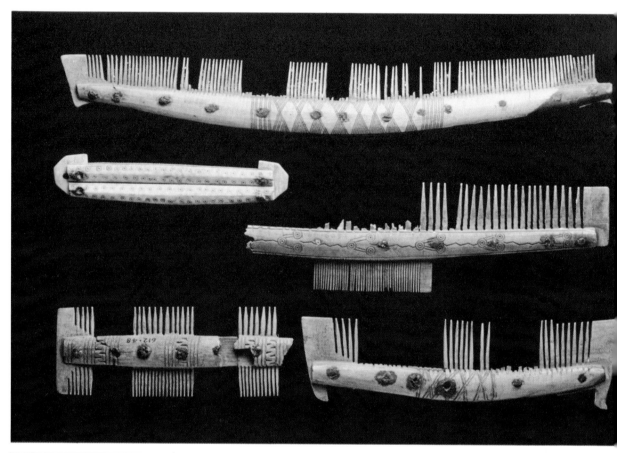

York craftsmanship in bone and antler
ABOVE *Four combs and a comb case – the combs are made of antler, the case from bone. They carry a variety of decoration. (YAB 5, 6, 10, 11, 13; see p 112/3.)*
LEFT *Two belt buckles both made of bone; the one on the right was dyed green. (YD32/33.)*

G1 Cast lead-alloy mount or blank
Flaxengate, Lincoln LAT [F74 Pb15]

It is trapezoid with a transverse slot at the narrow end, and three equally-spaced loops at each side. The front face is decorated with debased foliate ornament. On the reverse, the edge moulding and median moulding are decorated in punched dots, and the fields are filled with a disintegrated swirling pattern. L.8.1 × W.6.0cm.

G2 Incomplete iron slide-key
Flaxengate, Lincoln LAT [F74 Fe469]

It has a circular bit with an elaborate cruciform perforation, and a bulbous stem inlaid with a spiral copper-alloy wire. L.7.5cm.
  A similar key is known from York (no. YDL18), and this like the Lincoln example is probably a Scandinavian import. A key of this type from Lund is dated 1100–1150.

G3 Two half-manufactured copper-alloy garment hooks and a finished hook
Flaxengate, Lincoln LAT [F74 Ae169, F73 Ae294]

The completed hook has a sub-circular plate contoured with an incised line shouldered on either side of the broken underturned hook. There are two holes for attachment. L.2.7cm.
  Similar debris from the manufacture of garment hooks is known from the SE-Banken site, Lund. It is likely that the use of garment hooks was introduced to Scandinavia from Anglo-Saxon England where they were in use from as early as the ninth century (see no. C13).

G4 Two copper-alloy garment hooks one finished, one half-manufactured
Flaxengate, Lincoln LAT [F75 Ae485. F75 Ae546]

The half-made hook has a triangular plate, the plate of the finished example is shouldered on either side of the broken, under-turned hook, and is decorated with punched ornament. There are two perforations for attachment. L.2.2cm.

G5 Sub-rectangular two-sided sandstone mould
Flaxengate, Lincoln LAT [F74 M45]

On one side is a shape for casting a disc, now partially lost; on the other are the shapes for a similar disc and an ingot. 1.5 × 6.0 × 1.8cm.
  A large number of stone and clay moulds have come from Anglo-Scandinavian levels at Flaxengate, Lincoln, together with many crucibles and heating trays. Similar evidence for such extensive metalworking is known also from 16–22 Coppergate, York. (nos. YMW1–19).

G6 Sub-rectangular clay mould fragment decorated with a reticulated pattern
Flaxengate, Lincoln LAT [F73 M17]

L.4.2 × W.2.5 × 0.95cm.

G7 Group of glass beads
Flaxengate, Lincoln LAT [F73 G138, F74 G53, F75 G183]

It includes a brown triangular bead with rounded corners, decorated with blobs of green on yellow, a gadrooned dark blue bead and a yellow annular bead. D.c.1.3cm.

Beads similar to the yellow example were probably made in Lincoln; some of the Flaxengate crucibles were used for melting glass which has the same high lead content as that of the yellow bead. Similarly, green beads and finger rings (see no. G34) are thought to have been made in Lincoln. Blue gadrooned beads and yellow annular beads of the same form are known also from York (see nos. YAJG14–17).

G8 Stamford ware hanging lamp
Flaxengate, Lincoln LAT [F75 ST1]

The lamp has a globular body tapering towards the base, and a pouring lip. One side is fire blackened and splashed with glaze. H.8.5cm.

G9 Rim fragment of a flat shelly ware dish
Holmes Grainwarehouse, Lincoln LAT [HG22]

Inside it there are a series of concentric ridges. 11.7 × 6.3cm.
  A similar fragment is known from Århus, and both vessels have been identified as chicken feeders.

G10 Incomplete spouted jar in Lincoln sandy ware
Flaxengate, Lincoln LAT [F75 Q1]

There is a band of incised zig-zag decoration around the shoulder. H.c.36.0cm.
  Sandy wares of this type were probably made in Lincoln, although no kilns are yet known.

G11 Mis-shapen Lincoln sandy ware cooking pot
Flaxengate, Lincoln LAT [F75 Q16]

It has an everted rim and sagging base. H.c.13cm.
  This is presumably a waster; several were found on the Flaxengate site, but no kiln.

G12 Incomplete Lincoln sandy ware cooking pot
Flaxengate, Lincoln LAT [F74 Q7]

It has an everted rim. The exterior is fire blackened. H.c.25.0cm.

G13 Fragment of the rim and handle of an unglazed splashed ware jug
Flaxengate, Lincoln LAT [F74 SPL2]

It is decorated on the exterior with bands of combed ornament, and there is similar decoration inside the rim.

G14 Incomplete shelly ware basin
Flaxengate, Lincoln LAT [F75]

It has an ancient mend. D.c.44.0 × H.c.24.0cm.

G15 Shelly ware cooking pot
Lincoln LAT [un-numbered]

It has an everted rim and sagging base. H.20cm. This is a product of the Silver Street kiln, Lincoln.

G16 Badorf ware rim sherd
Flaxengate, Lincoln LAT [F73 F32]

Sherds of Badorf ware found beneath the first, late ninth-century buildings, on Flaxengate. Such sherds are also known in Lincoln from the Holmes

Grainwarehouse site and West Parade. Badorf ware was imported from the Rhineland (see no. YTC3) and with the sherds discussed below (nos. G17–21) illustrate the wide ranging nature of Lincoln's trading contacts in the Anglo-Scandinavian period.

G17 Body sherds in a fine, white fabric with a clear yellow glaze
Flaxengate, Lincoln LAT [F76 F29]

These were found in contexts dated to c.900, to the early tenth century, and were probably imported from the Low Countries.

G18 Shoulder sherd decorated with grooving
Flaxengate, Lincoln LAT [F75 Q409]

This is a sherd from the shoulder of a Slav pot made in the Baltic area and dating to c.950.

G19 Body sherds with an alkaline blue glaze
Flaxengate, Lincoln LAT [F76 F45]

Found in late ninth-century levels, these are sherds of Islamic blue-glazed pottery produced in Mesopotamia, Iran, or more probably north-east Syria. These are the first sherds of early Islamic pottery from north-west Europe, and presumably reached Lincoln by way of the Scandinavian trading routes through Russia from the Middle East.

G20 Part of the rim and neck of a collared jar
Flaxengate, Lincoln LAT [F76 F41]

The sherd with its buff/orange fabric and red painted decoration, has tentatively been identified as Spanish.

G21 Rim and base sherds of a stoneware bowl
Flaxengate, Lincoln LAT [F76 F44]

Found beneath the first, ninth-century timber buildings on Flaxengate, the sherds have been identified as Chinese Yüeh ware, produced in the eighth and ninth centuries in the north Chekiang province on the north-east coast of China. Similar sherds have been discovered at St Peter's Abbey, Ghent, in contexts sealed by Viking destruction levels. With the other Flaxengate fragments, these could have reached north-west Europe by way of the Middle East and the Russian rivers, but sherds of this type are known from Old Cairo, so possibly the vessels came via the Mediterranean.

G22 Two soapstone body sherds
Flaxengate, Lincoln LAT [F75 M15, F76 St51 (glued together), F74 M156]

The exterior is blackened by fire. L.5.8 × W.5.2 cm.
Soapstone sherds are known also from Anglo-Scandinavian levels in York, (see no. YTC8).

G23 Two copper-alloy ringed pins
Flaxengate, Lincoln LAT [E73 Ae290]
Broadgate East, Lincoln LAT [BE Ae164]

The pins each have a polyhedral head decorated with punched dots and a plain ring of square section. One of the rings is also decorated with punched dots. L.9.5 cm. For further discussion see no. YTC10.

G24 Bone fastening
Flaxengate, Lincoln LAT [F75 B53]

It is long and narrow with slightly rounded ends, and a swelling close to one. The perforation in the centre of the swelling is enclosed by an incised lentoid frame, which in turn is surrounded by a second lentoid frame developing at one end into a pair of incised lines which run down the length of the bone and enclose a narrow triangular field filled with a row of pellets. L.11.6 × W.1.8cm.
The bone appears to have pivoted on a pin through the perforation, and may have been used as a catch.

G25 Bone pin
Flaxengate, Lincoln LAT [F75 B40]

It has a flat, hour-glass shaped perforated head, and has an additional lobe at the top. L.8.0cm.

G26 Complete cooking pot
Birka, Sweden SHM, Stockholm

The pot has an everted rim and sagging base. Under the rim are four lines of rectangular stamps. H.22.0 × D.22.0cm.
The pot was found in a male cremation of the second half of the tenth century at the Viking site of Birka west of Stockholm. Over the pot were found the bones of a hen. Analysis of the fabric suggests that the pot is of English manufacture, and could have come from the same Lincoln kiln that produced the similar pot, no. G15.

G27 Curved antler point
Flaxengate, Lincoln LAT [F75 B69]

Of square section, and made from a single tine, the point is separated from the body of the tine by two collars. At the other end is a raised zone which is perforated. L.9.7 cm.
The function of the point is uncertain, but it has been suggested that such tines were associated with the splicing of rope (see no. YAB8). Similar tines from Birka have been identified as harness pins. Closely comparable pieces are known from Anglo-Scandinavian levels at 16–22 Coppergate, York.

G28 Bone mouth piece
Flaxengate, Lincoln LAT [F75 B44]

At the upper end are two roll-mouldings, below which is the blowing hole. It is decorated with a lightly incised basket-work pattern, the spaces between the strands being drilled. It is roughly broken at the lower end. L.5.5 × D.1.5cm.

G29 Bone pipe made from a swan's ulna
Flaxengate, Lincoln LAT [F75 B76]

There is a blowing hole near the upper end and a fingering hole near the lower. L.17.5 × D.1.3cm.
Similar bone pipes are known from Scandinavia and from Anglo-Saxon England. For further discussion see no. YDL26.

G30 Bone comb case with a runic inscription
Lincoln BM [67, 3-20, 12]

The case is composed of two black plates, each with a convex outer edge; inside are two straight inner plates. The pairs of plates are separated at each end by a narrow, sub-triangular end-plate, and held together by iron rivets. Incised on one of the back plates is a runic inscription in Old Norse which can be translated "Thorfast made a good comb". L.13.0cm.

ᚴᛏᚤᛒ: ᚠᚨᛈᛏᛏ: ᚦᛅᚱᚠᛏ ᛋᛏᚱ

G31   Half of a bun-shaped linen smoother of black glass
Flaxengate, Lincoln LAT [F76 G497]

There is a concavity in the underside. For the use of such objects see no. YT11.

G32   Group of crucibles
Flaxengate, Lincoln LAT [F74 P30, F76 P5, F73 P55]

They include a Stamford ware crucible with a lead lump, the base of a coil-made crucible, which has been re-lined and is covered with red and black glassy waste and copper corrosion and a Stamford ware crucible with possible tong marks, containing waste, possibly from the melting of copper.

The Flaxengate site has yielded extensive evidence for metalworking including large numbers of crucibles such as these, stone and clay mould fragments (nos. G6 and G7), and half-made objects such as the garment hooks (nos. G3, G4).

G33   Shallow shelly ware bowl-like crucible and a small dish in oxidized calcite-gritted ware
Flaxengate, Lincoln LAT [F76 P20, F75 P190]

Both vessels contain glassy waste of the same type as that used for the finger rings no. G34, and the yellow glass beads no. G7.

G34   Two yellow glass finger rings and an incomplete green glass finger ring
Flaxengate, Lincoln LAT [F75 G29 G444, F75 G31 G205, F75 F70 G244]

The rings have semi-circular sections. D.2.4cm.

G35   Globular Stamford ware hanging lamp
Lincoln LCCM [88.50/315/5]

H.7.0 × D.c.11.5cm.
This is similar to the hanging lamp no. G8, but its slightly flattened form suggests that it is later in date.

G36   Silver penny Viking issue of the Alfred period, c.890–900?
LM [Sir Francis Hill colln] SCBI Lincoln 2

Wt.1.43gm (22.1gr).
Obv: ERCENER Diademed bust facing right. Rev: Monogram of LINCOLLA (Lincoln).

G36a   Silver penny of the St Martin coinage of Lincoln, mid 920s
LM [Sir Francis Hill colln.] SCBI Lincoln 5

Wt.1.07gm (16.5gr).
Obv: SCI MARTI in two lines, sword between. Rev: INCOIA CIVT (for Lincoia Civitas). Cross within a cross.

G36b   Silver penny of Æthelred II, 978–1016. Crux type, c.991–997
LM [Sir Francis Hill colln] SCBI Lincoln 53

Mint: Lincoln. Wt.1.54gm (23.8gr).
Obv: AETHELRAED REX ANGLOR. Diademed bust left holding sceptre. Rev: STIGNBIT M-O LINCO. Crux in the quarters of a cross.

G36c   Silver penny of Æthelred II, 978–1016. Small cross type c.1009–1017
LM [Sir Francis Hill colln] SCBI Lincoln 289

Mint: Lincoln. Wt.1.19gm (18.4gr).
Obv: AETHELRAED REX ANGL. Diademed bust left. Rev: SUMERLETH MO LIN. Small cross in centre.

G36d   Silver penny of Cnut 1016–1035. Pointed helmet type, c.1023–1029
LM [Sir Francis Hill colln] SCBI Lincoln 422

Mint: Lincoln. Wt.1.15gm (17.7gr).
Obv: CNUT RECX. A bust left wearing pointed helmet and holding sceptre.
Rev: LIFINC ON LINCOLN. Cross, annulet in centre and in each quarter.

G36e   Silver penny of Olaf Kyrre, King of Norway, 1067–1093
Found in grounds of Usher Gallery, Lincoln. LM 1973; SCBI Lincoln 1937

Wt.0.76gm (11.7gr).
Obv: Crude head to right.
Rev: Cross enclosed in circle.

G37   Fragmentary cross-shaft
St Alkmund's Church, Derby DM (1–1872)

Made of gritstone, it was found in the demolition of St Alkmund's church in 1844. Decoration: Side A: two quadrupeds, one enlaced in its tongue extensions, separated by an arched frame from a third beast whose body is decorated with pellets. Side B: a bird, quadruped and backward-turning beast separated by arched frames. Side C: interlocked ribbon animals. Side D: a quadruped gripped in the jaws of a long-necked beast below knotwork. All beasts have contoured bodies. Late ninth or early tenth century. Ht. 75.0cm.

Though often cited as an example of insular Viking animal ornament, most of the decoration on this stone derives from earlier English art, which offers close parallels for the heraldic stance, the elongated necks, the pierced bodies and the pelleted ribbon beasts.

G38   Silver penny of Anlaf Guthfrithsson (in Derby 940–1)
BM [BMC 1098]

Wt.1.54gm (23.7gr).
Obv: ANLAF CUNUNCo Cross in centre.
Rev: SIGARES MOT (Mint of Derby).

G39   Copper-alloy disc
Leicester (?), Leics. M [33'1951]

This is similar to no. E5, except that it has a central perforation. D.3.0cm.

Leicester was one of the Five Boroughs along with Derby, Nottingham, Stamford and Lincoln. Unlike Lincoln, little archaeological evidence for Viking activities has been recovered from Leicester apart from casual finds (nos. G40–43).

G40   Copper-alloy ringed pin
Cank Street, Leicester, Leics. M [116'1962/680]

The pin has a baluster head and plain loose ring. The lower part of the shank is flattened and decorated with incised ornament. L.13.8cm.

G41   Copper-alloy openwork pendant decorated with an interlacing animal
Highcross Street, Leicester, Leics. M [18'1860]

L.5.2cm.

G42   Copper-alloy ringed pin
Jewry Wall, Leicester, Leics. M [JW89.14]

It has a looped head and plain loose ring. The upper part of the shank, just below the head, is flattened and the lower end is shouldered above the point. L.10.2cm.

The form of the pin closely resembles that of ringed pins made in Scandinavia, but based on Irish prototypes. The full-blooded Scandinavian type is exemplified by the pin from Meols, no. E13.

G43a   Torksey-ware cooking pot
Torksey, Lincs. NM [T68]

The pot has an everted mis-shapen rim, and a sagging base. H.20.5cm.

It is a waster from one of the seven kilns so far excavated in the Anglo-Scandinavian borough of Torksey near Lincoln. The range of vessels produced here includes cooking pots, bowls, cresset lamps (see G43b), storage jars and spouted pitchers. Production dated from the early tenth to the early twelfth century. Wares similar to those produced at Torksey were traded as far as York.

G43b   Torksey-ware lamp
Torksey, Lincs. NM [T68.K6]

The lamp has a deep dished bowl, a short stem and a flat base. H.7.5cm.

Like the cooking pot (G43a) this is a product of Torksey kilns. Similar lamps are known also in York-ware.

G44a   Incomplete cooking pot
Stamford, Lincolnshire SLAU

The pot has an everted rim and slightly sagging base. H.23.0cm.

The pot is from the Castle kiln, Stamford, and is of ninth-century date. Similar pottery from this and other kilns in Stamford was widely traded in the east Midlands in the Anglo-Scandinavian period.

G44b   Incomplete Stamford-ware storage jar
Stamford, Lincs. SLAU [Sta.76.EEXII.1417 and 1408]

It has an everted rim and originally had two handles. The body is decorated with applied thumbed strips and red-painted decoration.

This is a product of a Stamford kiln and can be dated to the ninth century. It is probably a copy of a north French import.

G45   Bone skate made from a horse left metacarpal
Holmes Grainwarehouse LAT [HG72 B30]

There is a perforation at the back end. The front end is pointed and has a transverse perforation. L.20.5 × W.4.5cm.

G46   Group of bone skates
Micklegate, York SCM [J93.1208]
Jubbergate, York SCM [J93.1209]

London Wall, London SCM
Token House Yard, London SCM

Each has a socket in the back end. L.26.0cm.
For similar skates from York see no. YAB48.

YORK DRESS

YD1 Silk cap in tabby weave
16-22 Coppergate, York YCC [YAT 1980. 7.8129]

Originally the cap had linen ribbons on either side, but only a few threads of these have survived. A repair patch has been cut from the inside of the dart and stitched over a hole at the back. The seam is stitched with silk thread, but the hemming was originally linen.

The silk tabbies from 16-22 Coppergate, 5 Coppergate, and Saltergate, Lincoln, are surprisingly similar; the latter two are so technically alike that they must be from the same bolt of cloth.

YD2 Silk purse reliquary embroidered with a Latin cross
16-22 Coppergate, York YCC [YAT 1977.7.1921]

The outer pouch is made from a compound twill, originally dyed red or purple and contains an inner purse made of two pieces of tabby. The stitching and cross are also of silk. L.3.0 × W.3.0cm.

The silk must have been imported from a Byzantine or Islamic weaving centre. The dyes used are *kermes*, the costly medieval dye 'grain', and another unidentified dye, possibly blue to give an overall purple colour. The reliquary contained nothing except traces of fibre resembling linen. These could represent a *brandea*, a strip of cloth which had been in contact with the relics of a saint, and which was itself, therefore, regarded as a relic.

YD3 Earring made of gold wire
16-22 Coppergate, York YCC [YAT 1979.7.4103]

The wire, of circular section, tapers to a point at each end. It was originally circular but has been pulled out of shape. L.3.3cm.

This earring, a piece of openwork interlace, and a group of gold threads are the only gold objects discovered during current excavations at 16-22 Coppergate, however, gold-working did take place on site (see YMW4).

YD4 Circular lead-alloy pendant with a wedge-shaped suspension loop and beaded frame
16-22 Coppergate, York YCC [YAT 1977.7.2213]

The central boss is surrounded by four outward-facing crescents, and is separated by a plain moulding from a border decorated with bosses alternating with outward-facing crescents. L.2.75cm.

Comparison with finds from Viking-Age graves in Scandinavia suggests that such pendants were strung on a necklace separated by beads.

YD5 Lead-alloy cruciform pendant
Clifford Street, York YM [1038.54]

The upper arm is extended and pierced for suspension, and bears the obverse and reverse impressions of a styca of Osberht, King of Northumbria, 847–67. L.5.1 × W.4.0cm.

The impressions were clearly made with coin dies. The pendant may have been while the dies were current, alternatively the dies may have been re-used after being discarded by the moneyer, as punches for ornamental metalwork. Osberht was one of the two rival claimants to the Northumbrian throne killed in an abortive attack on the newly-captured Viking city in 867.

YD6 Cast lead-alloy disc brooch
New Market Street, York YM [un-numbered]

It is decorated with a central boss, and with eight equally-spaced bosses around the edge just inside a billeted frame. The bosses are linked to each other and to the central boss by lentoid fields having billeted frames. The radiating lentoid fields are separated by plain false-filigree circles. D.5.3cm.

The disc brooch was a common type in England from the pagan Anglo-Saxon period onwards. In the late Anglo-Saxon period examples are known in silver although they are relatively uncommon. Base metal disc brooches are numerous and were apparently mass-produced. The decoration of this brooch is clearly related to that on a brooch from the Beeston Tor hoard (no. C10), which also uses a combination of bosses and lentoid fields. The hoard can be dated to *c*.873–5 on numismatic grounds.

YD7 Cast silver disc brooch
York (?) YM [701.48]

The brooch is decorated with a circular field imitating a coin of the Emperor Valentinian, surrounded by a series of beaded and plain concentric mouldings. On the reverse, the mouldings are crossed by four equally-spaced, narrow relief strips. D.4.5cm.

Coin brooches are known from the tenth century both in England and Scandinavia. This brooch is a cast version of examples, such as one from Canterbury, having a coin imitation in the centre, surrounded by concentric circles of twisted wire soldered together and supported at the back by transverse strips of metal. The cast relief strips on the back of the York piece imitate the functional strips of the Canterbury type.

YD8 Cast lead-alloy disc brooch
Near Mount, York YM [1921.21]

This has a plain frame inside which is an equal-armed cross having expanding arms and a central boss. D.4.3cm.

YD9 Cast lead-alloy disc brooch
Bishophill, York YM [YAT 1975.15.499]

The brooch is dished, the wide outer zone being decorated with bosses alternating with rectangular hatched fields. Inside is a bossed field within a beaded border, decorated with an equal-armed cross which has a central boss. D.4.6cm.

YD10 Cast copper-alloy disc brooch
Pavement, York YM [1951.52.3]

This has a beaded frame, inside which is a field having a central boss surrounded by six equally-spaced bosses. The bosses, each surrounded by a beaded collar, are separated by beaded mouldings. D.4.9cm.

YD11 Cast copper-alloy disc brooch
16-22 Coppergate, York YCC [YAT 1980.7.8803]

It is decorated with a backward-looking quadruped within a billeted border. There is a perforation near the animal's front leg. The catch survives but the pin and its attachment are lost. D.2.4cm.

This is an example of a well-known brooch type, the majority of which have come from East

YD6

YD7

YD15

Anglian sites, (see no. E10). No other specimen is securely dated and the early tenth-century date suggested for this piece by its context may serve to date the whole series. The brooch was, however, of considerable age when lost, as it is heavily worn; the perforation is placed next to the attachment for the pin and probably represents a repair.

YD12   Cast pewter disc brooch
York YM [652.48]

This brooch is decorated with a backward-looking quadruped which has a hatched and contoured body. The extended tongue interlaces with the body and rear leg. The whole is contained within a triple border, the two inner elements are billeted and the outer element diagonally hatched.

The brooch is decorated in the Scandinavian Jellinge style, closely paralleled on Norwegian pendants such as that from Nomeland, Valle, Aust-Agder. The suggestion that the brooch was made in York is strengthened by the recent discovery of a similar brooch from Coppergate, (no. YD13).

YD13   Cast lead-alloy disc brooch
16-22 Coppergate, York YCC [YAT 1980.7.9964]

This is similar to no. YD12 except that it has only a single billeted frame. The pin, its attachment, and the catch plate are lost. D.2.7cm.

YD14   Cast pewter disc brooch
16-22 Coppergate, York YCC [YAT 1977.7.1520]

The brooch is decorated with false-filigree conventionalized plant ornament. Inside the plain frame is an incomplete line of beading. D.3.1cm.

This is a base metal version of a type of gold filigree brooch known from Scandinavia and represented by an example from Hedeby. Pendants with similar ornament are known from Birka.

YD15   Cast lead-alloy disc brooch
16-22 Coppergate, York YCC [YAT 1980.7.7989]

It has a frame decorated with geometrical ornament. Inside is a series of bosses, each surrounded by a beaded collar. D.4.0cm.

The decorative scheme is related to that of no. YD10, and is derived from that of more elaborate bossed types, such as no. YD6.

YD16   Cast lead-alloy disc brooch
16-22 Coppergate, York YCC [YAT 1980.7.7548]

It is composed of six concentric plain mouldings surrounding a circular field decorated with an equal-armed cross having expanding arms. There is a boss in the centre of the cross and one in each of the arms. The pin is lost. D.3.8cm.

As with no. YD7, the ornament imitates the construction of such brooches as that from Canterbury, although here the concentric mouldings are further conventionalised.

YD17   Lead-alloy rectangular brooch with a three-element frame
Hungate, York YM [1971.321]

The inner and outer elements are plain, and the median element billeted. The brooch is decorated with a pair of saltires composed of a similar moulding, each with a boss at the crossing. L.4.1 × W.2.4cm.

The Viking man and woman
All the jewellery, household goods, ornament and weapons worn or carried by these two figures have been excavated and exist – many in this exhibition. Though we hear much about the Viking man, the woman ran the house and held the keys to it.

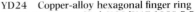

YD18   Lead-alloy bow brooch
16-22 Coppergate, York YCC [YAT 1980.7.8062]

This has an incomplete rectangular head and foot of the same width as the bow, separated from it by a double beaded moulding. There is also a beaded moulding around the edge of the brooch. In each of the fields is a boss surrounded by a beaded collar, with an additional small boss in each corner of the field on the bow. L.5.0 × W.1.7cm.

The brooch was probably made on or near the site at 16-22 Coppergate, since it appears to be a waster. This is suggested by the prominent casting flash on the front face, which has not been removed by secondary working. Moreover the ends of the brooch are not broken, but have the rounded edges characteristic of metal which has solidified in the mould before completely filling it. The closest parallel is in silver, from a hoard or grave group from Lerchenborg, Denmark.

YD19   Copper-alloy garment hook
6-8 Pavement, York YM [YAT 1972.21]

The hook has a sub-circular plate decorated with ring-and-dot. The plate develops at one end into an underturned hook, and at the other into two perforated lobed extensions. L.3.1 × W.1.9cm.

Hooks of this type are widely known from pre-Conquest sites in England, and appear to have originated in the ninth century (see no. C13). Their small size and relative weakness suggests that they are best identified as hooks for closing garments rather like the modern 'hook and eye'.

YD20   Copper-alloy garment hook with a circular plate
16-22 Coppergate, York YCC [YAT 1979.7.5176]

It has a circular plate decorated with a pair of incised, out-turned scrolls developing from the two perforations opposite the hook. L.2.1 × D.1.6cm.

YD21   Copper-alloy garment hook
York YM [718.48]

This has an oval plate decorated with an incised interlace triquetra. One end is drawn out to form the hook, and the other originally had three perforated, lobed extensions, now partially broken away. L.2.9 × W.1.7cm.

YD22   Iron garment loop
16-22 Coppergate, York YCC [YAT 1979.7.7374]

It is made of a rod of square section formed into a U-shaped loop with the ends brought together and turned outwards into tight spirals. Corroded to the loop is part of the opposing hook. L.2.2 × W.1.9cm.

The loop would be used like the eye of a modern "hook and eye" with a hook like nos. YD19-21, except made of iron.

YD23   Circular lead-alloy armlet
16-22 Coppergate, York YCC [YAT 1980.7.8502]

It is composed of a rod of circular section tapering towards the ends which are knotted together. D.4.6cm.

Such a small armlet or bracelet was presumably intended for the use of a child.

YD24   Copper-alloy hexagonal finger ring
16-22 Coppergate, York YCC [YAT 1980.7.7797]

The ring has each of the sides composed of an undecorated lozenge-shaped field. D.2.1cm.

The closest parallels to this ring are the ninth-century gold rings from Llysfaen, Anglesey, and the Trewhiddle hoard, Cornwall. The latter is now lost.

YD25   Copper-alloy finger ring of triangular section
16-22 Coppergate, York YCC [YAT 1980.7.7590]

Each facet is decorated with a pair of interlacing strands. D.2.4cm.

YD26   Cast lead-alloy finger ring
16-22 Coppergate, York YCC [YAT 1980.7.8500]

This damaged ring is decorated around the circumference with three parallel rows of beading. D.2.3cm.

YD27   Copper-alloy finger ring
16-22 Coppergate, York YCC [YAT 1979.7.7806]

It is composed of a wire tapering towards the ends which are knotted together. D.2.3cm.

The use of a knot to link the ends of a ring was a common feature in Viking-Age Scandinavia, where it was used for finger rings, arm rings and more everyday objects such as suspension loops.

YD28   Plaited gold finger ring
Hungate, York YM [726.48]

It is composed of several plaited rods. These rods taper towards the ends, where they are hammered together. D.2.6cm.

The ring is very similar to that from Soberton, Hants. (no. E17).

YD29   Copper-alloy tweezers
16-22 Coppergate, York YCC [YAT 1979.7.6901]

They are made from a single narrow bronze strip bent in half. The ends of the strip are turned inwards to form the grip. The collar which serves to lock the tweezers closed is corroded so that it no longer moves freely. There is a knotted suspension loop L. (excluding loop) 5.0cm.

Tweezers were common in the Viking Age and were presumably used for depilation, although they may have had a secondary use, such as for handling precious metal threads for embroidery.

YD30   Copper-alloy tweezers
16-22 Coppergate, York YCC [YAT 1979.7.6956]

Similar to no. YD29 except that these are decorated with ring and dot. The inturned ends of the tweezers and the locking collar are lost. There is an opaque white glass bead on the suspension loop. L. (excluding loop) 4.5cm.

YD31   Copper-alloy ear spoon
16-22 Coppergate, York YCC [YAT 1980.7.8027]

It has a tapering stem of ovoid section and a long, narrow, upturned bowl. L.5.0cm.

An ear spoon of similar form belongs to a set of toilet implements from Hedeby. More elaborate versions are known also from Birka, Sweden.

YD30   YD29

YD32 Buckle made from a single piece of bone
York YM [618.48]

The rectangular plate is decorated with a pair of interlacing lentoids and was attached to the belt by a notched projection which engaged in a hole at the end of the belt. L.4.7 × W.3.7cm.

YD33 Buckle made from a single piece of bone and dyed green
York YM [617.48]

The belt fitted into a split in the end of the undecorated plate, and was held in place by two copper-alloy rivets. The tongue is lost. L.4.2 × W.2.7cm.

YD34 Copper-alloy buckle
Hungate, York YM [1971.321]

This has an undecorated rectangular plate and a loop enriched with conventionalised plant ornament. L.4.1 × W.3.1cm.

Similar small buckles with plain plates and interlace-decorated loops are widely known from Scandinavia, for example from Birka. The plant ornament on the York piece, and a closely related example from a Viking grave at Alfsstadir, Skeidahreppur, Iceland is, however, more reminiscent of Anglo-Saxon ornament, and both buckles may be of Anglo-Saxon manufacture.

YD35 Copper-alloy suspension loop
Bishophill I/Skeldergate. York YM [YAT 1974.14.823]

It has a sub-triangular openwork attachment plate decorated with animal ornament and was originally fixed to a strap by four rivets. L. (excluding loop) 3.9 × 3.5cm.

The use of an animal mask and paws gripping parts of the design suggests that the ornament is derived from the Scandinavian Borre style.

YD36 Copper-alloy strap-end
16-22 Coppergate, York YCC [YAT 1980.7.7501]

This is in the form of an openwork, conventionalised vine scroll, developing from the rectangular upper end, which is split to accommodate the end of the strap; it was held in place by two rivets. The strap end is decorated all over with ring-and-dot. L.5.8 × W.2.6cm.

The piece can be compared with openwork, acanthus-decorated strap-ends such as those from Ixworth (Suffolk), Winchester (Hants.), and Buccombe Down (Isle of Wight), which are dated to *c.*1000 A.D. The York piece is probably rather earlier in date as it uses the vine scroll which, in the course of the tenth century, was replaced by acanthus as the predominant form of plant ornament in English art.

YD37 Hour-glass shaped, tinned-iron strap-end
16-22 Coppergate, York YCC [YAT 1980.7.7801]

The rectangular upper and lower zones are separated by a deeply recessed concave zone. The mineralised remains of the leather strap are inserted into a split at the upper end and held in place by a single iron rivet. L.2.7 × W.1.7cm.

Iron strap-ends are unusual both in Anglo-Saxon England and Viking-Age Scandinavia, and the tinning may be an attempt to imitate silver.

This strap-end forms part of a large group of tinned iron objects from Coppergate.

YD38 Copper-alloy strap-end decorated with a Borre-style ring chain
16-22 Coppergate, York YCC [YAT 1979.7.5976]

The undecorated upper end is split to accommodate the end of the strap, and there is an animal head terinal. L.4.7 × W.1.2cm.

The form of the strap-end is characteristic of ninth and early tenth-century Anglo-Saxon examples, although the ornament is in Scandinavian taste. Typologically, the strap-end is earlier in date than the similar strap-end, no. YD39, which has a rounded end, more characteristic of the tenth century, and the animal head terminal reduced to two dots representing the eyes.

YD39 Copper-alloy strap-end decorated with a Borre-style ring chain
St Mary Bishophill Senior, York YM [1973.24]

The belt fitted into a split in the upper end and was held in place by two rivets. The lower end is rounded. The reverse has an incised contour and is decorated with ring-and-dot. L.4.9 × W.1.7cm.

The discovery of two such similar objects from York (see YD38) suggests that they may have been made there. The discovery of the trefoil brooch mould (no. YMW13) and the mould master (no. YMW12), both of which are also decorated in Borre style, helps to substantiate this suggestion.

YD40 Interlace-decorated lead-alloy strap-end with animal-head terminal
16-22 Coppergate, York YCC [YAT 1979.7.7306]

The damaged upper end was originally split to accommodate the end of a leather strap. L.4.9 × W.1.3cm.

The discovery of this piece in York strengthens the hypothesis that a closely comparable example from Aggersborg, Denmark, is in fact an Anglo-Scandinavian product, probably made in York.

YD41 Cast copper-alloy chape
Coppergate, York YM [551.49.47]

The chape is decorated in openwork with a Jellinge-style animal having a hatched and contoured ribbon-like body contorted into a reversed-S shape. L.8.6cm.

This is one of a group of similar chapes most commonly found around the Baltic, but occurring as far east as Danilovka in the Lower Volga region, and as far west as Iceland.

YD42 Tri-lobate iron sword pommel
16-22 Coppergate, York YCC [YAT 1979.7.6807]

There is a circular raised field in the centre of each face, and a raised field at each end of the pommel. H.4.4 × W.6.2cm.

The closest parallel to this pommel is on an Anglo-Saxon sword from the River Escard at Hensden, Belgium. In each case the silver which originally covered the raised fields has been lost. The Hensden sword is of the same type as the swords from Gilling (no. D3) and Fiskerton (no. D2) and the York pommel must have belonged to a similar weapon.

YD38

YD35

YD36

YD40

YD43   Iron scramasax
16-22 Coppergate, York YCC [YAT 1979.7.7784]

The weapon has a tang of square section. The cutting edge is slightly curved. L.22.2 × W.2.6cm.

Scramasaxes – single-edged knives – of this type range in date from the ninth to the eleventh century. Similar examples have been recovered from the Thames at Fulham, Wandsworth and Brentford. For an inlaid example see no. D4.

YD44   Iron knife
York YM [620.48]

It has a long tang of square section which projects beyond the end of the bone handle. The handle, of flattened ovoid section, is decorated with ring-and-dot and is encircled by a zone of hatched ornament close to each end. L.13.6 × W.1.7cm.

YDG45a   Iron knife
York YM [627.48]

The knife, its blade partially broken away, has a bone handle of ovoid section decorated with ring-and-dot. L.13.6 × W.1.5cm.

YD45b   Copper-alloy pin
16-22 Coppergate, York YCC [YAT 1979.7.5672]

It has a flat hour-glass shaped head with two narrow extensions from the upper end perforated to take loose rings. The head itself is perforated twice, each perforation surrounded by a punched ring. L.9.2cm.

YD46   Copper-alloy pin
York YM [H.200]

The pin has a flat expanding head with the upper corners cut away. It is decorated with ring-and-dot; and dots are pierced. L.8.3 × W.1.4cm.

YD47   Copper-alloy pin
York YM

It has a polyhedral head decorated all over with punched dots. L.10.6cm.

YD48   Two copper-alloy pins with lozenge-shaped heads
16-22 Coppergate, York YCC [YAT 1979.7.6294]
Museum Gardens, York YM [YAT 1975.4.911]

The points of the lozenges have small bulbous extensions. The head of one has a border of stamped zig-zag ornament. L.6.8cm.

A similar pin was found in the grave of Archbishop Wulfstan of York, and, therefore, probably dates to the eleventh century. Pins of similar form are known also from Ireland.

YD49   Copper-alloy pin
16-22 Coppergate, York YCC [YAT 1977.7.1600]

The upper end of the shank has been divided and formed into a pair of tight inward-facing spirals. L.5.5cm.

Pins of this type are widely distributed in Anglo-Saxon contexts, over half the known examples coming from pagan graves. This pin, however, is securely stratified in a tenth-century level.

YD50   Grave group consisting of an iron knife, a rectangular buckle plate and a whetstone
St Mary Bishophill Junior, York YM [1975.27, 2-4]

1 The corroded iron knife has a broken tang of rectangular section. L.10.2 × W.2.1cm.
2 Copper-alloy buckle plate made from a single sheet of metal bent in two and held together at the open end by two rivets. It is decorated with repoussé bosses. L.3.7 × W.2.2cm.
3 Pendant schist whetstone. L.6.5 × W.1.2cm.

These objects, together with a St Peter's penny, accompanied a male burial. The grave was one of four excavated in the churchyard of St Mary Bishophill Junior. The other three contained female burials, one with grave goods (no. YDS1). These are the only burials of the Anglo-Scandinavian period from York which are accompanied, and must represent the graves of early Scandinavian settlers who were buried in the pagan tradition, but in a pre-existing Christian graveyard (see no. E26).

YD51   Grave group – silver armlet and ring
St Mary Bishophill Junior, York YM [1975.27.1]

The armlet is made of a single rod of lozenge-shaped section tapering towards the ends which are hooked together. It is decorated with rows of punched dots. D.6.8cm.

The silver ring, made of a single rod of circular section, is damaged. D.2.0cm.

The armlet was found at the wrist of one of the female burials. The small ring was threaded through the larger.

YORK DAILY LIFE

YDL1   Ovoid stone net-sinker decorated with an interlace plait
Clifford Street, York YM [C658]

There is a perforation through the upper end and another running from the base to the back. H.12.2 × W.6.2 × T.5.3cm.

YDL2, 3   Two iron fish-hooks
6-8 Pavement and 16-22 Coppergate, York YM [YAT 1974.21.5409; 1978.7.3347]

Each is made from a single piece of iron of square section, and having a barbed tip and flattened bulbous end. L.7.0cm.

Iron fish-hooks from the Thule excavations, Lund, dated to 1000–1050, are of basically similar form, except that the end of the hook is turned back to form a suspension loop.

YDL4, 5, 6   Cylindrical edge grindstones, each with a central perforation
16-22 Coppergate, York YCC [YAT 1979.7.6065, 7249, 7348]

D.7.6 × W.4.8cm.

The function of these objects is unclear but they may have been used for grinding materials in connection with an industrial process.

YDL7   Top of a millstone grit rotary quern
16-22 Coppergate, York YCC [YAT 1980.7.8846]

The handle originally fitted into a central hour-glass shaped perforation. D.36.0cm.

YDL8   Iron double-pronged socketed implement
16-22 Coppergate, York YM [551.54.48]

It has a plain bronzed moulding towards each end of the socket. L.15.2 × D. (socket) 2.3cm.

The object was recovered from tenth- to eleventh-century levels in Coppergate. Comparable objects are known from 16-22 Coppergate, York, Birka (Sweden), Hedeby and Dorestad. Their function is not known, but they may have been eel-spears.

YDL9   Cylindrical limestone lamp
16-22 Coppergate, York YCC [YAT 1980.7.7774]

The lamp tapers from the upper end towards a slight waist before expanding again towards the base. In the top is a circular tapering hollow with a flat base, and in the bottom is a narrow tapering circular socket. D.9.6 × L.14.1cm.

Stone lamps are well known from other English sites, such as Southampton. The socket in the base would presumably have fitted over a spike to prevent the lamp being overturned.

YDL11   YD44   YAB27   YDL12

YDL10   Four sherds of Stamford ware: two rims of glazed spouted pitchers, a glazed lamp base, an unglazed cooking pot/jar rim sherd
6-8 Pavement, York YM [YAT 1972.21]
Ebor Brewery, Aldwark, York YCC [YAT 1974.5]
Parliament Street, York YCC [YAT 1977.11]

Pottery of this type was made at Stamford, Lincs. and imported into York.

YDL11   Wooden spoon
Clifford Street, York YM [C629]

It has a narrow bowl and flat handle shouldered above the bowl and expanding towards the end where it terminates in a fan-shaped projection. The handle is decorated with an incised step pattern, the units alternately plain and hatched. L.22.0cm.

Wooden spoons with incised ornament on the stem are known from a number in Scandinavia.

YDL12   Wooden spoon
Clifford Street, York YM [C628]

Similar to no. YDL11, this spoon however lacks the fan-shaped end to the handle, which is decorated with an angular three-strand plait terminating in a knot. The plait is confined between frames of interlocking triangles alternately plain and hatched. L.22.0cm.

YDL13   York ware cooking pot
16-22 Coppergate, York YCC [YAT 1980.7.]

The pot has external sooting and a carbonised deposit on the interior. H.16.5 × D. (rim) 13.0cm.

YDL14   Torksey-type ware tubular spouted pitcher
16-22 Coppergate, York YCC [YAT 1979.7]

It has multiple handles and thumbed strip decoration. H.44.0 × D. (rim) 24.0cm.

YDL15   Incomplete stone lamp
16-22 Coppergate, York YCC [YAT 1980.7.9594]

This is part of the bowl, biconical knop and foot of an hour-glass shaped stone lamp with incised ornament. L.11.2 × 6.25cm.

There is a late Anglo-Saxon stone lamp of closely comparable form from Saxon Southampton.

YDL16   Incomplete York ware lamp
Pavement, York YM [552.5.48]

This has a hemispherical bowl and short stem which expands towards the flat base. There is a conical socket in the base. H.8.0 × D.7.6cm.

The socket in the base would prevent cracking during firing, likely if the base were solid. It would also allow the lamp to fit over an iron spike to prevent it being knocked over.

YDL17   Iron pricket
16-22 Coppergate, York YCC [YAT 1979.7.7458]

It is made of a rod of square section, pointed at each end. On to each two opposed sides has been welded a separate sheet of iron, its thickness divided into two for half its length, and the two halves pulled out in opposing directions. At each end is an inward facing spiral. L.10.2 × W.4.8cm.

The heavier end would be driven into a timber; a candle or taper would fit into the other.

YDL18

YDL18 Iron sliding key with a loose suspension ring
16-22 Coppergate, York YCC [YAT 1977.7.1612]

The bulbous stem is decorated with a spiral copper-alloy inlay. The elaborate bit is incomplete. L.10.0cm.

Sliding keys of similar form are known from both Scandinavia (graves 759 and 1142A at Birka) and England, (St Peter's Street, Northampton). The English examples are, however, probably imports from Scandinavia. Keys of this type were used with box padlocks with T-shaped slots (see no. YDL25).

YDL19 Iron sliding key
16-22 Coppergate, York YCC [YAT 1978.7.3265]

The flattened upper half of the stem expands and the upper end is drawn out and turned back to form a suspension loop. The lower half of the stem is of square section and the circular bit is brought forward at right angles to it. L.16.4 × W.3.0cm.

Such a large key was probably used with a chest or door lock.

YDL20 Iron sliding key
16-22 Coppergate, York YCC [YAT 1977.7.2390]

The stem is of square section and flattened into a lozenge shape at the upper end. The circular bit is bent forward. L.10.7 × W.1.5cm.

YDL21 Iron sliding key
16-22 Coppergate, York YCC [YAT 1977.7.1184]

Similar to no. YDL18, except the inlay on the stem is largely lost. L.8.0cm.

YDL22 Iron twist key
16-22 Coppergate, York YCC [YAT 1980.7.8146]

It has a circular loop, undecorated stem of square section, and narrow bit bent into an S-shape. L.19.3 × W.3.6cm.

YDL23 Iron hasp
16-22 Coppergate, York [YAT 1979.7.5338]

The hasp is composed of three twisted, curved rods terminating at one end in a copper-alloy animal head decorated with ring and dot. From the underside of the head projected a loop, now lost, on which the hasp could pivot. At the other end is a similar animal head from the mouth of which issued a loop, now broken away. L.11.7 × W.1.6cm.

Similar hasps are known from chests or caskets in graves 854, 845 and 839 at Birka, Sweden and from Lejre, Denmark.

YDL24 Hour-glass shaped iron hasp
16-22 Coppergate, York YCC [YAT 1978.7.2648]

It is composed of a twisted rod of circular section. L.13.9 × W.3.1cm.

Such a hasp would have been used on a small casket of the type well known from Viking-Age graves in Scandinavia.

YDL25

YDL25 Iron box padlock
Hungate, York YM [1971.321]

The sides are framed by twisted iron rods and decorated with three similar equally-spaced vertical rods. The bottom, top and ends are undec-orated. One end is hinged at the top and opens to reveal the inverted T-shaped slot for the key. There are the ends of chains fixed to the top and one side. H.6.0 × W.3.8 × T.2.7cm.

Box padlocks are relatively well-known both in England (as from St Peter's Street, Northampton), and from Scandinavia (as from Trelleborg, Denmark). They were probably used for locking small chests or caskets.

YDL26 Bone pipe
16-22 Coppergate, York YCC [YAT 1979.7.5316]

Probably made from a goose ulna fractured at both ends, it has two blow holes, one close to each end. L.18.2 × 0.1.1cm.

Two bone pipes of similar form are known from Clifford Street, York. Comparable examples are known in England from Southampton and Thetford, and in Scandinavia from Hedeby and Birka.

YDL27 Pan pipes made from a rectangular piece of box wood
16-22 Coppergate, York YCC [YAT 1979.7.5083]

In the edge is bored a row of five holes of increasing depth, the first of which is partially broken away. There is a pierced hole for suspension. L.9.8 × W.8.1cm.

This unique instrument is still playable; the notes produced range from top E to top A.

YDL28 Lignite bridge made for a six- or seven-stringed instrument
16-22 Coppergate, York YCC [YAT 1979.7.6876]

L.2.9 × W.2.2cm.

Such an instrument bridge was probably intended for use with a lyre of the type illustrated as being played by King David in the eighth-century Vespasian Psalter, and known from the seventh-century Sutton Hoo ship burial, Suffolk.

YDL29 Wooden pipe
Hungate, York YM [1971.321.353]

This has an expanding end and is now in two pieces. Four fingering holes separated by transverse ridges survive out of an original five. Below the last fingering hole is a panel of incised ornament. L.9.6 × D.2.0cm.

YDL30 Group of playing pieces of sub-conical form
16-22 Coppergate, York YCC [YAT 1979.7.4949, 7332; 1980.7.7592, 7611, 7656, 7630, 7667, 7668, 8169, 8243]

The white pieces are made from chalk and the dark pieces from antler. Most are roughly shaped with a knife, but one is lathe-turned and has a bulbous extension on the top. W.2.2 × D.2cm.

The playing pieces are not a set, being found separately, but all are probably pieces for playing *hnefatafl*, a Viking board game. The bulbous top identifies the lathe-turned piece as a *hnefi* or 'king'. Such playing pieces were common in the Viking Age, made from a variety of materials including bone, amber, jet and glass.

YDL31 Group of five discoid gaming pieces
16-22 Coppergate, York YCC [YAT 1979.7.6765, 1980.7.7525, 7607, 7628, 7707]

Three are made from a dark micaceous sandstone,

one from a lighter coloured sandstone, and one from a re-used Roman pottery base. 5.7 × 5.4cm.

Such gaming pieces in stone or re-used Roman tile and pottery are known in all periods in York, and these are attributed to the Anglo-Scandinavian period on the basis of their tenth-century contexts.

YDL32   Part of a wooden gaming board
16-22 Coppergate, York YCC [YAT 1979.7.6609]

The full width of 15 squares survives three ranks deep. A raised strip is nailed round the edge. L.51.0 × W.11.6cm.

Although gaming pieces are abundant in the Viking world, the boards are less common, presumably since they were made of perishable materials. The best surviving example is from Ballindery Crannog, Ireland, its Scandinavian affinities suggested by the use of Borre style ornament around the edge.

YDL33   Iron snaffle bit with inverted Y-shaped cheek pieces
Coppergate, York YM [551.52.48]

The incised decoration may originally have been inlaid. L.25.5 × W.9.8 × H.9.7cm.

A closely comparable bit is known from the Merovingian and Viking period cemetery at By, Løten, Hedmark, Norway from a tenth-century male cremation. Fragments of comparable bits are known in England from London and Winchester.

YDL34   Tinned iron prick spur
16-22 Coppergate, York YCC [YAT 1980.7.8589]

The loop is of triangular section and decorated with incised ornament. One of the attachments for the leather strap survives. L.14.8 × W.8.2cm.

Spurs of very similar form are known from Birka although apparently not tinned. One example is, however, bronze plated. Tinning of iron objects was a common practice in Viking-Age York, see nos. YD37 and YDL35.

YDL35   Tinned iron prick spur
16-22 Coppergate, York YCC [YAT 1979.7.5618]

This has a loop of semi-circular section decorated on each side with three equally-spaced mouldings. One of the attachments for the leather strap survives. L.17.0 × W.8.7cm.

YDL36   Two bone skates made from horse metatarsals
16-22 Coppergate, York YCC [YAT 1980.7.10629, 10993]

Each has a circular socket in the back end, and a pointed front end. L.25.0cm.

For further discussion see no. YAB48.

YORK ANTLER/BONE WORKING

YAB1   Red deer antler sawn into lengths ready for use, and an antler burr still attached to a piece of skull
Clifford Street, York YM [C657, C603, C612, C610, C615]

L.3.9cm.

The burr still attached to a piece of skull suggests that some antler came from dead animals, although the majority was shed naturally.

YAB2   Rectangular antler blanks for the tooth-plates of a single-sided composite comb
16-22 Coppergate, York YCC [YAT 1976.7.85, 1979.7.4724, 5038, 5331 and 5444]

Two retain the rough outer surface of the antler on one face. Fine saw marks are visible on the cut surfaces. L. (largest) 4.4 × W.2.8cm.

The discovery of such tooth-plate blanks, and the rough-outs for the comb backs, indicates that there was a comb-making industry of considerable size in Viking-Age York. Similar manufacturing debris is known from Ribe, Hedeby and Dublin.

YAB3   Three antler comb-back rough-outs illustrating the stages in manufacture
York YM [1014.54, 1020.54, 1011.54]

L.15.0 × W.2.0cm.

Manufacture started with a length cut from the beam of the antler. The rough outer surface was then removed by trimming with a knife, possibly a draw knife. Finally the facetted surface was rubbed smooth.

YAB4   Single-sided composite antler comb with a curved back
16-22 Coppergate, York YCC [YAT 1980.7.8445]

The final tooth plates project slightly beyond the ends of the back plates and have curved upper edges, giving the comb-back upturned ends. There are six tooth plates and two back plates linked by five iron rivets. Each of the back plates has simple incised decoration originally inlaid with a black material (see no. YAB12). L.16.4 × W.4 × 1.3cm.

YAB5   Single-sided composite antler comb, like YAB4
16-22 Coppergate, York YCC [YAT 1980.7.8033]

The outer edges of the end plates have a double carved profile. Each of the back plates has three longitudinal facets, the median facets being undecorated, and the flanking facets decorated with groups of oblique incised lines. A number of teeth are lost. L.12.6 × W.5.4cm.

YAB18

YAB6 Damaged single-sided composite antler comb, like YAB4
York YM [583.48]

There are twenty-one tooth plates linked by thirteen iron rivets. The incised decoration on the back plates may originally have been inlaid. L.28.7 × W.3.8cm.

YAB7 Damaged single-sided composite antler comb, like YAB4
York YM [586.48]

The upturned ends are greatly exaggerated. Five of the original seven tooth plates survive, and are held in place by six iron rivets. L.16.8 × W.4.6cm.

YAB8 Single-sided composite antler comb, like YAB4
16-22 Coppergate, York YCC [YAT 1980.7.8481]

There are six tooth plates and two back plates held together by seven iron rivets. The back plates have simple incised ornament. L.12.2 × W.3.2cm.

YAB9 Single-sided composite bone comb, like YAB4
16-22 Coppergate, York YCC [YAT 1979.7.5704]

There are seven tooth plates and five iron rivets. The ends of the connecting plates have vertical grooving, possibly originally inlaid. L.10.7 × W.3.6cm.

This is one of the few single-sided composite combs from York made of bone. With the comb case no. YAB13, it illustrates the overlap between the antler workers' and bone workers' crafts. This comb is of particular interest, as microscopic investigation of the soil removed from between the teeth has revealed the presence of sheep nits, suggesting that the comb was used for combing wool before spinning.

YAB10 Damaged two-sided composite antler comb
York YM [609.48]

It has ten surviving tooth plates held in place by seven surviving iron rivets. It is similar in construction to the single-sided combs except that four of the tooth plates in the middle of the comb project beyond the comb back, and are cut into finer teeth than those of the main comb. L.18.9 × W.5.6cm.

YAB11 Damaged, two-sided composite antler comb, similar to YAB4
York YM [612.48]

Four tooth plates survive from the original seven, and the two connecting plates are held together by five rivets surviving from an original seven. The connecting plates are decorated with vertical frets flanked by groups of incised lines, the whole probably originally inlaid. L.12.5 × W.4.6.

YAB12 Antler comb case
16-22 Coppergate, York YCC [YAT 1979.7.7284]

It is composed of two back plates having a convex outer edge, inside which are two straight inner plates. The pairs of plates are separated at each end by a narrow end plate, and are held together by five iron rivets. All the plates have deeply incised decoration filled with inlay, now partially lost. L.16.0 × W.3.8cm.

Single-sided composite combs often had a matching case to protect the fragile teeth, particularly when the comb was intended to be worn suspended from the belt. The use of inlay on antler seen here is unusual. The material may be niello.

YAB13 Bone comb case
York YM [571.48]

This is similar to YAB12 except that it is held together by four iron rivets, and is decorated with ring-and-dot. L.12.3 × W.2.1 × D.0.7cm.

YAB14 Two sub-rectangular antler wasters, each with a single row of perforations
Clifford Street, York YM [C564]
Hungate, York YM [1971.321]

L.9.8 × W.2.0 × D.0.6cm.
Such plates are the refuse from the manufacture of antler beads, (no. YAB15).

YAB15 Three disc-shaped antler beads
16-22 Coppergate, York YCC [YAT 1979.7.6266 and 7356, 1980.7.7589]

D. (largest) 1.2cm.

YAB16 Undecorated antler finger ring of D-shaped section
16-22 Coppergate, York YCC [YAT 1980.7.7505]

D.1.1cm.
Similar plain rings are known from 16-22 Coppergate in a variety of materials including jet, amber, and glass, as well as metal.

YAB17 Two Y-shaped antler pendants
Clifford Street, York YM [C667]
York YM [619.48]

They are decorated with incised ornament, and small relief animal heads. L.9.2cm.
These are utilised waste tines from antler working. The small animal heads are similar to those used on the metalwork of the ninth- and early tenth-century Anglo-Saxon Trewhiddle style.

YAB18 Group of worked antler tines
Clifford Street, York YM [C583.4, C585, C591, C604]

They are decorated with incised saltires or spiral grooving. Two are perforated. L.30.0cm.
Objects of this type are common in York; possibly they were used to separate the strands of rope for splicing. Such tines are known from Bergen, Norway, associated with lengths of rope.

YAB19 Antler die
16-22 Coppergate, York YCC [YAT 1979.7.7051]

The numbers are indicated by ring-and-dot. The six is placed opposite the one, and the five opposite the two. L.1.1 × W.1.0cm.

YAB20 Antler strap-end
16-22 Coppergate, York YCC [YAT 1980.7.8146]

This has an animal-head terminal and is decorated with an incised four-strand interlace plait. The end of the leather strap fitted into a split in the upper end and was held in place by two iron rivets. L.11.5 × W.1.3cm.
The strap-end may be unfinished since the

animal head has only a single incised eye and the interlace is only lightly cut. It is possible that the craftsman had sketched out the basic design intending to deepen and widen it.

YAB21 Bone toggles made from the metacarpi of juvenile pigs
16-22 Coppergate, York YCC [YAT 1979.7.5683 and 7075]

L.6.1 × W.1.5cm.

Except for the perforations the bones are unworked. Such toggles may have been used for fastening clothing although they have been identified as musical instruments or amulets. Similar toggles are known in England from late tenth/eleventh-century contexts in Saddler Street, Durham and in Scandinavia from the Thule excavation, Lund. The manufacture of such simple objects did not require specialist craftsmen, and they were probably made from domestic food bones as and when required.

YAB22 Double-pronged bone implement made from a bovine nasal bone
16-22 Coppergate, York YCC [YAT 1979.7.4107]

L.10.0cm.

The wear on the prongs and the polishing from handling indicates that the bones were used. Other examples are known from 6-8 Pavement, York, the Church Street Roman sewer, York and from later medieval levels at Jarlshof, Shetland. Their function is uncertain but they can be compared with yarn twisters (see no. YT10). Alternatively they could have been used as forks for eating.

YAB23 Socketed bone point
16-22 Coppergate, York YCC [YAT 1980.7.7620]

L.13.2 × W.5.3cm.

Similar unstratified objects are known from London, and from Anglo-Scandinavian levels at 6-8 Pavement, York, but their function is uncertain. The wear marks are not those characteristic of awls, and the suggestion that they formed the tips of ice skating poles is unconvincing.

YAB24 Bone awl
16-22 Coppergate, York YCC [YAT 1980.7.7557]

It is made from a jaw bone and has a sub-triangular upper end which tapers to a long narrow point. L.8.4 × W.5.8cm.

The marks of wear on the point indicate that it has been used.

YAB25 Two spindle whorls
16-22 Coppergate, York YCC [YAT 1979.7.5280]
York YM [566.48]

Each is made from the head of an ox femur; one is decorated all over with incised dots. D.4.1cm.

YAB26 Incomplete scoop made from a scapula
6-8 Pavement, York [YAT 1972.21.5302]

L.13.2 × W.7.2cm.

YAB27 Iron knife
Clifford Street, York YM [C662]

This has a bone handle of ovoid section decorated around the circumference with pairs of grooves and geometrical ornament separated from each other by plain bands. The blade is incomplete. L.14.3 × D.1.3cm.

YAB28 Bone point
16-22 Coppergate, York YCC [YAT 1979.7.6412]

The handle of ovoid section expands towards a slight shoulder from which develops a shallow hook. The inner edge of the hook has a double curved profile and like the outer edge is cross-hatched. There are wear marks on the tip. L.11.5cm.

A similar object is held by the scribe in the portrait page of the Eadwine Psalter, (Trinity Coll., Camb. MS. 171.f.67). The wear marks on the tip suggest that it was used for ruling lines, or laying out the ornament of a manuscript. Alternatively it may have been used for burnishing gold lettering or decoration.

YAB29 Undecorated, five-lobed whalebone sword pommel
16-22 Coppergate, York YCC [YAT 1979.7.4752]

W.7.1 × H.4.1 × T.2.1cm.

Although found in twelfth-century levels, the form of the pommel suggests a rather earlier date. Perhaps used with a bone guard like YAB30.

YAB29

YAB30 Undecorated bone sword guard
Clifford Street, York YM [C560]

L.8.6 × W.2.0 × T.1.8cm.

YAB31 Bone dress pins made from pigs' fibulae
16-22 Coppergate, York YCC [YAT 1979.7.5534, 5629, 7163]

The expanding ends, formed by the natural distal ends of the bone, are perforated. One has additional rudimentary shaping of the head. L.10.9cm.

Similar pins are well known from other English pre-Conquest sites such as Southampton, where manufacturing debris has been found. They also occur in Scandinavia at Hedeby, and the Thule and PK-Banken sites, Lund. They are frequently identified as needles rather than as dress pins, but against this is the lack of wear in the perforations which might be expected on needles, the occurrence of unperforated examples, and the marked expansion of many of the heads.

YAB32 Bone pin
York YM [C643]

It has a perforated spatulate head separated from the shank by a cross bar. L.11.5cm.

It may be related to cross-head types dated at Jarlshof, Sheltland, to the eleventh century.

YAB33 Bone pin
Clifford Street, York YM [C533]

It has a perforated square head with notched edges. L.11.4 × W. (head) 1.3cm.

Similar pins are known from Hedeby.

YAB34 Bone pin
Clifford Street, York YM [C675]

This has a perforated annular head separated from the shank by a raised collar. L.19.6cm.

Pins of this type are known from Birka, Hedeby and Jarlshof.

YAB35   Bone pin
16-22 Coppergate, York YCC [YAT 1977.7.2276]

It has a spherical head divided into vertical zones decorated alternately with incised hatching and ring-and-dot. L.5.5cm.

YAB36   Bone pin with a facetted head
Bedern, York YM [1951.21]

L.10.6cm.

YAB37   Bone crutch-headed pin
16-22 Coppergate, York YCC [YAT 1977.7.1763]

L.10.0cm.

YAB38   Three animal-headed bone pins
York YM [1955.10.6]
Clifford Street, York YM [C505 and C528]

L.11.2cm.
   Animal-headed pins like this are known elsewhere in Britain only from Jarlshof, Shetland, but are widely distributed in Scandinavia. An eleventh-century date is proposed for the type.

YAB39   Bone styliform pin
Clifford Street, York YM [C504]

The upper end is carved in the form of a winged beast from whose open mouth protrudes an expanding tongue of square section. L.8.0cm.
   This object has been identified as a stylus for writing on wax tablets but it is very small and slight for this purpose. Moreover on a stylus such as that from Whitby (no. C4) the expanding end is flat to smooth down the wax for re-use. The animal's tongue here is unsuitable for such a purpose being of square section. The piece is better identified as a styliform pin related to the animal-headed pin no. YAB38.

YAB40   Bone copy of a bronze ringed pin
Clifford Street, York YM [C.529]

The pin has a crutch head, and an incised fret decorating the lower part of the shank. (Compare with no. YTC13). L.11.9cm.
   Bronze staining in the hollows in the ends of the head indicates that the pin originally had a bronze ring, like the similar pin from York now preserved in the Castle Museum, Norwich.

YAB41   Fragment of a jaw bone used as a trial piece
16-22 Coppergate, York YCC [YAT 1979.7.5692]

It is decorated on one side with five randomly-placed quadrupeds, and an interlace triquetra knot, and on the other with a single quadruped above a panel of interlace, together with a mass of more lightly incised designs. L.9.8 × W.5.2cm.
   Trial pieces seem to have been used to practise drawing or carving designs, or for working out designs which were subsequently to be transferred to other objects, either to bone or other media such as metal. The random nature of the sketches on this piece suggests that it belongs to the former category. Trial pieces are known from Ireland and from London and York in England, but they are not known from Scandinavia.

YAB44

YAB42   Fragment of a cow's rib, used as a trial piece
16-22 Coppergate, York YCC [YAT 1980.7.8016]

On each face there are two irregularly-shaped carved areas placed side by side. Each is decorated with a pair of interlacing Jellinge-style animals. L.18.2 × W.3.2cm.
   The four fields are probably successive attempts to work out the same design, and the unusual shape suggests that the craftsman had in mind a particular object for which he was working out this design.

YAB43   Narrow rectangular bone plaque
York YM [658.48]

At one end it has the rough-out for an openwork rectangular panel. L.15.7 × W.3.6cm.
   The piece is important as it provides several clues about the techniques of bone working. The decorated panel was first sketched out freehand, and the openwork begun, using a drill. The holes were then extended to the required shape. Surface detail would have been added later.

YAB44   Bone strap-end
16-22 Coppergate, York YCC [YAT 1979.7.6833]

It has a rounded lower end and a horizontal slot in the upper end for the attachment of the strap. It is decorated on one face with a conventionalised plant, and on the other with a six-strand plait, the interlace having a median billeted zone. L.6.2 × W.2.4cm.
   The piece comes from an early tenth-century context, a date supported by its form, the rounded end being typical of tenth-century strap-ends.

YAB45   Bone pin head
16-22 Coppergate, York YCC [YAT 1979.7.5734]

It consists of a shank of ovoid section issuing from a mouth shared between two animal masks, one on either side of the stem. The shank terminates in a pair of outward-facing animal heads. L.4.3 × W.1.4cm.
   The identification of the piece as a pin head is tentative. The flat end, and the nature of the break below the animal masks suggests that a turning action may have been applied to the object, and it is possible that it was used as a tuning peg.

YAB46   Narrow rectangular bone plaque
York YM [582.48]

At one end is a narrow vertical slot, now partially broken away, and at the other is an irregular ovoid perforation impinging on the figure-of-eight interlace plait which decorates the front face. L.11.1 × W.2.0cm.

YAB47   Curved, tapering bone handle of circular section
Jubbergate, York SCM [J93.719]

The body of the handle is decorated with bands of incised interlace, and at each end there is an animal head terminal. In the broad end is a socket with a rivet hole on either side. L.9.3cm.

YAB48   Two bone skates made from horse metacarpals
16-22 Coppergate, York YCC [YAT 1979.7.6456, 7360]

Each has a circular socket in the back end. L.22.5cm.

Such skates were tied to the feet by leather thongs passing through iron or wooden loops in the socket at the back end. Sometimes an additional thong was passed through a perforation at the front. Bone skates are widely known in Scandinavia and appear to have been introduced into England at the time of the Viking settlement.

YORK METAL WORKING

YMW1   Two pieces of the lead/silver ore, galena
16-22 Coppergate, York YCC [YAT 1980.7.7673 and 7902]

L.9.7 × W.8.3 × D.7.4cm.

Galena is a lead sulphide ore, usually mixed with a small percentage of silver sulphide. The nearest source to York is in the Pennines, some 45kms. away. Before smelting, the ore was crushed and roasted to convert the lead sulphide into lead oxide.

YMW2   Lead spillages
16-22 Coppergate, York YCC [YAT 1979.7.6032; 1980.7.7641, 8333]

They incorporate plant remains carbonised on contact with the molten metal. L.7.8 × W.4.9cm.

During the smelting and manufacturing process spillages of molten metal were inevitable. Lead seems to have been so abundant that such spillages were not immediately remelted for use. Spillages of other metals are not found.

YMW3   Two bi-conical open clay crucibles
16-22 Coppergate, York YCC [YAT 1980.7] York YM [551.41.48]

Each has the rim pulled out to form a pouring lip. Both are vitrified and glazed from use. D.4.6 × H.3.3cm.

Among the crucibles discovered at 16-22 Coppergate bi-conical crucibles were the commonest. They were used for melting silver.

YMW4   Two fragmentary open clay crucibles of the "thumb pot" type
16-22 Coppergate, York YCC [YAT 1979.7.5722, 1977.7.2137]

Both are glazed and vitrified from use.

Analysis suggests that they were used for melting of copper and gold. Crucibles of similar type are known in Scandinavia from Hedeby, Birka, Lund and Kaupang (Norway) and at Southampton and Cheddar, where they were also used for melting gold.

YMW5   Hemispherical open clay crucible with the rim pulled out to form a pouring lip
York YM [un-numbered]

Glazed and vitrified from use. D.5.8cm.

YMW6   Incomplete circular clay dish
16-22 Coppergate, York YCC [YAT 1980.7]

Glazed and vitrified from use. D.5.3cm.

The heating trays were used for working both gold and copper. Similar trays are known from Hedeby, Rike, Birka, Trelleborg and Fyrkat, where they were associated with a gold and bronze smith's workshop. The trays were used for refining gold, and heating jewellery during the application of filigree and granulation.

YMW7   Two incomplete stone ingot moulds
16-22 Coppergate, York YCC [YAT 1979.7.5479; 1980.7.7660]

Each is of square section with a slot for casting different-sized ingots in each of the long faces. L.7.7 × W.3.7 × T.3.4cm.

Casting an ingot was the first stage in the manufacturing process. Pieces were then cut off either to be cold-worked into objects, or remelted in a crucible for casting. Such moulds are widely known from Scandinavia, at Hedeby and Fyrkat, as well as English town sites – Southampton, Lincoln and Chester (E19).

YMW8   Incomplete soapstone ingot mould
16-22 Coppergate, York YCC [YAT 1980.7.9645]

It has a rectangular section, with a flat underside and five slots distributed among the remaining three faces. L.8.5 × W.5.2 × T.4.7cm.

YMW9   Damaged stone ingot mould
16-22 Coppergate, York YCC [YAT 1980.7.9987]

Originally of square section, it has five slots for casting ingots distributed among the four long faces. L.15.0 × W.10.2 × H.3.3cm.

YMW10   Ingot mould of re-used Roman tile
16-22 Coppergate, York YCC [YAT 1980.7.8708]

There are three slots for casting ingots, or the basic shapes of objects, cut into each face. L.15.2 × W.10.5 × T.3.1cm.

Once the basic shape of the object was cast in such a mould, it would then be cold-worked into its final form.

YMW11   Length cut from a copper-alloy ingot
16-22 Coppergate, York YCC [YAT 1980.7.8219]

The narrow, slightly tapering ingot has a trapezoid section. L.1.4 × W.1.4 × T.0.6cm.

Ingots of this form would be cast in a mould like YMW7. The piece has been cut from an ingot prior to re-melting for casting, or cold-working into an object.

YMW12   Lead ingot
16-22 Coppergate, York YCC [YAT 1979.7.5897]

This has a sub-rectangular form and D-shaped section. L.9.9 × W.2.9 × T.1.7cm.

An ingot of such irregular shape would have been cast in a sand-box rather than an ingot mould.

YMW13   Sub-cruciform lead-alloy matrix
York YM [702.4.48]

Decorated in the Borre style, it has an expanding

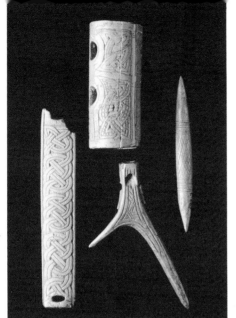

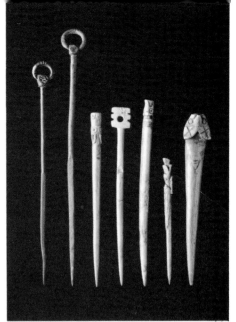

RIGHT *Decorated bone objects of York. The top cylinder (E9) displays designs reminiscent of the Scandinavian Mammen art style.*
FAR RIGHT *A selection of bronze and bone dress pins.*
BELOW *Animal bones have been used by craftsmen to work out trial designs in patterns of interlace and animals. The upper one is Scandinavian in style, the lower two pieces (B41 and C7) have been carved with Anglo-Saxon Trewhiddle motifs.*

suspension loop in the form of a bird's head. L.4.7 × W.4.1cm.

Such a matrix was probably used for making moulds, from which pendants could be cast. Silver pendants of similar form are known from the Tolstrup hoard, Denmark, (see no. H6), and this matrix provides important evidence for their manufacture in Scandinavian taste in York.

YMW14 Incomplete upper part of a two part clay mould for a trefoil brooch
Blake Street, York YCC [YAT 1975.6.448]

There is an animal mask at the junction of the two surviving arms, and a similar mask in the centre of each arm below a pair of outward-facing but inward-looking birds or winged bipeds. L.10.7cm.

Trefoil brooches were introduced into England from Scandinavia, but the ornament here combines the animal mask derived from the Scandinavian Borre style with the bird or winged biped whose ancestry is English. No brooch which could have been cast in this mould survives.

YMW15 Two circular lead-alloy badges
16-22 Coppergate, York YCC [YAT 1977.7.1071; 1979.7.4950]

Inside the beaded border is a plain zone surrounding the main field, which is raised and decorated with an openwork design based on a saltire superimposed on two concentric circles. At the end of each cross arm is an animal mask. At each side of the object is a U-shaped loop for attachment. The second brooch is damaged. D.4.3 × W.3.2cm.

The animal masks suggest that the ornament is related to the Borre style. The gaps in the openwork are flaws in the casting, and this, coupled with the discovery of two almost identical objects within a restricted area, suggests that they were made on or near the site of discovery.

YMW16 Circular lead-alloy pendant
16-22 Coppergate, York [YAT 1980.7.8323]

Cast in one piece with an unpierced suspension loop, it is decorated with a runic inscription surrounding a central boss. Casting flashes survive around the edges. L.2.7 × D.2.0cm.

The runic inscription is not yet read. The unpierced suspension loop, and the presence of casting flashes, suggest that the pendant is unfinished and was made on or near the site.

YMW17 Several pieces of the iron ore haematite (red ochre)
16-22 Coppergate, York YCC [YAT 1980.7.7532, 7845, 8111, 8150, 8249, 8599]

L.3.1 × W.2.4 × T.2.0cm.

Haematite is an iron oxide. Before smelting, the ore was broken into small pieces and the impurities removed by washing. They were then roasted to remove the water. Haematite is, however, such a rich ore that additives would be needed for effective smelting and it is possible that it was intended for some other purpose since it can be used as a pigment, a cosmetic or jeweller's rouge.

YMW18 Two haematite fragments
16-22 Coppergate, York YCC [YAT 1980.7.8949, 9775]

One is roughly worked into a wedge shape. Both show the marks of rubbing. L.4.5 × W.2.5cm.

The rubbing suggests that the pieces were used for jeweller's rouge, for polishing, not smelting.

YMW19 Fragmentary furnace bottom of iron slag, originally circular
16-22 Coppergate, York YCC [YAT 1980.7]

D.26.0 × T.12.0cm.

For iron smelting, a furnace was constructed by digging a small hollow, and building the superstructure of the furnace around it. After firing, waste products solidified in the hollow to form the furnace bottom.

YORK LEATHER WORKING

YL1 Iron awl
6-8 Pavement, York YCC [YAT 1974.21.5403]

It is of rectangular section, with a cylindrical wooden handle. L.9.7cm.

Several similar awls were recovered from 6-8 Pavement, associated with abundant evidence for leather-working.

YL2 Iron scraper
16-22 Coppergate, York YCC [YAT 1978.7.2673]

This has a straight blade turned up at each end to form a narrow, tapering tang. The cutting edge is on the side opposite the tangs. L.13.0cm.

The tool is a scraper for removing the flesh and hair from the hides prior to tanning.

YL2a Lunate iron scraper
Pavement, York. YM [1316]

It has a short tang developing from the middle of the concave edge.

Such scrapers were used for stripping the hair and flesh from the hide prior to tanning.

YL3 Alder-wood shoe last
6-8 Pavement, York YCC [YAT 1972.21]

It has a rounded toe and a squared heel. In some places it has been made up with leather strips secured by iron nails. L.21.5 × W.8.0 × D.7.5cm.

The last would have been used in the making of shoes like nos. YL5–7 and is shaped for the left foot. Similar lasts are known from Hedeby, Oslo, and Wolin, Poland.

YL4 Group of leather offcuts
6-8 Pavement, York YCC [YAT 1972.21]

Excavation at 6-8 Pavement, York has produced abundant evidence for leather working, including a leather stretcher, a shoe last (no. YL3) and a mass of offcuts.

YL5 Two leather shoes
16-22 Coppergate, York YCC [YAT 1980.7.9116, 9558]

Each has a rounded heel and toe. The one-piece uppers have a seam on the inside of the foot and were blind stitched to the single thickness soles. One of the soles has a separate piece stitched on to reinforce the heel. L.27.0 × W.10.2cm.

Simple slip-on shoes of this form are known also from Hungate, York, Hedeby, and Lund where they occur as late as the twelfth century. Like the

YMW13

YMW16

YL10

other shoes from York, they were probably made by the turnshoe method in which the sole and upper were assembled inside out, and turned the right way round only after softening by soaking.

YL6   Leather shoe with a rounded heel and toe
16-22 Coppergate, York YCC [YAT 1971.7.4650]

The two-piece upper has a seam along the instep which turns at right angles to run down the inside of the foot. It is blind stitched to the one-piece sole.

YL7   Leather shoe with a rounded heel and toe
16-22 Coppergate, York YCC [YAT 1978.7.2581]

The back of the sole is pointed and upturned to fit into a triangular slot in the heel of the one-piece upper, which has a seam down the inside of the foot and a triangular dart in the instep. L.19.0cm.

The shoe would have been tied by a thong running round the heel and over the instep and tied at the ankle. Shoes with pointed backs are widely known from Frisia, Scandinavia and Russia between the seventh and the fourteenth centuries. The type may have been introduced to England by Scandinavian settlers in the ninth and tenth centuries.

YL8   Child's ankle boot
16-22 Coppergate, York YCC [YAT 1977.7.4422]

The one-piece upper, which is blind stitched onto the single thickness sole, has a seam down the inside of the foot, and a triangular flap over the front of the ankle. This was closed by a thong passing round the heel and over the instep, and tied at the ankle. L.15.5 × W.4.0cm.

YL9   Child's shoe, like no. YL8
16-22 Coppergate, York YCC [YAT 1978.7.5286]

It has an added strengthening piece over the back of the heel. L.15.3 × W.6.0cm.

YL10   Leather scabbard
Parliament Street, York YCC [YAT 1976.11.73]

It has a row of rivet holes along one edge. The throat is damaged, possibly by the loss of a mount for suspension, and there is a second suspension point half-way along the length of the scabbard. On the front face are two long, narrow interlace-decorated fields separated by a coiled animal. Alongside them is a zone of hatched triangles. On the back are two long panels similar in shape to those on the front and decorated with a net pattern. L.34.0cm.

The scabbard was intended to take the whole knife except the pommel, and the layout of the ornament reflects the shape of the knife inside the scabbard. The two panels of interlace represent the blade and handle, and the coiled animal, the guard. The mode of suspension, from the throat and half-way along the scabbard, is like that seen on the warrior panel on one of the crosses from Middleton, Yorks. A similar, fragmentary scabbard from Gloucester may be from the same workshop.

YL11   Leather scabbard
Parliament Street, York YCC [YAT 1976.11.47]

There are stitch holes along the edge, and a large rectangular suspension hole near the throat. The decoration is laid out like that on no. YL10, reflecting the shape of the knife inside the scabbard. On the front, the handle is decorated with small interlace-filled panels and the blade decorated with a fret. On the reverse the blade is filled with a conventionalised plant scroll, and the handle with a fret. Each side, remaining space is filled with rows of pellets. L.17.5 × W.4.4cm.

YORK TEXTILES

YT1   Group of stone spindle whorls
16-22 Coppergate, York YCC [YAT 1980.7.7678, 7950, 8085, 8484, 8609]

D.4.1cm.

Spindle whorls were used to weight the spindle when spinning yarn for weaving. The heavier the whorl, the finer the finished yarn, which explains the wide variation in the weight of the whorls (from 21–38 grams in this group).

YT2   Part of a plain annular steatite (soapstone) spindle whorl
16-22 Coppergate, York YCC [YAT 1980.7.8355]

D.6.8cm.

Similar whorls occurred in phases I and II of the Viking-Age settlement at Jarlshof (Shetland) dated to the early and mid ninth-century respectively.

YT3   Two annular and one bun-shaped undecorated lead spindle whorls
16-22 Coppergate, York YCC [YAT 1980.7.7873, 8485, 8070]

D.2.8cm.

The weights of the lead spindle whorls fall into the same range as those of the stone whorls, but being made of a heavier material, are much smaller in size. Given the amount of lead-working debris at 16-22 Coppergate, it is possible these objects were made there.

BELOW *A group of York objects all employed in the Viking Age for the manufacture of textiles. The group includes spindles and whorls, shears, a loom weight, antler tines for braiding, a glass linen smoother, and the finished material which has survived a thousand years.*

York finds LEFT *A decorated chape designed to protect the bottom of a scabbard. Its ornament carries a Jellinge-style animal and a human face (YD41).* RIGHT, *a copper alloy strap-end (YD39) with Scandinavian Borre-style decoration.* FAR RIGHT, *a cast pewter disc brooch with a backward-looking animal in the Jellinge style (YD12).* BELOW, *an unfinished limestone slab carved in Jellinge style found during Coppergate excavations (YS1).*

YT4   Three spindles, two of bone and one of wood
6-8 Pavement, York YCC [YAT 1972.21, 5232]
York YM [555.8.48]
Goodramgate, York YM [Goodramgate 4]

L.21.8 × D.1.0cm.

YT5   Three undecorated baked clay loom weights
16-22 Coppergate, York YCC [YAT 1979.7.6723, 1980.7.8291]
Hungate, York YM [1971.321.35]

D.8.7cm.

Weights from warp-weighted looms are common finds in Anglo-Saxon and Viking-Age settlements, and are usually made either of clay or stone. Stone was more usual where a soft stone such as steatite was available; the Old Norse name for soapstone was *heberg*, *he* meaning loom weight and *berg*, stone. Some clay loom weights, such as those from Hedeby and Fyrkat, have simple decoration, but most are plain.

YT6   Bone pin-beater
Clifford Street, York YM [C665]

It has a circular section and pointed ends. The central portion is cross-hatched with incised lines, the zone of hatching separated from the undecorated points by groups of parallel incised lines around the circumference. L.8.9cm.

Pin-beaters were used to make minor alterations to the weft during weaving. The hatched zone would have provided a good grip.

YT7   Bone pin-beater
16-22 Coppergate, York
YCC [YAT 1980.7.10306]

It has a flattened ovoid section with pointed ends. There are zones of hatched ornament around the circumference close to each end. L.10.7 × D.1.0cm.

YT8   Rectangular antler tablet with a perforation at each corner
16-22 Coppergate, York YCC [YAT 1980.7.8476]

L.2.7 × W.2.4cm.

Weaving tablets are widely known both from Anglo-Saxon England and from Scandinavia, for example from the Oseberg ship burial, Norway. Such tablets were used principally for manufacturing elaborate braids (like those known from the Birka graves) which were used to edge garments.

YT9   Double-pronged bone implement decorated with a lightly incised interlace sketch
16-22 Coppergate, York YCC [YAT 1979.7.7408]

L.5.2cm.

Similar implements are known in England from Portchester (Hants.) and in Scandinavia from the Thule excavations, Lund. One of those from Lund has a runic inscription which identifies it as a thread maker.

YT10   Y-shaped antler tine
16-22 Coppergate, York YCC [YAT 1980.7.9931]

It has one point longer than the other. Except for the points which are of circular section, the surfaces have been trimmed flat, giving the tine a square section. The faces are decorated with incised ornament. A triangular perforation has been made at the junction of the branches, and the end has been carved into a stylized animal head. L.9.2 × W.4.5cm.

Experiments suggest that this can tentatively be identified as a lucet: an instrument for making braids like the modern 'French' knitting. The knitting would be done on the points and the finished braid would have passed through the triangular perforation. The Y-shaped tines, no. YAB17, may also have served the same function.

YT11   Black glass linen smoother with a damaged example in opaque white glass
Clifford Street, York YM [1948.6.4, C656]

On the underside of each is a central depression, which is a manufacturing scar. D.7.0cm.

Such objects are believed to have been for smoothing the seams on linen, and are common on Viking-Age sites. It has been suggested that they were continental imports.

YT12   Small iron shears with a U-shaped bow
16-22 Coppergate, York YCC [YAT 1980.7.9876]

L.18.0cm.

Such shears would be used for needlework, and some examples, such as a pair from grave 4 at Fyrkat, were so highly prized that they had their own wooden case.

YT13   Fine worsted (combed yarn) three shed diamond twill stitched to a coarse woollen tabby (plain weave). The twill has been dyed red
6-8 Pavement, York YM [YAT 1972.21.5272, 5054]

*c.*80.0 × 71.0cm.

YT14   Fragment of light brown cloth
6-8 Pavement, York YM [YAT 1972.21.5268]

This was intended to be a 2/1 diamond twill with accurate meetings, but a mistake was made during weaving. L.12.0 × W.6.0cm.

YT15   Group of short lengths of woollen yarn
6-8 Pavement, York YM [YAT 1974.21.5331]

These are probably weak pieces cut out of the yarn when preparing the warp for weaving.

YORK WOODWORKING

YW1   Two iron axes
16-22 Coppergate, York YCC [YAT 1980.7.7991]
York YM [551.47.48]

One has a slightly asymmetrical expanding blade with the hafting hole largely broken away. The other has a much heavier hafting hole and wider neck with a marginally asymmetrical expanding blade. L.15.8 × W.8.0cm.

Both these axes were probably woodworking tools rather than weapons.

YW2   Iron T-shaped axe
York YM [642.48]

Both ends of the blade are broken away. L.16.5 × W.8.7cm.

The T-shaped axe was the main carpenter's axe in the late Anglo-Saxon period. It is represented in both the Hurbuck (Co. Durham) and Crayke

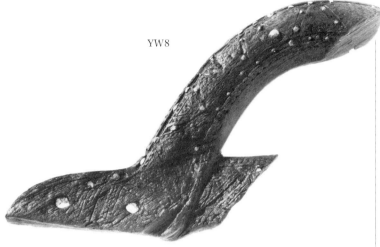

YW8

been finished, and the knob removed from the base. D.12.2 × W.9.5cm.

After turning, a small column of wood (into which the chuck of the lathe had fitted) remained in the centre of the bowl's interior. This was then snapped off and the interior rubbed smooth. The turning cores are the waste pieces of wood. Similarly, a small knob of wood into which the opposing chuck had fitted remained on the exterior and had to be removed. Wood-turning was apparently practised at 16-22 Coppergate where one of the workshops has yielded unfinished bowls, turning cores and wood shavings. The street Coppergate is probably named after the wood turners who worked there, the name deriving from the Old Norse *koppari* – a joiner or turner.

YW7   Small turned wooden bowl, and a shallow platter
16-22 Coppergate, York YCC [YAT 1977.7.1384, 1333]

D.11.0 × H.8.0cm.

Excavations at 6-8 Pavement and 16-22 Coppergate have produced fragments of turned vessels which include lids, mugs and deep bowls, as well as the more common shallow bowls. Such bowls are known from a number of other sites in York including Hungate, King's Square and Parliament Street, and from other late Anglo-Saxon sites such as Gloucester. Similar bowls are known from Hedeby.

YW8   Wooden saddle bow
16-22 Coppergate, York YCC [YAT 1977.7.1745]

It is decorated with a series of small interlocking triangular fields filled with interlace, and divided from each other by beaded mouldings, and with strips of horn. L.31.0cm.

Few decorated pre-Conquest wooden objects survive, and this piece, therefore, provides valuable insight into decorative techniques on wood. The use of small triangular fields in the decoration are reminiscent of the Trewhiddle style. Similar interlace-filled fields can be seen on the scabbard (no. YL11).

YW9   Cylindrical wooden box
16-22 Coppergate, York YCC [YAT 1980.7.9974]

The base is made of a single thin flat disc of oak, around which is wrapped a thin ash strip which forms the box sides. The ends of this strip overlap and are fixed together with two parallel vertical rows of stitching. Between these is a square field decorated with incised geometrical ornament. The rest of the exterior is decorated with a single large field, part of which is filled with a basket-work effect and part with a looped strand. D.20.0 × H.8.2cm.

The best parallels for the box are from Hedeby, where three of similar construction were found.

(Yorks.) hoards, and in the Bayeux tapestry. A hafted example has been found in an eleventh-century context from Milk Street, London (no. D26).

YW3   Two iron spoon bits
16-22 Coppergate, York YCC [YAT 1980.7.8542] Parliament Street, York YM [YAT 1976.11.17]

Each has a narrow triangular butt and a shank of square section. L.32.5cm.

Such bits were used for drilling holes, and were the standard form of drill bit in late Anglo-Saxon England, examples being known from Brundall (Norfolk), Hurbuck (Co. Durham), Thetford (Norfolk), and Westley Waterless (Cambs.). The bits vary greatly in size; every carpenter would have presumably had a range. Spoon bits are also known from Scandinavia, as for example from Trelleborg and Lund.

YW4   Iron shave
16-22 Coppergate, York YCC [YAT 1979.7.7278]

The semi-circular blade develops at each end into a narrow, tapering tang of square section, turned at right angles to the blade. The cutting edge is on the same side as the tangs. 12.5 × 9.6cm.

The tangs of the shave were linked by a wooden handle, and the shave was used for hollowing out large wooden vessels.

YW5   Iron chisel
16-22 Coppergate, York YCC [YAT 1980.7.10108]

It has a fan-shaped blade tapering towards the cylindrical socket. L.15.4 × W.6.7cm.

The tool would have had a wooden haft, and was used to plane down the surface of the wood. No other example is known from England, but several are known from Viking-Age Norway, and one from the Thule excavations, Lund.

YW6   Small turned wooden bowl and a group of cores
16-22 Coppergate, York YCC [YAT 1977.8.980; 1977.7.640, 849, 998]

The bowl was discarded before the interior had

OVERLEAF *The map shows Denmark with important monuments of the tenth century when the country's first Christian king, Harald Bluetooth, ruled. It displays some burial sites △, the four great fortresses ⊕, and the newer towns of Aarhus, Odense, Roskilde and Lund.* RIGHT *An aerial view of the circular fortress at Fyrkat on Jutland.*

NORWAY

SWEDEN

NORTH SEA

Aggersborg ⊕

△ Lindholm Høje

Fyrkat ⊕

JUTLAND

Aarhus •

SKANE

Ravning Enge bridge ⊢⌐ △ Jelling

Vorbasse •

Saedding •

△ Baekke

Roskilde •

Lund •

△ Glavendrup

• Ribe

Odense •

ZEALAND

Nonnebakken ⊕

⊕ Trelleborg

FUNEN

Danevirke •⌐ Hedeby

BALTIC SEA

Eider

• Hamburg

FRISIA

Elbe

Weser

YORK TRADE AND COINAGE

YTC1   Two fragmentary lava querns
16-22 Coppergate, York YCC [YAT 1979.7.4706 and 6077]

The larger has the remains of a central hour-glass shaped perforation. L.17.0 × W.12.0cm.
    Lava querns of this type are widely known in pre-Conquest England, and were imported from the Mayen region of Germany, possibly via Dorestad.

YTC2   Four sherds from a Tating ware pitcher
Skeldergate, York YM [YAT 1974.14]

The sherds show traces of adhesive for the original tinfoil decoration which has not survived.
    The place of manufacture of Tating ware is not known, but is thought to be in the Rhineland, North France, or east Belgium. The vessels, probably associated with the wine trade, are well known from both England and Scandinavia in the ninth century.

YTC3   Two sherds from a Badorf ware relief-band amphora, decorated with roller-stamped clay strips
16-22 Coppergate, York YM [1979.7]

Large amphorae of this type were produced in the Rhineland probably associated with the wine trade. The sherds are from tenth-century levels.

YTC4   Three sherds of Pingsdorf-type ware, with red-painted decoration
6-8 Pavement, York YM [YAT 1972.21]
16-22 Coppergate, York YCC [1979.7.19807]

Red painted wares of this type were made at Pingsdorf and other centres in the Rhineland. The main form appears to be the pitcher, and, like Tating and Badorf wares, the vessels may be associated with the wine trade.

YTC5   Copper-alloy brooch in the form of an equal-armed cross with expanding arms
16-22 Coppergate, York YCC [YAT 1980.7.7808]

There is a boss in the centre and a smaller boss at each corner at the ends of the arms. The pin and its attachment are lost but the catch survives. L.3.4 × W.3.3cm.
    The form is closely paralleled by material of German manufacture, such as the gilt-bronze cross brooch found in Ireland and now in the British Museum. Small cross brooches are, however, known from England, but usually the ends of the arms are convex, and their sides concave.

YTC6   Copper-alloy bow brooch
16-22 Coppergate, York YCC [YAT 1980.7.9209]

It has a tapering head and foot separated from the bow by pairs of transverse mouldings. In the middle of the bow is a group of three transverse mouldings. The catch and hinge plate survive but the pin is lost. L.4.1 × W.0.7cm.
    Bow brooches of this type were common on the continent from the seventh to the ninth century, but are rare in England although other examples are known from 16-22 Coppergate, York, Old Erringham (Sussex), Southampton (Hants.) and Totternhoe (Beds.) all obviously imports. The two

York examples may provide evidence for the existence of the elusive colony of Frisian merchants, mentioned in the literature as being active in York in the ninth century.

YTC7   Group of complete and fragmentary hones, many showing marks of heavy use
16-22 Coppergate, York YCC [YAT 1979.7.5942, 4621, 6048, 6930; 1980.7.7780]

L.33.8 × W.3.4 × H.2.8cm.
    Such hones, made from schist quarried in the Eidsborg region of Norway, were imported into England in bulk in the Viking Age.

YTC8   Group of soapstone bowl fragments, including rim and body sherds
6-8 Pavement, York YM [YAT 1972.21.5050]
16-22 Coppergate, York YCC [YAT 1979.7.7280; 1980.7.9935]

L.13.4 × W.11.1cm.
    Although imported pottery was available in Scandinavia in the Viking Age, vessels of wood, metal, or soapstone – a crystalline talc – were preferred. Soapstone occurs naturally in both Norway and the Shetlands, and these fragments may derive from either source.

YTC9   Part of the rim of a soapstone bowl with a U-shaped iron handle
16-22 Coppergate, York YCC [YAT 1980.7.7723 and 7565]

The exterior is heavily fire-blackened. 21 × 7.5cm.
    Soapstone bowls from the Shetlands, presumably made locally, do not usually have iron handles. It is, therefore, possible that this bowl was imported from Norway where iron-handled examples are well known.

YTC10   Copper-alloy ringed pin
16-22 Coppergate, York YCC [YAT 1977.7.774]

This has a polyhedral head decorated with punched dots, and a plain loose ring of square section. L.8.8 × D. (ring) 1.3cm.
    The type originated in Ireland but became popular with the Vikings. Those with polyhedral heads are of principally tenth-century date, having a wide distribution in western Britain, the Northern Isles, the Faroes, and Iceland. A single example is known also from Newfoundland. Pins with baluster heads are of slightly later date, while pins with crutch heads have been found from eleventh- and twelfth-century contexts in Dublin.

YTC11   Two copper-alloy ringed pins
York YM [555.5.48, 622.48]

Each has a polyhedral head, and a ring fitting into hollows in the side of the head, decorated with groups of transverse incised lines. The lower part of the shank is flattened and decorated on both faces with an incised fret. L.13.1 × D. (ring) 1.8cm.

YCT12   Copper-alloy ringed pin
16-22 Coppergate, York YCC [YAT 1979.7.7388]

This pin has a plain loose ring and baluster head decorated with punched dots. L.13.1 × D. (ring) 1.8cm.

YTC5

YTC14

YTC17

YTC18

YTC13   Iron ringed pin
All Saints Pavement, York [YAT 1976.19.92]

This has a crutch head and plain stirrup ring with tenons at the ends which fit into hollows at either side of the solid head. The lower half of the shank is flattened and decorated with punched ornament. The pin was originally covered with a layer of soft solder which is now heavily rubbed. L. (excluding ring) 14.1 × D. (ring) 2.4cm.

YTC14   Copper-alloy penannular brooch terminal
16-22 Coppergate, York YCC [YAT 1979.7.7159]

It is essentially square with cusped sides, and is decorated with an equal-armed cross having a central setting originally filled with a blue glass stud of which only a small fragment survives. There is a boss in each of the angles of the cross and the cross arms are filled with interlace. The broken hoop develops from one corner of the terminal. L.6.0 × W.4.0cm.

This terminal formed part of one brooch in a group which has been identified as Pictish. It is probably of ninth-century date, but was found in a tenth-century context and was obviously of some age when lost. Its presence reflects Viking activity in Scotland, which is well documented both historically and archaeologically. The layout of the ornament closely parallels that on the base of the Ormside bowl (no. C8).

YTC15   Selvedge of silk tabby (plain weave) which has been tied into a slip knot
6-8 Pavement, York YM [YAT 1972.21.593]

L.163.0 × W.1.5cm.

Like the silk for the reliquary, this piece must have come from a Byzantine or Islamic weaving centre. The silk would have been imported as cloth and made up into articles such as the reliquary (no. YD2) or cap (no. YD1) in England. This selvedge is probably an offcut from such manufacture.

YTC16   Iron bell
16-22 Coppergate, York YCC [YAT 1979.7.6599]

This is made from a single metal sheet having a narrow waist bent in half and joined down each side. There is a semi-circular suspension loop. The original plating of copper-alloy is largely lost. L.3.6 × W.2.1cm.

Similar but larger bells of bronze or iron, made in the same way, are known from Ireland. Many of them are associated with early Irish saints, and some have been elaborately enshrined in precious metal as relics. A small bell like this, however, is more likely to have been functional; it may have been used as an animal bell. A similar bell of bronze is from Nordre Ferang, Sandeherred, Norway.

YTC17   Copper-alloy strap-end
16-22 Coppergate, York YCC [YAT 1980.7.11100]

The strap was held in place at the upper end by four iron rivets. The lower end is rounded. The front face is decorated with a central rosette having a projection at each of the cardinal points. Each of the fields thus created is filled with an acanthus spray developing from the outer edge of the field. L.5.1 × W.3.1cm.

The strap-end's shape is typical of Carolingian workmanship; the piece may, therefore, be an import. During the tenth century, however, under Carolingian influence, this form of strap-end replaced the normal ninth-century Anglo-Saxon type (see nos. J10 and J11). At the same time acanthus ornament was introduced into Anglo-Saxon art. It is, therefore, conceivable, but unlikely, that this is an Anglo-Saxon copy of a Carolingian strap-end.

YTC18   Banded slate whetstone
16-22 Coppergate, York YCC [YAT 1980.7.11114]

The whetstone is black with grey-purple oblique bands and tapers towards the top, which is perforated to take a copper-alloy suspension loop with knotted ends. L.4.8 × W.1.1cm.

Similar whetstones are known from Birka in Sweden, and this example is almost certainly an import from Scandinavia.

YTC19   Copper-alloy balance beam
16-22 Coppergate, York YCC [YAT 1978.7.3716]

The arms are of circular section and taper towards the ends, which are perforated to take suspension loops for the chains. From the middle of the beam rises a narrow triangular pointer perforated at the base to take the elaborate suspension mechanism. L.12.6 × W.4.5cm.

Portable balances with either rigid or folding arms (see no. YTC20) were in common use in the Viking-Age. The pans would have been suspended on three chains linked at the top, and suspended on a single chain from the end of the beam. Such scales were possibly used to weigh silver bullion, the principal means of exchange (apart from barter) before the Vikings began to use coins.

YTC20   Two copper-alloy folding balance beams
16-22 Coppergate, York YCC [YAT 1980.7.7576]
9 Blake Street, York YM [YAT 1975.6.82]

These are similar to no. YTC19 except that the inner ends of the arms are hinged so that the arms can fold upwards. L.15.1cm.

YTC21   Two lengths of copper-alloy suspension chains
16-22 Coppergate, York YCC [YAT 1977.7.743]

Perhaps for a balance these are made of interlocking S-shaped links. One has a circular suspension loop at one end. L.9.2cm.

YTC22   Shallow circular copper-alloy scale pans, each with three equally-spaced holes for suspension
16-22 Coppergate, York YCC [YAT 1978.7.3378; 1980.7.8569]

D.5.1cm.

YTC23   Three lead weights
16-22 Coppergate, York YCC [YAT 1980.7.8012, 8411 and 8475]

One is semi-conical with a hole in the base, another is cylindrical, and the third a truncated pyramid. D.2.4 × T.2.0cm.

Weights of this type were used with portable balances.

ABOVE *The Christian and the pagan. To the left, a silver cross-pendant (H8) part of the Bonderup hoard and buried between 1060 and 1070 when the Church was well established in Denmark. And right, a Thor's hammer (H2), part of the Sejrø hoard.*
RIGHT *A gold chain (H13) from Fæsted in south Jutland with animal-head terminals. And far right, a gold disc-brooch (H14) decorated with Borre-style gripping beasts in fine filigree work.*

YTC24   Fragment of a silver penning, Danish, *c*.800
Coppergate, York YCC [1980.7 I 22714/10614]

Mint: Attributed to Hedeby. Wt.0.107gm (1.65gr): the fragment has been oxidized.
Obv: Portion of border (which surrounds a mask), itself showing a tiny male face, with moustaches, flanked by circular snakes. (This could be from either right or left of the central head.) Rev: Neck of backward-facing stag (top right-hand quarter of design); the snake under the belly, on the full coin, is likely to have been the circular, rather than spiral, variety which is dated from about 850).

The fragment was found in a tenth-century context, where it was obviously residual. The mask/stag type is known to have survived in pendant form once the coin had ceased to be current in its home-land. It is possible that the Coppergate fragment is from a piece that was looped for suspension.

YTC25   Copper dirhem: contemporary forgery of an Islamic silver coin; A.H. 290–295 (A.D. 903–907/8)
Coppergate, York, YCC [1980.7]

Obv: The Arabic is the closest approximation possible.

لا اله الا

الله وحده

لا شريك له

Inner margin:

بسم الله ضرب هذا الدرهم بسمرقند

سنة [١١١] وتسعين ومائتين

Outer margin: intended to be the usual *Qur'an* XXX, 3,4; lettering bungled and largely illegible.
Rev:

[الله]

محمد

[رسول الله]

[المكتفى بالله]

اسمعيل بن احمد

the second and third lines are bungled, possibly even transposed. The name is that of the Samanid prince Isma'il ibn Ahmad.
Margin: traces of *Qur.* IX, 33.
Mint: Samarqand. Wt.3.534gm. Analysis: (by X-ray fluorescence, at Oxford): Copper: 77.7%; Zinc: 3.3%; Lead: 6.0%; Tin: 13.2%. The lead and tin will have been deliberate additions; the zinc is probably present unintentionally. There was no trace of silver.

The coin was intended to pass as a silver dirham, not as a copper *fals*, because of its general appearance and broad, thin flan; the four-line

reverse inscription occurs only on the dirhems of Samarqand at this period; the final 'm' of 'dirhem' can just be seen. The obverse margin gives the date: A.H. 29 x; the quality of the engraving is not of the normal Samarqand standard at this time, so it is not possible that dirhem dies were used in error on a copper blank.

This coin may be related to the eastern dirhems found together with English coins and jewellery at Goldsborough, near York (E15). Of the nineteen identified Islamic coins, sixteen were of Isma'il ibn Ahmad, several from Samarqand from precisely this period. It would certainly seem possible that this coin started on its journey from the East along with the Goldsborough coins, its lead and tin element giving it a silvery tone that became less and less convincing as time went on.

YTC26   Iron die, *c*.910–19?, for obverse of St Peter's Penny; second issue, with sword
Coppergate, York, YCC [1980.7 I 25630/9351 P1.00]

Wt.463gm; D. (face) 2.8cm, (of die) 2cm. L. (total) 9.1cm.
Face: o+o / SCIPE /   / TR IIo / o o, the letters retrograde and inceus, above and below a sword, to left; Thor's hammer between lower half of legend.
Collar: only one (the top) of the 4 control points (see trial-pieces, below) is now clearly defined.
Body: cylindrical, flaring slightly above rect-angular tang, which is now broken.

This is the only known specimen of a die for coinage of the Anglo-Saxon period and its discovery at Coppergate, inside a building which is now being interpreted as a die-cutter's workshop, widens our knowledge of the mint at York at this period. No coin struck from this die has yet been traced; the example (no. YTC38) is one of four struck from very similar obverse dies.

YTC27   Lead trial-piece, uniface, bearing a reverse die for the regal moneyer of York, Regnald, BMC v, *c*.928–39
Coppergate, York, YCC [1980.7 I 25350/8563]

Wt.6.20gm (96gr).
Rev: + REGNALD MO EFo RPI. Collar: 4 pellets, one at each quarter.

No coin struck from this die has been traced. The coinage of Regnald, the sole moneyer for this type at York, was prolific and some eighty specimens recorded by C. E. Blunt all have the mint signature rendered as EFORPIC. It is possible that the die with which this trial-piece was struck was rejected for further use because the legend was not wholly correct.

YTC27

YTC26

Eadwig, 955–59

YTC28 Lead trial-piece, recording obverse and reverse dies for the moneyer Frothric, BMC i d
Coppergate, York, YCC [1979.7 I 7692/4622. Pl.00]

Wt.71.952gm (1077gr). L.15.3 × W.4.4cm. T.0.2cm.

Without mint-signature; a leaf-shaped strip of lead which, when found, was folded in two. On the outside of the folds is the obverse, almost obliterated; this is repeated on the other side, together with the reverse.

Obv. die: + EΛDVVICRE, small cross in inner circle. Rev. die: FROĐ / RICM, retrograde, in two lines; rosettes above and below, o+o between.

Collars: 4 pellets on each, one at each quarter; the arcs inscribed within the dies from these centre-points can faintly be seen and be recognized as the guide-lines for the spacing of the legends.

This trial-piece varies from the examples of Æthelstan's reign in its shape and size and in recording both obverse and reverse dies. No coins from the dies have been traced. Frothric is a moneyer associated in mint-signed issues with Chester; the occurrence of this piece at York cannot yet be fully explained. Eadwig's reign itself was most unsettled and there may have been some reason for maintaining a record of Mercian dies at York at a time when his power in Mercia was uncertain.

The English coinage at York might not then have achieved uniformity of regional style, after the expulsion of the Scandinavian regime, and some issues may have simulated Mercian style. The reverse die is itself irregular, and it could be suggested that the piece belongs to the known series of blundered imitations connected with this period.

COINAGE IN YORK

Unless otherwise stated, all the specimens are owned by the YM or YCC.

Coins from kingdoms other than Northumbria.
The two below illustrate that the coinage circulating in ninth-century York was not entirely of local manufacture.

YTC29 Wessex: Æthelwulf, *c.*838/9–56/8; silver penny, BMC type i
Clementhorpe, York, YCC [1976.3 110/42]

Moneyer: Wealheard. Wt.1.06gm (16.3gr).

OVERLEAF The vast bay called The Wash on the east coast of England. Tidal waterways thread a passage through the sea marshes of what was once part of the Danelaw – a familiar flat expanse to a Viking who only three days before had sailed from Jutland.

Obv: +EĐEL + VVLF + REX; DORIBI in inner circle. Rev: +VVEΛL HHE ΛRD; CANT in inner circle.

YTC30 Mercia: Burgred, 852–74, deposed; silver penny, BMC type d
Bishophill I, York, YCC [1974.14 1682/1009]

Moneyer: Diarwulf. Wt.0.74gm (11.4gr): the weight is low because of the coin's present condition.
Obv: BURGRED REX, bust to right. Rev: FMON / DIARVL / ETA in three lines.

The Anglian Kingdom of Northumbria: mid-ninth century issues.
The styca coinage, whose regular issues were in the names of the kings of Northumbria and the archbishops of York, followed the eighth-century spasmodic issues of base silver sceattas. Itself being largely of copper, and the flans being of small module, it is totally anomalous in comparison with the contemporary coinage of other kingdoms. The series is currently the subject of research; chronology is still uncertain: both traditional dates and, in brackets, proposed revised dates are quoted above.

One is still far from being able to introduce a typological sequence of issue or, indeed, to suggest a second mint in addition to York. A large proportion of the material is, in varying degrees, irregular in style; nonsense legends are many. It is not yet possible to determine which of these groups may be contemporary imitations, produced throughout the series (perhaps regionally), or which may be associated with the civil war at the time of the Danish occupation of York in 866.

YTC31 Æthelred II, *c.*841–44, deposed; restored *c.*844–849/50 (*c.*854–8; *c.*858–62). Copper styca, first reign?
Coppergate, York, YCC [1979.7 IV 6789/6232]

Moneyer: Alghere. Wt.0.80gm (12.35gr).
Obv: +AEDILRER, round central cross. Rev: +ALDHERE, round central cross.

YTC32 Wulfhere, Archbishop of York, *c.*854–900/2 (dates uncertain). Copper styca, *c.*860?
Bishophill I, York, YCC [1974.14 1647/967]

Moneyer: Vvlfred. Wt.1.03gm (15.9gr).
Obv: +VLFHERE ABED, retrograde; cross in circle of pellets. Rev: +VVLFRED, retrograde, round central cross.

YTC33 Irregular, of uncertain date and attribution. Copper styca
Coppergate, York, YCC [1980.7 IV 21143/8644]

Moneyer: fictitious. Wt.0.85gm (13.15gr).
Obv: +ΛNTED:, retrograde, round central cross of pellets. Rev: +PER ΛVĐ, round central pellet-in-annulet.

This is the first record of this particular irregularity having been found in the York area. Excavations at Bamburgh Castle, Northumberland (1971, as yet unpublished) recovered two other specimens, each with the same reverse die but each with different obverses whose legends attempt to record the name of Æthelred.

The Scandinavian Kingdom of York: Anglo-Danish coinage

YTC34   Silver penny, c.895–c.903
Coppergate, York, YCC [1980.7 II 27440/9862]

Wt.0.89gm (13.8gr), the coin is heavily oxidized and much underweight.
Obv: +CVNNETTI; small cross with pellets in two angles, within inner circle. Rev: +CNVT REX round a patriarchal cross.

The extensive coinage of the Vikings of Northumbria, of which this is representative, is largely known from the major hoard found at Cuerdale, Lancashire, in 1840 (E25). The Coppergate provenance is one of the few recorded for single finds.

In view of the tight die-linking with other mint-signed coins the whole coinage is attributed to the York mint where it was put out by the largely Christianised Danes who derived the range of religious legends and symbols from Continental prototypes.

Imitations of the coinage of Ælfred (King Alfred of Wessex), c.900

YTC35   Silver penny, BMC Ælfred, type xviii
CM, Leeds. [Purchased, 1968, ex F. Banks. Collection; ex Spink, 1965] SCBI Yorkshire, 38

Mint: 'Orsnaforda'; moneyer: Bernvald. Wt.1.36gm (21gr).
Obv: ORSNΛ / ELFRED +/ FORDI. Rev: BERNV / + + +/ ΛLRMO.

YTC36   Silver penny, BMC Ælfred, type xviii
CM, Leeds. [ex Lockett, 1960, 3647; ex Bruun I, 1925, 66b] SCBI Yorkshire, 39

Mint: 'Orsnaforda'; moneyer: Bernvald. Wt.1.36gm (21gr).
Obv: ORSNΛ / ELFRED / FORDΛ. Rev: BERNV / + / V ŒMO.

This issue has been attributed to a mint in the York area, but recently it has been suggested that certain coins of this type are of better style and should be given to a southern mint. Both the coins listed here can be identified as Northumbrian Viking copies of the coinage of King Alfred.

St Peter's coinage of York

The St Peter coinage of York, whose obverse legends abbreviate the Latin *Sancti Petri Moneta* (St Peter's money) was issued in two phases, of which the latter, with sword, is considered to be the prototype of the St Martin's coinage of Lincoln.

The chronology of the series has been much discussed. The most recent proposals suggest that the coinage as a whole was over by the time that the Norse Regnald captured York in 919. That the second, less prolific, issue was the sole output of the York mint in the period 910–19 may reflect the local economic straits after the Danes had been defeated by Wessex and Mercia at the battle of Tettenhall near Wolverhampton, in 910. It should also be noted that the second issue (with sword, appropriate to St Peter, and with Thor's hammer) reflects an uncertainty, then current, about the new faith in relation to the old paganism.

YTC37   Silver penny, c.905–10?; first issue, without sword
Coppergate, York, YCC [1980.7 I 22416/7600]

Wt.0.65gm (10.1gr).
Obv: ·/ SCIE / +·+ / TRN /·. Rev: +EBORΛCI round small cross.

YTC38   Silver penny, c.910–?; second issue, with sword
CM, Leeds [ex Thornton Collection, 1924] SCBI Yorkshire, 48

Wt.1.04gm (16gr).
Obv: o+o / SCIPE /   / TR IIo / oo, above and below a sword pointing to the right; Thor's hammer between lower half of legend. Rev: +EB◇RΛCEI, with annulets between each letter; evangelistic cross (:÷:) within inner circle.

Scandinavian kings of York: I. Sihtric Caoch, 921-6

YTC39   Silver penny, contemporary imitation of the Sword issue
Coppergate, York, YCC [1980.7 I 26247/9539]

Wt.1.07gm (16.5gr).
Obv: SITEI (retrograde) / ЯCDIX, above and below sword pointing to left. Rev: +IIEBIΛI IOEIX; inner circle enclosing Thor's hammer (?) with a trefoil of pellets on either side.

This is the first certain record of a coin of Sihtric having been found in York. The piece can be compared with two other imitations of the reign from the Skye Hoard, 1891 (*SCBI Edinburgh*, 70–71). It is now thought that most of Sihtric's regular coins were produced south of the river Humber; it is possible, however, that the imitations were struck in the king's northern territory.

YTC40   Silver penny, BMC via, c.939?
Coppergate, York, YCC [1980.7 I 22803/7996]

Mint: Chester; moneyer: Wulfstan. Wt.1.41gm (21.8gr).
Obv: +EÐELSTΛNRE + TOBRT, rosette in inner circle. Rev: +VVLFST Ƞ M ·o LEGCF, small cross in inner circle.

The regal title on the obverse is the abbreviation of the Latin *rex totius Britanniae*; Æthelstan adopted this term for the coinage after 927, when he had recovered York from the Vikings and could be styled king of all Britain.

YTC41   Silver penny, BMC i, c.939?
Coppergate, York, YCC [1980.7 I 22803/7997]

Moneyer: Willuf. Wt.1.42gm (21.85gr).
Obv: +/EÐEL STAN REX, small cross in inner circle. Rev: ·.· / VVIL / + + + / LVFM / ·.·

The coin is of a style that is recognized as having distinct links with the coinage of the Scandinavian kings of York.

Norse Kings of York – II

Anlaf Guthfrithsson, 939–41

YTC42   Silver penny, c.939–40
Coppergate, York, YCC [1980.7 I 22803/7995]

Mint: York; moneyer: Æthelferd. Wt.1.24gm (19.2gr).
Obv: ' + A'Hl'Λ'FCVNVNCX, raven with out-stretched wings, in inner circle. Rev: +'A'ÐEL' FERDMINETI', small cross in inner circle.

YTC43   Silver penny, c.939–40
Coppergate, York, YCC [1980.7 I 22803/7999 P1.00]

Mint: Lincoln?; moneyer: Odeler. Wt.1.22gm (18.8gr).
Obv: +OHLΛFCVNVNC +, raven with out-stretched wings, in inner circle. Rev: + ODELER. MONETΛ.

Hitherto, Æthelferd, striking at York, has been the only moneyer known for the Viking Raven issue of Anlaf, in which the king's title is rendered as *cununc* (ON *konungr*). Odeler, whose name is Germanic in origin, has been recorded as a moneyer for Edmund (940–6) but never before for Anlaf. In view of the fact that the king's name on Odeler's coin is rendered as ONLAF, it is likely that the moneyer was striking south of the Humber, most probably at Lincoln.

Regnald II, Guthfrithsson, 943–4

YTC44   Silver penny, 943–4
HM, Glasgow: Hunter Collection; SCBI Glasgow, 523

Mint: York; moneyer: Avra. Wt.1.30gm (20.1gr).
Obv: +REGNALD CVNVC, cross moline in inner circle. Rev: + AVRAMONITRE, small cross (pattée) in inner circle.

Eric Bloodaxe: second reign, 952–4

YTC45   Silver penny, 952–4
HM, Glasgow: Hunter Collection; SCBI Glasgow, 526

Mint: York; moneyer: Ingelgar. Wt.1.35gm (20.8gr).
Obv: ERIC / REX, above and below sword, pointing to right. Rev: + INEGELGAR, small cross within inner circle.

Kings of England

Eadred, 946–55

YTC46   Fragment of a silver penny, BMC i
Coppergate, York, YCC [1980.7 I 22423/7755]

Moneyer: Werstan ?. Wt.0.32gm (4.9gr).
Obv:] ═ DR [. Rev:] :/ RZ / + + [
Werstan is the only moneyer's name for Edmund, Eadred and Eadwig, which includes the letters . . . . RS . . . . , but is is so far unrecorded in the main type, appearing on the variety, *BMC* i d.

Edgar, 959–75

YTC47   Silver penny, c.959–73
Coppergate, York, YCC [1979.7 15472/4349]

Moneyer: Fastolf. Wt.1.30gm (20.1gr).

Obv: +EADGAR' REX)', small cross in inner circle; small pellet in field. Rev: +FA ' STO 'L' FIMoN, small cross in inner circle.
The obverse is that used also by the moneyer Durand: cf. *SCBI Edinburgh*, 523–24.

YTC48   Silver penny, c.959–73
Coppergate, York, YCC [1979.7 15550/4439]

Wt.1.10gm (16.9gr).
Obv: +EADGAR' REXI', small cross in inner circle. Rev: +FASToLF . MoN, small cross in inner circle.

Æthelred II, 978–1016.

YTC49   Silver penny, 978–9
Coppergate, York, YTC [1977.7 8801/2372]

Mint: York; moneyer: Styr. Wt.0.70gm (10.8gr); the coin is exceptionally thin.
Obv: +AEÐELRED REX ANGLOR, but to left. Rev: +ST [V] RMOИE [T] AEEORPIC, small cross in inner circle.
This is the first recorded instance of this moneyer striking at York in this type; he is known for the First Hand issue which follows.

YTC50   Silver penny, 979–85
Coppergate, York, YCC [1980.7 I 26240/8715]

Mint: York; moneyer: Fastolf. Wt.0.98gm (15.2gr); the coin is heavily oxidized.
Obv: + 'EDELREI + DE + AN, bust to right. Rev: +FASTVLFM – OEFOI, hand between alpha and omega.

YTC51   Silver penny, 975–85
Coppergate, York, YCC [1977.7 8225/1078]

Mint: York; moneyer: Outhgrim. Wt.0.82gm (12.7gr); the coin is heavily oxidized.
Obv: +EDELRED REX AN, bust to right. Rev: +OVÐGRIMM · OEFER, hand between alpha and omega; pellet at wrist.
This is the first recorded instance of this moneyer striking at York in this type; he is known for the Crux issue which follows.

Cnut, 1016–35

YTC52   Silver penny, 1029–35
Coppergate, York, YCC [1979.7 V 17103/4838]

Mint: York; moneyer: Thurgrim. Wt.0.64gm (9.8gr).
Obv: +CNV T RECX, bust to left. Rev: +Ð VR [G] RIM ONEOFE, short cross contained by circle.

Harold I, sole king, 1037–40

YTC53   Large fragment of silver penny, 1038–40
Bishophill II, York, YCC [1973.15 10428/337]

Mint: York ?; moneyer: Ucede ?. Wt.0.7128gm (11gr).
Obv: uncertain legend, bust to left. Rev:] + VC :/ DE '·' / O ? [, *fleur-de-lis* within angles of long cross.

Edward the Confessor, 1042–66

YTC54   Silver penny, 1062–5
Clementhorpe, York, YCC [1976.3 23/21]

Mint: York; moneyer: Outholf. Wt.0.99gm

ABOVE *A painting of the St Paul's stone (119) as it appears now when, for study purposes, the surface is dampened to bring out the colours. It carries fine English Ringerike ornament. (Painting by Eva Wilson.)*
RIGHT *The Gosforth Cross as it stands in its Cumbrian churchyard. It is 4.42 metres high and displays scenes from Scandinavian legends (F24). And, below, the Mildenhall book mount (127).*

(15.3gr); the coin is worn.
Obv: +EDPΛRD REX . . . , facing bust. Rev: +OV-
ÐOLFONEOFFR, small cross within inner circle.

Norman coinage

William I, 1066–87

YTC55   Silver penny, 1083–6?
CM, Leeds [ex Thornton Collection, 1924; ex Spink, 1922] SCBI Yorkshire, 788

Mint: York; moneyer: Aleif. Wt.1.31gm (20.2gr).
Obv: +PILLELMREX, facing bust. Rev: +
ΛLEIFONEFRPIC; P ΛX S, each within an annulet,
within angles of a cross.

Towards the end of Edward the Confessor's
reign, the number of moneyers at each mint was
considerably reduced; York at the time retained as
many as twelve. It was during the early years of the
Norman regime that the harrying of the north
brought to an end the pre-eminence of Anglo-
Danish York. By 1083–6 the mint at York was
reduced to a complement of four moneyers who
shared a small quota of dies in order to produce
coinage for an impoverished city.

YORK AMBER/JET/GLASS

YAJG1   Group of unworked pieces of amber
Clifford Street, York YM [C598b, C599a-d, h, m]

L.4.4 × W.2.5cm.

Amber – fossilized resin – may have been collected from east coast beaches. Alternatively it
could have been imported from the coasts of south-
west Jutland or the south Baltic, where it is much
more abundant.

**YAJG2   Semi-manufactured wedge-shaped
amber pendants, and a finished pendant of
similar form**
Clifford Street, York YM [C601c, f, h. C602b]

L.4.3 × W.1.3cm.

The pendant was first roughed out from an
amber lump, before being perforated for suspension and polished. The perforation was made
with a drill of small diameter, here 0.37cm.
Finished and semi-manufactured pendants of this
form are known in York from 6-8 Pavement and
16-22 Coppergate, and from Hedeby and Birka.

**YAJG3   Debris from the manufacture of
annular amber beads, including rough-outs and
wasters broken during manufacture**
*Clifford Street, York YM [C617b, d. C618b, c, d.
C620f. C625a. C660a]*

D.2.3cm.

As with the pendants YAJG2 the shape of the
bead was first roughed out. It was then perforated
using a fine drill, here 0.46–0.5cm. in diameter.
The perforation allowed the bead to be held in a
lathe for final shaping and polishing.

**YAJG4   Waste from the manufacture of amber
finger-rings, including rough-outs and pieces
broken during manufacture**
*Clifford Street, York YM [C617a, 618a, C626e-g, j,
k, l]*

D.3.5cm.

A flattish disc of amber was first roughed out,
then perforated using a fine drill, here of 0.57cm
diameter. The perforation allowed the rough-out
to be held in a lathe for finishing.

**YAJG5   Wedge-shaped amber pendants,
annular beads and a large wedge-shaped
pendant, its long edges chamfered, arranged as a
necklace**
*16-22 Coppergate, York YM [YAT
1976.7.302,606; 1977.7.893, 1697, 2116,
2160; 1979.7.4201, 5224; 1980.7.8564]*

L.4.3 × W.1.3 × T.1.0cm.

The components of the necklace were not found
together, but have been arranged on analogy with
necklaces from Viking-Age graves in Scandinavia
which often have a series of pendants separated by
beads. Grave 835 from Birka, Sweden, has yielded
an amber necklace of similar construction.

YAJG6   Three pieces of raw jet
*16-22 Coppergate, York YCC [YAT 1979.7.4825,
4247; 1980.7.7907]*

L.5.6 × W.4.0 × T.2.0cm.

Jet occurs most abundantly in western Europe
at Whitby, Yorkshire, where it has been exploited
since prehistoric times. There was a considerable
jet industry in Roman York, but the craft probably
ceased in the post-Roman period, and was revived
in the Viking Age. Jet also appears to have been
worked in Lincoln in this period.

**YAJG7   Fragment of worked jet, a damaged
rough-out for a Latin cross, a wedge-shaped
rough-out and the rough-out for a spindle whorl
or jet finger ring**
*16-22 Coppergate, York YCC [YAT 1978.7.3267,
3406; 1980.7.8267, 9181]*

L.5.4 × W.2.0 × T.1.4cm.

The discovery of these rough-outs suggests that
jet was being worked in the Coppergate area in the
Viking Age, although evidently not on a large
scale. Both the cross and wedge-shaped rough-
outs were probably intended for use as pendants.

YAJG8   Two complete jet finger rings
*16-22 Coppergate, York YCC [YAT 1979.7.5381,
7080]*

D.3.1cm.

YAJG9   Circular jet pendant
Railway Station, York YM [H110]

The pendant is in the form of a coiled snake with
the head in the centre. There is a cylindrical
suspension loop with the snake's tail coiled twice
round it. D.4.5 × H.5.2cm.

Pendants in this form are well known in metal
from Scandinavia. A jet example has come from
the early Viking Age burial at Longva, Haram,
Sunmøre, Norway.

YAJG10   Jet equal-armed pendant cross
16-22 Coppergate, York YCC [YAT 1979.7.5163]

It is decorated with ring-and-dot inlaid with the
yellow mineral orpiment (arsenic trisulphide).
L.3.3 × W.2.1cm.

The cross comes from a post-Conquest context
and may not, therefore, be of Anglo-Scandinavian
date. The use of orpiment for inlay was probably

known in the Anglo-Scandinavian period since pieces of the mineral have been found in Viking-Age contexts at 16-22 Coppergate. Orpiment occurs naturally in France and Germany and must have been imported into York.

YAJG11   Jet playing piece
16-22 Coppergate, York YCC [YAT 1979.7.4941]

It is of heptagonal section with a rounded top. D.1.6 × W.2.0cm.
  The piece is probably for playing *hnefatafl*.

YAJG12   Small jet spindle whorl with a central perforation
Clifford Street, York YM [C579b]

D.3.1cm.

YAJG13   Two jet dice
16-22 Coppergate, York YCC [YAT 1978.7.3696; 1979.7.4954]

The numbers are indicated by ring-and-dot inlaid with silver. On one the six is opposite the five, on the other the six is opposite the one. L.1.2 × W.1.2cm.

YAJG14   Group of yellow glass annular beads and finger-rings
7-13 Pavement, York YM [1951.52]

A number of the beads are mis-shapen and clearly represent manufacturing debris. Similar beads are known from 16-22 Coppergate, Flaxengate (Lincoln), Hereford and Gloucester, where as at Lincoln, manufacturing debris has also been discovered. Glass of this type is characterised by a high lead oxide content – up to 70% – which gives the glass a more brilliant appearance. This brilliance, allied with the yellow colour, may suggest an attempt to imitate amber.

YAJG15   Yellow glass conical playing piece
16-22 Coppergate, York YCC [YAT 1977.7.2269]

D.2.0 × H.1.3cm.
  The piece is apparently made of the same type of glass as the beads and finger rings.

YAJG16   Group of dark green annular beads
7-13 Pavement, York YM [1951.52]

Dark green glass beads and finger rings are also known from tenth-century levels at Flaxengate, Lincoln, and are characterised by a high lead oxide content.

YAJG17   Group of glass beads
16-22 Coppergate, York YCC [YAT 1976.7.289, 308, 393, 426; 1977.7.1234, 1545; 1980.7.8550]

These include a dark blue quadrilobate, gadrooned and cuboid bead, a blue/black annular bead decorated with white trails and yellow blobs, a colourless segmented bead, two gilded beads and an opaque red cylindrical bead.
  Similar blue glass quadrilobate and gadrooned beads, colourless segmented beads and gilded beads are known also from Scandinavian sites.

YORK STONE-WORKING

York   *Before 1969 little pre-Viking sculpture was known from the city; chance finds and excavations since then (notably at the Minster) have confirmed what was long suspected – that York was a lively centre of Anglian carving. The art continued to flourish in the Viking period, absorbing and transforming the animal styles of Scandinavia whilst, at the same time, capable of near-classical figure sculpture.*

YS1   Fragmentary, unfinished carved slab
16-22 Coppergate, York YCC [YAT 1977.7.2115]

Made of magnesian limestone, the slab was found in 1976, incorporated in a layer of limestone rubble surface provisionally dated *c*.950–960. Decoration: Side A: two interlocked animals, with contoured bodies, bound in strands issuing from head lappets; one beast has a spiral joint and curled lip. Side B: Head and foreleg of a beast. Early or mid-tenth century. H.22.3cm.
  This securely-dated fragment was rejected before completion. Details of the Jellinge animals and its mode of cutting suggest that it is by the same hand as the Newgate stone (no. YS2).

YS2   Fragmentary cross-shaft
Newgate, York YM

Made of magnesian limestone, it was found in the masonry of a house in Newgate in 1963. Decoration: all panels have an arched frame, gripped by

YS2

winged angels set at the upper corners of the shaft. Side A: Christ with a cruciform nimbus. Side B: ribbon animals with contoured bodies linked to confronting scrolls; Side C: bird motif; Side D: two beasts with contoured bodies enmeshed in strands issuing from lappets. Early to mid-tenth century. H.63.3cm.

This stone combines the Anglian tradition of well-modelled naturalistic portraits with the flatter styles of insular Jellinge art. Traces of red paint and of marking-out lines still survive on the sides; the hole on the top was for the retaining rod of the cross-head. There is a close parallel for the motif of gripping angels on a shaft at Nunburnholme, 23 km. to the east of York.

YS3   Fragmentary recumbent slab
Clifford Street, York YM [1979.52]

Made of magnesian limestone, it was found under the Mechanics Institute in 1883. Decoration: two beasts occupy the (original) upper quadrants of a slab divided into panels by a raised cruciform motif which is decorated with knotwork and terminates in animal heads; the two animals have contoured bodies and are bound in strands issuing from their back legs and ear lappets. Tenth century. L.43.2cm.

Like some of the slabs from the Minster, the Clifford Street slab has been sawn up for re-use as a headstone.

YH1   A Viking house of York; a reconstruction

The reconstruction is based on a house discovered on the Viking Coppergate site at York. The original house (only partly excavated – some of it lay beneath a main road) was a maximum 4 metres long where uncovered, and 3.60 metres wide. It was built largely of oak, and would have been, it is estimated, twice as long as its width.

The building here is a first attempt to show how one of the tenth-century structures excavated at 16–22 Coppergate, York, may have looked when complete. Buildings of this basic type, used both as houses and workshops, were found on each of the four tenements investigated, and between them provided sufficient detail for the lower 1.8m of this replica to be constructed with confidence.

The building's most notable feature is its floor sunk more than 1.5m below the surrounding ground surface. It is not obvious why this building method was chosen, but the choice clearly influenced how the structure was assembled, for substantial revetment walls were required to stop the earth outside from collapsing into the building. The bases for these walls were sometimes provided by massive squared foundation-beams which had raised lips along their innermost upper edges to stop the other elements which rested on them from slipping off.

Sometimes, however, there was no foundation-beam, and the squared uprights which were the second major element in the construction were set directly into the ground. They, like all the excavated timbers from these buildings, were of oak; they were carefully finished, probably with an axe, and were positioned quite closely together at regular intervals, facing each other in pairs across the building. They in turn supported the horizontally-laid planks which rested edge upon edge behind them and which held back the earth.

Perhaps the strangest feature of the building remains surviving to be excavated was the total absence of any nails, pegs or joints except at the very tip of the tallest surviving uprights: below this height (1.8m) it was only the transferred pressure of one timber on another which kept the building upright. Above this point, however, the nature of the building must have differed radically, for without the pressure of earth behind them, the type of walls found below the contemporary ground surface could not stand upright. Clearly the traces of jointing and the associated peg-holes which survive at the top of the tallest uprights must have been of crucial importance to the building's superstructure, and it seems possible that a horizontal timber at this level, jointed to each of the uprights, served to keep them the correct distance apart and to provide rigidity.

One of the most difficult questions to answer with assurance is whether the building was heightened by additional uprights above this hypothetical horizontal beam, or whether a roof capped the structure at this height. A single-storey structure seems to have sufficient headroom without further heightening, but it is possible that an upper storey or loft was created. The roof itself is also problematic – wooden shingles, turf or thatch might have been used, although at present thatch seems most likely.

Further research may well suggest refinements to the reconstruction presented here, but it gives at least a broad idea of the building traditions of tenth-century York.

R. A. HALL

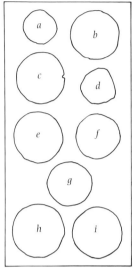

a   A copper styca of Wulfhere, Archbishop of York c.860. The obverse shows a cross in a circle of pellets.

d   Northumbrian copper styca of uncertain date and attribution.

c   Silver penny of Sihtric Caoch 921–6. The obverse displays a pointed sword.

b   The reverse shows a Thor's hammer.

i   A Cnut silver penny c.895–c.903. The obverse bears a cross with two pellets.

e   The reverse displays a patriarchal cross.

g   A Cnut silver penny 1029–35. The obverse has a bust facing left.

f   The reverse shows a short cross.

h   A silver penny of Anlaf Guthfrithsson c.934–40. The obverse carries a raven with outstretched wings.

All the coins here have been enlarged.

KINGS AND THEIR COINAGE

D URING THE LAST QUARTER OF the eighth century, a regular English coinage based on the silver penny was established by Offa of Mercia. Although initially confined to the south and east of England, it was virtually the only denomination south of the Humber for the next 500 years. Small dumpy pieces – called by numismatists 'stycas' – continued to be struck in Northumbria by the king and archbishop of York. Large quantities of these, increasingly debased with copper, have been found in hoards in Yorkshire and Northumbria, their loss occasioned, it is thought, more by civil strife than by raids from Denmark.

Circulation of the penny gradually extended over a wider area of England, but in Northumbria it was left to two Danish kings, Siefred and Cnut, to introduce in the last years of the ninth century a silver penny coinage of their own. The types were distinct from the English coinage and it is clear from the evidence of finds that it had for the most part a local circulation. That the coins of these two kings are relatively plentiful today is due to the discovery of a great treasure at Cuerdale in Lancashire, clearly Viking loot, in which there were some 3,000 specimens.

Besides this strikingly independent coinage, there is good reason to attribute to the Vikings at this time a substantial number of coins that imitate, more or less closely, the coinage of Alfred, and they generally bear his name. There were large numbers of these, too, in the Cuerdale hoard. Parallel with these two issues, East Anglia produced a quite distinct coinage of its own that bore the name of St Edmund, the English king who had been murdered by the Danes in 870 and canonized soon after. This again bore designs that marked it apart from the coinage of England proper.

Alfred died in 899 and the Siefred/Cnut coinage ceased about then, to be replaced by one bearing the name of no ruler but instead those of the mint of York, and its patron saint, St Peter.

The recovery of Northumbria by the English king Athelstan in 927 brought temporarily to a close the Viking coinage in England, but the coinage as a whole developed substantially and more than thirty minting places can be identified in his reign. It is worth noting that, whereas in most parts of England these coins were widely distributed, the former kingdoms of Northumbria and East Anglia, that had earlier been under Scandinavian domination, were both served by a single mint – at York and Norwich respectively.

Following Athelstan's death in 939, the Vikings were in and out of Northumbria, and occasionally further south as well, until the final ejection of Erik Bloodaxe in 954. The history and the coinage of this period is complicated, but mention must be made of the initial issues which have as designs the Scandinavian emblems of a raven, a standard or a triquetra. Their later issues, however, conformed in type to the English coinage, a reflection perhaps of increasing intercourse between the two communities.

The year 954 effectively brought to an end the Viking coinage in England. In the last years of Edgar's reign, which ended in 975, a major reform of the coinage was undertaken, and coins began regularly to bear the names of both mint and moneyer, a second consequence led to a periodical change in the design of the coins which regularly depicted a representation of the king – sometimes bare-headed, sometimes crowned or wearing a diadem or helmet and, under Edward the Confessor, as a full-length figure seated on his throne.

Within two years of Æthelred's accession, raiders from Scandinavia appeared again, but it was not until 991 that the first major operation took place, the English were then forced to pay the intruders £10,000 in gold and silver, the first of a number of such payments designed to secure peace. This Danegeld resulted in turn in the great number of English coins of Æthelred, Cnut, Harold and Harthacnut that have been unearthed in Scandinavia, so that today the collections in Copenhagen, Stockholm and Oslo far out-number those available in Great Britain.

CHRISTOPHER BLUNT

DENMARK'S MONEY

THE VIKINGS, IT IS FREQUENTLY CLAIMED, did not properly understand the use of coins before they learnt it in England, and that even then they were slow to accept this medium of exchange, preferring to use weighed silver. Certainly, the large mixed silver hoards containing hack-silver, rings, ingots and coins are the most conspicuous. But modern investigations have revealed that the hack-silver often had a coinweight corresponding to Arabic dirhems and to European pennies. Halved and quartered coins must also be taken as usual means of payment in minor transactions.

Finds of eighth-century Merovingian deniers and English and Frisian sceattas in several places in southern Jutland are evidence of trade and early use of coins; and the many sceattas found in Ribe on workshop floors and among refuse are an indication of an incipient coin-economy. The most common coin type in these finds is the Frisian Wodan/monster sceatta (no. B21). This evidence is substantiated by the oldest Danish coin from c. 800, which closely imitated the sceatta's face-mask and – a little more freely – its backward-looking animal. Another type in the earliest group imitated Charlemagne's Dorestad coin and is evidence of trading links with the Carolingian Empire. The Charlemagne/Dorestad legend was revived on the coins minted at Hedeby during the late tenth century. Another group of coins with cross-motifs and a seated man minted by Harald Bluetooth about the year 975, possibly in Jelling, show Byzantine inspiration.

The earliest Danish coin to bear the name of a Danish king was, however, clearly inspired by Viking contacts with England. Svein Forkbeard's coin with the legend ZΛEN (Svein) REX AD DENER imitated the crux-type which Æthelred II struck for the payment of Danegeld between 991 and 997. The English moneyer Godwine travelled to Denmark (perhaps from Lincoln) and journeyed on to Sweden and Norway to strike coins for the kings there.

Cnut the Great, Svein Forkbeard's son and successor, found a well-organized royal coinage in England. This he transferred to Denmark with the help of English moneyers, and mints were established in many towns across the country. The most important was at Lund in Skåne, a town which grew and flourished precisely because Cnut had established a mint at the crossing of old trade routes. Cnut's large issues in England consisted of three main types, two of which – quatrefoil and pointed helmet – were created for him by English moneyers, while the short cross, with its sceptre-carrying king on the obverse, imitated the coin type of Æthelred II, one of Cnut's English predecessors.

By means of a simple and primitive line, the engravers of the pointed helmet succeeded in emphasizing a genuinely characteristic Viking feature: the pointed helmet which we find on, *inter alia*, the Gotland picture stones and a small bone sculpture from Sigtuna in Sweden. The picture on the coin cannot be ascribed to chance – it represents Cnut, *the Viking king*. Otherwise Anglo-Saxon coins bear a portrait-head dressed with a diadem, an echo of the Roman representation of emperors.

Danish mints produced all three of Cnut's English types and also other imitations of Æthelred's coins: his small cross, his Hand type – with the Hand of God emerging from the cloud, the long cross with a cross reaching the edge of the coin, and the Agnus Dei – with the Lamb of God and the Dove of the Holy Ghost. These religious motifs were there to emphasize that Denmark was a Christian country.

During the reign of Harthacnut, Cnut's son, the close contact between English and Danish coinage continued. In Denmark he revived the crux-type of Æthelred and Svein Forkbeard and, like Cnut, he minted the pointed helmet, short cross, long cross and Agnus Dei. Several highly decorated crosses on the reverses are identical on English and Danish coins. Under the succeeding kings and beyond the close of the Viking Age, England continued to exert a strong influence on Danish coins. Coinage was a royal prerogative and Denmark, like England, had only one denomination: the penny, made of good quality silver, weighing about one gramme. (During the reign of Cnut the penny bought one *skæppe* – 17.39 litres – of corn.)

The many tenth- and eleventh-century hoards demonstrate that some Anglo-Saxon coins also circulated in Denmark alongside Arabic, German and Danish issues. There are few from before the year 1000, but in the Over Randlev hoard, for example, which contains mostly Arabic coins, there is a St Edmund coin of *c*.900. The Sejrø hoard contained ten English coins from the first half of the tenth century, struck by the Viking kings in York, and by Athelstan, Edmund and Eadred, kings of England. Æthelred II's large Danegeld payments are naturally clearly reflected in Danish finds. Cnut's English coins also appear frequently, as for example in the St Jørgensbjerg hoard at Roskilde. Not until Harald Hen's reform of Danish coinage around 1075 did foreign coin cease to circulate.

KIRSTEN BENDIXEN

TOP ROW *left: A Frisian silver sceatta from Ribe, c.750, showing Wodan and a monster. Right: Denmark's oldest coin from Hedeby, c.800. It bears faces and a backward-looking beast.*

SECOND ROW *left: Harald Bluetooth, Jelling? c.975, with cross motifs and a seated man. Right: Svein Forkbeard shortly before 1,000. It shows a portrait and a cross, and is an imitation of the Æthelred coin below.*

THIRD ROW *left: Silver penny of Æthelred II, 991–997. This is a Danegeld coin with portrait and cross. Right: Silver penny of Cnut the Great showing the pointed-helmet type of 1023–29. And, below, the Danish version of this coin. It has a confused legend.*

BOTTOM ROW *left: A silver penny of Anlaf Sihtricsson, 941–43, a Viking king of York.*

H4

GROWTH OF A DANISH KING

BY THE BEGINNING OF THE tenth century, Danish raids in western Europe were diminishing and the Viking kingdoms of England were gradually falling under the control of the kings of Wessex. The last mention of Danegeld on the Continent is made in 926, and Rollo, a Danish or Norwegian Viking, had already in 911 received Normandy in fief from the King of France; place-name evidence shows that many Danes settled there.

The half-century that followed when western Europe was more or less left in peace was not, however, a period of decline in Denmark. Many of the greatest finds and monuments of the Danish Viking Age are from these years. Among them are a number of large hoards containing jewellery, ingots and coins, hacked-up as well as whole. The metal in these finds is generally silver, rarely gold. The hoards were mostly buried during times of unrest, and represent substantial fortunes. They also show that silver had become a common means of payment, even in minor transactions, and they provide important evidence for tracing the directions taken by trade and other foreign contacts. Most coins in the hoards deposited before 970/980 were Arabic, finding their way to Scandinavia via Russia. After that, this eastern source of silver stops. Was this one of the reasons that the Vikings renewed their interest in the westward raids?

Rich tenth-century Vikings were buried in great splendour, the men with horse equipment, weapons, hunting-dogs and games; the women with fine textiles, jewellery boxes, implements for needlework, lapdogs – all ready to continue their lordly lives in the Hereafter. In these pagan graves we meet the upper classes – and among them, very likely, some of those known to us from the sagas and histories of later ages.

The tenth century, and the beginning of the eleventh, saw the flowering of runestones in Denmark. Generally raised to honour the dead, though rarely on their grave, the stones were sometimes decorated with pictures and ornament which, like the runes themselves, were painted in strong colours. At times, the runestones were part of ship-settings – standing stones arranged to make the outline of a boat – as for example at Glavendrup on Fyn (generally known as Funen in England) and Bække in central Jutland.

LEFT A panel from Tamdrup in central Jutland (a replica is shown in the exhibition – H4). With other panels it illustrates incidents from the history of the Christian mission to Denmark. Here, it is said, a bishop blesses King Harald Bluetooth as he is baptised after his conversion. For reasons not known, the figure of the bishop is an overlay and it covers the image of an archbishop.

Ship-settings could also surround graves, generally cremation graves, where the dead and his grave-goods had all been burnt together.

Grave-goods and hoards are our main source of knowledge of the outstanding artistic craftsmanship of the period – axes, spurs and stirrups with inlaid patterns in contrasting metals, harness-bows for wagon horses with gilt and ornamented bronze mounts, textiles, gold and silver jewellery with filigree animals and interlace, silver cups and much else.

During the tenth century, building works were undertaken on a scale never before seen in Denmark. Several of these were the first, largest and most splendid of their kind and still dominate the Danish landscape. Some of these structures have been dated to a precise year by dendrochronology and many were built by Harald Bluetooth, who succeeded his father to the throne and ruled c. 940–986.

King Harald's most magnificent monument is the Jelling complex: an architectural display of power centering on Harald's parents, King Gorm and Queen Thyre and on his own achievements. The core of this monument is Denmark's largest burial mound (the North Mound) with a diameter of 65 m. and a height of 8·5 m. It contains a timber-built grave-chamber in which were found the remains of very resplendent grave-goods, among them the small Jelling cup. But there were no human remains and it is clear that the grave had been emptied of most of its contents in ancient times. Part of a huge stone-setting survives, probably a ship-setting. This is associated with the North Mound where probably King Gorm and possibly his Queen were buried in sumptious pagan fashion. Thyre died before Gorm and was commemorated by him on the smaller Jelling stone. The second Jelling mound (the South Mound) does not contain a grave, but was probably a cenotaph or a cult or assembly place. Having a diameter of 77 m. and a height of 11 m. it is the largest of Denmark's ancient mounds.

Recent excavations below the present church in Jelling, which lies between the two huge mounds, have revealed traces of a large wooden church from the Viking Age. Associated with this was a grave which contained parts of a male skeleton (and possibly of a female) as well as gold threads from textiles and two strap-mounts of unusually beautiful work- manship; these are closely related in style to several objects from the North Mound grave-chamber. The bones were obviously moved to this grave from elsewhere. It seems most likely that they came from the North Mound, transferred at the time of King Harald's and Denmark's official conversion to Christianity around 960. This doubtless made it desirable to give the Jelling complex a Christian character; and so another, Christian, burial in the large new church was given to the father (or possibly both parents) of the new Christian king. Perhaps Harald inaugurated the large Jelling stone at the same time. The world's most magnificent runestone, its three sides are covered partly by a proud animal entwined with a serpent, partly by Christ, and partly by a memorial to Harald himself and his parents: "King Harald ordered these memorials made to Gorm his father and Thyre his mother; that Harald who won for himself all Denmark and Norway and made the Danes Christian".

In about 979 a bridge, almost three-quarters of a mile (one kilometre) long, was built across the broad valley of the Vejle River in Ravning Enge some six miles (ten kilometres) to the south-west of Jelling. It was constructed with engineering precision – all vertical posts, four in each section, were carefully cut one-foot square, and it has been calculated that about 2,500 immense oak posts were used just for the supporting parts of the bridge. Sunken roads were dug to facilitate access to it. A work of such dimension must be attributed to a king, and he must be Harald Bluetooth.

The tenth century saw repeated border-fighting with the German realm. One such encounter was anticipated in 968, the year when, probably, an immense extension of the Danevirke took place, enlarging it into a continuous wall nearly nine miles (fourteen kilometres) long – Harald Bluetooth's greatest building-work. The war did not break out until 974 and Harald lost. But in 983 the Danes took revenge and captured a fortress which the German emperor had established in the border country. The opportunity was taken at the same time to harry Holstein and burn Hamburg. During this period of unrest Hedeby was fortified by its huge semi-circular rampart; and Århus, which in the tenth century emerged as Denmark's third town and bishopric, acquired its defences. By means of these walls, the towns were adapted to function also as strongholds.

Fortresses as such are known only in Denmark for a very brief moment of the Viking Age. Four in all, they were probably all constructed around the year 980 – Trelleborg on Zealand, Nonnebakken on Fyn, Fyrkat in eastern Jutland, and Aggersborg in northern Jutland by the Limfjord. They differ greatly in size, but are all built to the same strict geometric pattern: a circular wall, with gates at the four points of the compass, and houses set in all four quarters. The fortresses were situated close to important land-routes, but had little or no access to the sea, apart from Aggersborg which guarded the Limfjord traffic and fjord crossing. They can have been built only by the king, and their primary purpose must have been to safeguard his internal power. They were probably also centres for managing his financial and administrative rights and duties.

King Harald also encouraged the minting of coins and ordered the building of a church in Roskilde, the first predecessor of Roskilde Cathedral where Danish royalty is buried today. Harald was killed in c.986 in a rebellion led by his son Svein Forkbeard and he was himself the first king to be buried there.

No royal monuments are known from the remainder of the Viking Age. Much of King Svein's energy was directed towards his English adventures; and Cnut the Great spent most of his time in England, ruling Denmark by proxy and only visiting to settle pressing problems.

But Denmark flourished in many other ways. Coinage became of increasing importance and was regulated on the English pattern; bridges were built and fords improved to facilitate communications; the number of towns increased considerably – all manifestations of the growing importance of trade and the stability of a united realm. Christianity gradually penetrated everywhere, more bishoprics were established and church organization became more effective. The first stone buildings – churches – appeared during the eleventh century. In this, as in many other fields, European culture was making itself felt.

In 1028, Cnut the Great conquered Norway, where once both his father and his grandfather had ruled; he also claimed to be king of part of Sweden. But the realm collapsed after his death and the passing of his son Harthacnut in 1042 meant the end of the North Sea Empire. In the following years there were problems with both Norway and Sweden, now unified each under its own king, and with the Slav tribes south of the Baltic.

Danish interventions in the northern English revolts against William the Conqueror in 1069, 1070 and again in 1075 mostly took the form of raids for plunder and when finally King Cnut the Holy (St Cnut) in 1085 organised a large expedition to conquer all England, he was delayed by problems on his southern border. The fleet dissolved and the levies which he had collected for the offensive enflamed the people to revolt in 1086. Cnut himself was killed in Odense, in the church dedicated to the English Saint Alban, and became Denmark's first royal saint. The Viking Age was long since past. With this Cnut there also died the dream of a Danish England.

ELSE ROESDAHL

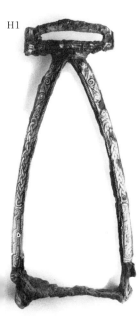

H1

H1　The grave goods of a wealthy Viking: weapons, horse trappings and personal belongings
Brandstrup, central Jutland. FHM [336]

1　Double-edged sword in the remains of a wooden scabbard. The upper and lower guards are straight, the pommel tripartite. The covering of the grip is poorly preserved; rest of the hilt is decorated with silver wire. Shanks of two nails or rivets on the scabbard, 65cm and 70cm from the tip, indicate suspension-points. Towards the tip of the scabbard are traces of binding. Total length 97.5cm; length of blade and scabbard 81.5cm; grip 9.4cm.
2　Spearhead of iron. L.53.0cm.
3　Iron horse-bit. A fragmentary two-link bit with side-bars and cheek-pieces. There are traces of a whitish metal on the cheek-pieces. L. of longest side bar, 17.5cm.
4　Two D-shaped buckles of iron. Internal width at thorn, 5.3cm.
5　Two rectangular buckles of iron. Internal width at thorn 5.2cm.
6　Two trapezoid iron strap-mounts with a bronze-covered plate. The short sides have loops, in one of which is a small ring. W. (maximum) 5.6cm.
7　Two iron stirrups decorated with designs in silver and copper. H.24.3cm and 24.5cm; W. (foot-plate) 8.4cm.
8　Two iron spurs decorated with designs in silver. On one spur much of one arm is missing. Length from end of prick to point equidistant between the end plates, 18.5cm.
9　Two spur buckles? Bronze. Rectangular, 4.3 × 2.4cm.
10　Knife with a wooden handle and the remains of a leather sheath. L.13.8cm.
11　Whetstone of greenish striped slate, perforated for suspension. Square cross-section. L.7.6cm.
12　Iron shears, incomplete. L.22.4cm.
13　Iron bucket-handle, incomplete. It has a flat central portion with twisted ends. The span of the handle is about 27.0cm.
14　Wooden gaming-board. Strengthened at the corners and transversely by metal mounts. Nails decorate the edges. It is reconstructed on a modern board. Rectangular, 30 × 60cm.
15　The grave also contained a few bones and teeth of a horse as well as an awl, three Danish silver coins from the first half of the tenth century and some pieces of iron and mounts.

The objects in the grave were for use in life after death. The horse and riding equipment would allow the dead man to arrive in comfort at his destination, probably Valhalla, where Odin reigned and time was spent in fighting and feasting.

H2　Silver Thor's hammer on a chain
Sejrø, isl0nd off N.W. Zealand; part of a hoard (see H10)

The hammer is cast and undecorated. It is suspended from a ring of thin twisted wires and attached to a plaited chain. H.3.7cm. W.3.3cm. D. (ring) 2.9cm. L. (chain) 62.0cm.

Such hammers, the symbol of the god Thor, are comparatively common in tenth-century hoards in Denmark. When Scandinavia became Christian in the eleventh century they were replaced by crosses (see H8).

H3　The Jelling Cup (replica)
Jelling, central Jutland; from the royal burial NM I [CCCLXXII]

The original cup is of silver, the inside gilt. The engraved lines of the ornament contain traces of gold and niello in many places. The bowl of the cup is slightly conical, the short stem has a nodus and the foot is circular and almost flat. The bowl is encircled by engraved lines and a design of Jellinge-style animals. Repair work at some time in the past involved soldering the foot into a bored hole in the bowl. H.4.3cm.

The cup was found in 1820 in the grave chamber of the North Mound at Jelling where King Gorm, and perhaps also Queen Thyre, were buried with grave-goods in the pagan tradition. It has been suggested that the cup is a Christian chalice, but it is more likely that this is an ordinary secular cup for strong drink. The ornament of the cup has given its name to the Jelling style. After the introduction of Christianity in 960, it is believed that Harald Bluetooth removed the bones from the grave in the mound and re-interred them in a new grave in the church he had built between the two mounds at Jelling.

H4　'King Harald's baptism'; twelfth-century gilt panel (replica)
Tamdrup, central Jutland. Once displayed on a pulpit with other panels. NM II [D801]

Gilt and chased bronze plate refashioned from an earlier panel. To the right a man half submerged in a barrel. To the left a bishop with raised arm on a smaller, separate plate which covers the original figure of an archbishop. H.19.3cm. W.15cm.

The plate is from a so-called 'golden altar' or from a reliquary. Together with other panels from Tamdrup it illustrates incidents from the history of the Christian mission to Denmark, including Poppo's miracle which led to the conversion and baptism of Harald Bluetooth about 960. When this panel was produced, stories about Poppo and the conversion of the Danes were numerous. It is likely that the man in the barrel represents King Harald.

H5　Mould for casting ingots, a Thor's hammer and two crosses
Trendgården, north Jutland; single-find. NM I [C24451]

Rectangular soapstone mould with grooves for ingots on three sides and on the fourth the cut-shapes of two crosses and a Thor's hammer. It was probably re-used as a weight. L.9.8cm.

H1

The conversion to Christianity was a gradual process in Denmark, apparently without serious confrontations between the new faith and the old. This mould illustrates the peaceful transfer from one religion to another.

H6 Silver cross-pendant

Tolstrup, north Jutland; part of a hoard. NM I [C6670]

The cross is stylized and designed in the Borre style. The loop is in the shape of a bird's head. The pendant is produced in the same technique as the brooch, H14. H. (now) 4.2cm. W. (tip of left arm missing) 3.9cm.

The coins found with this pendant indicate that it was buried about 1000. There can be no doubt that the pendant was produced in the second half of the tenth-century when Christianity was officially introduced into Denmark. Like the later cross from Bonderup (no. H8), it was designed in a Scandinavian art-style.

H7 Four Danish silver coins of cross-type

Pihuse, central Jutland; part of hoard. NM VI [FP 1990: 26, 41, 45, 47]

Weights 0.33g, 0.40g, 0.39g and 0.22g respectively.

Date *c*.975. Probably struck for Harald Bluetooth, possibly at Jelling. The design of this coin type is derived from Byzantine coins.

H8 Silver cross-pendant on a chain

Bonderup, Zealand; part of a hoard. NM II [14190]

Silver, with traces of niello on the cross. Both sides of the cross are basically identical: the arms are designed as tendrils with pear-shaped lobes in the Ringerike style. It is suspended from a plain ring which is attached to the plaited chain by animal-head terminals in the Urnes style. H. (overall) 5.4cm. W.4.1cm. D. (ring) 2.4cm. L. (animal-heads) 2.5cm. L. (chain) 76.5cm.

The cross and chain were part of a hoard; coins found in it indicate that it was deposited between about 1060 and 1070. By this time the Church was well-established in Denmark and the country was divided into stable dioceses.

H9 Two harness-bows

Mammen, central Jutland: ? grave find NM I [C1063]

Gilt bronze mounts applied to a modern wooden base. Corresponding mounts on the two bows are basically identical, although they may vary in detail. There are nine mounts on one bow and seven on the other. The end mounts have some details picked out in silver and niello and consist of animal-heads in the round: inside the gaping mouths are small gripping-beasts. On the ridge of each bow are three mounts with crests. The round hole for the reins on the central ridge-mount (which show no signs of wear) is surmounted by bearded human masks. The crests of the ridge-mounts on either side terminate in animal-heads with gaping jaws. Both ridges and sides are decorated in the Jellinge-style with animals, snakes, interlace and human figures. One each side of the harness-bows were two curved, band-shaped mounts decorated with Jellinge-style animals; on each bow one mount is incomplete and on one side they are missing altogether. Total length 41cm and 42cm; height at the centre (including the human mask) 9.0cm.

Harness-bows are known from several Danish graves; they occur in pairs and formed part of the harness of the wagon horses of the rich: their function was to hold the reins. They are re-constructed on the basis of known examples in which the wood is preserved.

H10 Silver hoard containing complete jewellery, hack-silver, coins, ingots, half-finished jewellery and silver scrap

Sejrø, island off N.W. Zealand. NM I [17270, 18112-19, 18192-205, 18583, C4810]

1 Rings: three plaited neck-rings; two smooth arm-rings, one with four small rings appended; a moulded arm-ring with nine small rings; two twisted arm-rings; a plaited arm-ring; a band-shaped finger-ring and a crescent-shaped ear-ring of Slav origin.

2 Brooches: a circular brooch with a soldered-on animal in Jellinge style; three circular brooches with a symmetrical ornament in the Borre style in

RIGHT *The only known contemporary representation of Cnut the Great is found in the* Liber Vitae *of the New Minster in Winchester. This 'Book of Life' was begun about 1031 and shows Cnut and his Queen, Emma, presenting an altar cross to the religious community, members of which are seen below the king and queen. The queen's name is given as Ælfgyfu, as she was generally known in England. (See 116, p 162.)*

H6

H9

filigree and granulation. Suspended from a ring on one of these are three chains, each terminating in a ring: one of these is empty, the second carries a ring with two silver beads and the third a small knot-shaped ornament.

3 Pendant: an Arabic coin with a loop.

4 Unfinished jewellery: two circular discs with stamped ornament, five round blanks, probably for jewellery.

5 Hack-silver: fragments of ingots and jewellery (including the round terminal of a penannular brooch, a Slav ear-ring and a perforated Arabic coin) and silver scrap.

6 Coins: the hoard contained 143 complete and fragmentary coins including 97 Arabic coins, one German, one Bohemian, 10 English and 34 Danish coins (according to an account dated 1942). Of these approximately 60 Arabic coins and 9 English coins are exhibited. For the English coins (see H11); the Thor's hammer (see H2). The latest coin in the hoard was struck 953–65.

The hoard was presumably laid down in the 950s. It was brought into the National Museum piecemeal over a period of time and now represents in all probability only a part of the original hoard. With the exception of a number of coins, the whole surviving portion of the hoard is exhibited. The content of the hoard, which includes complete and fragmentary jewellery etc., and a large percentage of Arabic coins, a much smaller number of Danish coins and only a few western European coins (including the English coins), is characteristic of this period.

H11   Nine English silver coins

Sejrø, island off N.W. Zealand; part of hoard (see H10). NM VI [FP 187, 191]

1 Anlaf Sihtricsson (Norse king of York), 941–43. Moneyer, AVRA. Weight 1.30g.

2 Æthelstan, 924–39. Moneyer, ABONEL. Weight 1.47g.

3 Edmund, 939–46. Moneyer, INGELGAR. Weight 1.47g.

4 Edmund, 939–46. Moneyer, LIVFINC. Weight 1.09g.

5 Edmund, 939–46. Moneyer ?, WIGEARIN. Weight 1.26g.

6 Eadred, 946–55. Moneyer, CRISTIN. Weight 1.31g.

7 Eadred, 946–55. Moneyer, INGELGAR. Weight 1.50g.

8 Eadred, 946–55. Moneyer, THEODMAER. Weight 1.40g.

9 Eadred, 946–55. Moneyer, THEODMAER. Weight 1.5g.

A fragment of a tenth English coin is not exhibited. It was struck for Anlaf Guthfrithsson (Viking king of York) 939–41.

H12   Four Danish silver coins of Carolus/Dorestad type

Pilhuse, central Jutland; part of a hoard. NM VI [FP 1990: 1, 10, 12, 14]

Weight, 0.40g, 0.41g, 0.31g and 0.40g respectively.

Date about 900–975. The coin type is reminiscent of one of the earliest Scandinavian types from about 800 which was inspired by the coins struck for Charlemagne in the Frisian town of Dorestad.

H13   Gold chain

Fæsted, south Jutland; single-find. NM I [$\frac{90}{11}$]

Knitted chain with animal-head shaped ends terminating in loops (one is missing) and decorated in filigree and granulation. L. (total) 62cm. L. (animal-head with loop) 2.1cm. Weight 67.1g.

A ring was presumably threaded through the loops of the animal-heads from which a jewel was suspended, cf. H8 below.

H14   Gold disc-brooch

Sperrestrup, Zealand; single-find NM I [20540]

The brooch has a plain back-plate, and a dished top-plate embossed in relief and decorated within a border with Borre-style gripping beasts in filigree and granulation – a small portion of the border is missing. The heads of the animals meet at the centre. The back is decorated with spiral patterns. The pin is missing. A ring is suspended from a loop at the back. D.4.6cm; weight 24.3g.

The brooch belongs to a group of gold and silver disc-brooches which were fashionable in the second half of the tenth century and in the period around 1,000.

H18

H15

H18

A close-up of the decorative detail to be seen on the spear far left.

H15   The Mammen axe; iron inlaid with silver
Bjerringhøj in Mammen, central Jutland; grave find. NM I [C133]

The butt of the axe-head is flat. Much of the spurs at the shaft-hole are missing; the upper tip of the edge is reconstructed. The surface is decorated with inlaid silver wire; only the edge, the upper and lower faces of the blade and the grooves for the binding in the shaft-hole area are unornamented. The groove which separates the shaft-hole from the blade is encrusted with a yellow metal. One side of the blade is decorated with a backward-looking bird, the other side bears a restless pattern of interlaced tendrils. Other parts of the axe-head are decorated with geometric patterns, triquetrae, spirals, a tetragram and a mask. L. (right angles from centre of butt) 17.5cm; edge about 10.5cm.

The Mammen axe represents one of the high points of Viking-Age art. The Mammen style takes its name from the bird included in the design.

H16   Two iron shield-bosses
1 Valbygård, Zealand; grave find. NM I [C3795]
2 Hald, north Jutland; grave find. NM I [C6295]

1 Shield-boss with a pointed dome and flat flange. D.16.0cm. H.7.5cm.
2 D.13–13.5cm. H.4.5cm.

The shield-boss covered the hole cut in the board of the shield to receive the grip.

H17   Four iron arrow-heads
FHM [1188]

Iron leaf-shaped blades with off-set tangs. L. (longest) 14.5cm.

H18   Two iron spear heads
1 Tissø, Zealand; single-find. NM I [C5336]
2 Rønnebæksholm, Zealand; grave find. NM I [C9488]

Iron with ornamented sockets.
1 The socket is encrusted with silver decorated with geometric and interlace designs. L.35.2cm.
2 The socket is encrusted with copper and silver decorated with geometric designs and a ribbon interlace pattern. L.47.0cm.

H19   Two iron spear-heads
1 Hald, north Jutland; grave find. NM I [C6299]
2 Trelleborg, Zealand, from civil settlement or fortress. NM I [Q19f]

L.45.0 and L.35.8cm. respectively.

H20   Axe-head; iron with silver inlay
Trelleborg, Zealand; grave find. NM I [Q1613]

The axe-head is T-shaped; the lower tip of the edge is slightly bent. There is a split in the shaft-hole. Both sides are decorated with patterns of inlaid silver wire of which only few traces survive. L.16.5cm. W. (edge) 31.5cm.

H21   Two iron axe-heads with expanded blades
1 Trelleborg, Zealand; from civil settlement or fortress. NM I [Q254]

L. (at centre of shaft-hole) 23.0cm. Edge 19.2cm.

2 Johannisminde, Lolland; grave find. NM I [C8040]

L. (at centre of shaft-hole) 21.5cm. Edge 21.0cm.

H22   Two double-edged iron swords
1 Sjørring, north Jutland; single-find. NM II [D1031]
2 Tissø, Zealand; single-find. NM II [D111/1957]

1 The blade is pattern-welded with a flat fuller. The upper and lower guards are straight; the pommel (made in one piece with the upper guard) is low and tripartite. The covering of the grip is missing. The rest of the hilt is decorated with brass bands and wire, of which only few traces remain. L. (total) 91.8cm. L. (blade with tip missing) 77cm. Grip 9.5cm.
2 The blade has a flat fuller and traces of an indecipherable inscription. The lower guard is straight; there is no upper guard. A lengthwise section through the pommel is roughly semi-circular. The covering of the grip is missing. L. (total) 94.2cm. L. (blade) 80.2cm. Grip 10.5cm.

H23   Coin of Svein Forkbeard (copy) and two Æthelred II coins of crux type
1 Purchased. NM VI [G.P.3425]
2 and 3 No provenance. NM VI

1 Silver. Svein Forkbeard's coin has on one side a portrait and the inscription ZΛEN REX AD DENER, and on the other a cross and the inscription CRUX, GODWINE M AN DNER. Weight 1.65g.
2 and 3 Æthelred II's coins were both struck in London. 2. Moneyer ÆLFGAR. Weight 1.45g. 3. Moneyer EADMVND. Weight 1.24g.

Date of Æthelred II coins, 991–997. These coins poured into Denmark in large quantities as Danegeld. They became the prototype of Svein Forkbeard's coins – the earliest Danish coins to carry the name of the king. The moneyer of these coins had an English name. Svein's coins are dated to shortly before 1000.

H24   Fifteen Æthelred II coins (Danegeld)
No provenance. NM VI

Enormous quantities of silver coins left England under Æthelred II as he tried in vain to buy off the Vikings. Many more of his coins have therefore been found in Scandinavia than in England.

DANEGELD AND CNUT

IN THE REIGN OF ÆTHELRED, who ruled between 978 and 1016, England was once again attacked by Vikings. The first raids in 980 were widespread, affecting Thanet and Cheshire as well as Southampton, and in the next two years Cornwall, Devon and Dorset suffered in their turn. Attacks of this kind seem to have been feared for some time, that at least is implied by the attention paid to naval defence by Æthelred's father, King Edgar, and it was probably the political confusion following Edgar's death in 975 that gave a new generation of Scandinavians an opportunity that they eagerly seized. Some of the raiders, especially those who attacked the western parts of England, were descendants of Norwegians who had settled in Ireland, Man and the Hebrides in the ninth century, but many came directly from Denmark, Norway or Sweden. Scandinavian chieftains and their followers, whose appetite for silver had been whetted by the flood of Arabic coins that reached the Baltic during the tenth century, now found an alternative source – in England.

The first raids were on a small scale; Southampton was attacked in 980 by seven ships and the raid of 982 on Portland was made by three, but the fleets were soon much larger. The vulnerability of England to such attacks was quickly demonstrated and the English proved able, and willing, to pay large amounts of silver as the price of peace, however temporary. Ninety-three ships raided the south-east in 991 and forced the English to pay £10,000 of silver. Three years later a similar fleet, led by the same men, failed to take London and then resorted to general violence in Essex, Kent, Sussex and Hampshire until the English agreed to pay an even larger sum, £16,000.

One of the leaders of these attacks was the Danish king, Svein Forkbeard, who returned several times in 1003 to attack the south coast, including Exeter and Wilton, and in the next year to East Anglia, where he plundered Norwich and Thetford. The great raids of 1006–7 and 1009–12 were led by others but were probably encouraged by Svein.

When in the summer of 1013 he came for the last time his purpose was not the extortion of tribute but the conquest of the kingdom. The demoralised English could offer little resistance and after a swift campaign "all the nation regarded him as full king". Æthelred fled to Normandy, but Svein did not enjoy his triumph long, for he died on the 3rd February, 1014. Æthelred returned but the attacks continued, and within three years of Svein's death his own son Cnut had been accepted by the English as their king.

The detailed account of these events was the work of a chronicler who wrote in the years of defeat. His interpretation, coloured by that failure, has been the basis for most judgements of Æthelred as a disastrous king, but we should in fairness recognise, as the chronicler did not, the magnitude of the problems Æthelred had to face. The English had some notable successes but to defeat or even buy off one fleet did not ensure peace, for other fleets were assembled. There were also great internal problems. England had only recently been united under one king, Northumbria having finally submitted to the rule of the West Saxon dynasty in 954.

In areas remote from Wessex, and rarely if ever visited by the king himself, his authority depended on the loyalty of his agents and of the local aristocracy. In the Danelaw these men were predominantly of Scandinavian descent, but in all parts of England some of them, English as well as Danish, came to think that their interests might be better served by supporting Viking invaders rather than opposing them; the rule of Alfred's dynasty was not accepted by everyone as inevitable or even desirable.

As early as 991 Æthelric of Bocking, in Essex, was suspected of supporting Svein, and accusations of treachery were freely made and readily reported by the chronicler. It is hardly surprising that the loyalty of men of Scandinavian descent was doubted. Widespread hostility to Danes settled in England was shown on St Brice's day (13th November) in 1002 when, according to the *Anglo-Saxon Chronicle*, the king ordered all the Danes in England to be killed. This cannot have been directed against the inhabitants of the Danelaw; the victims were probably men who had more recently settled in other parts of England, including Vikings who had retired or agreed to help the English. The reality of this massacre can be glimpsed in a charter that describes Danes in Oxford seeking sanctuary in a church.

Æthelred was nevertheless forced to recruit Vikings to reinforce his defences, even though they could not always be relied on. Svein's brother-in-law, Pallig, was one such leader who was generously treated by Æthelred with land and treasure but changed sides in 1001 to join a fleet raiding in the south-west. In 1012 forty-five ships commanded by a Dane, Thorkell the Tall, agreed to serve Æthelred and were based in the Thames – a remarkable development, for Thorkell had been the leader of the army that dispersed in 1012 after almost three years in England, having been paid the unprecedented sum of £48,000.

There were, therefore, different ways in which a Scandinavian warrior could share England's wealth; by plunder, as tribute or as payment for service. The coin-hoards of Scandinavia show that large quantities of English pennies must have been taken home by men like the Swede commemorated on a rune stone at Yttergärde in Uppland: "And Ulv has in England taken three gelds. That was the first which Tosti paid. Then Thorkell paid. Then Cnut paid". The men who gained most were, of course, the leaders, some of whom used the newly-won wealth and enhanced reputations to support their ambitions in Scandinavia.

Two Norwegian kings were Vikings in England before gaining power at home: Olaf Tryggvason was a leader in 991 and 994; while Olaf Haraldsson, later known as St Olaf, took part in Thorkell's invasion of 1009–12. Cnut is an even more striking example. It was only after establishing himself as king of England that he was able, after his brother's death in 1018, to assert his claim to rule Denmark, and ten years later his attempt to conquer Norway was undertaken with a fleet of fifty ships from England.

Cnut's interest in Scandinavia was naturally great, but the basis of his power lay in England, and it was there that he spent most of his time. He married Æthelred's widow, reissued Æthelred's laws as his own, and maintained the system of coinage and taxation that his predecessor had developed. He ruled as a Christian king, went on pilgrimage to Rome, was well served by English bishops and when he died, in 1035, he was buried at Winchester. What little unity there was in his so-called 'North Sea Empire' was personal, and after his death Denmark and England were separate kingdoms apart from a brief interval (1040–42) when the English invited Harthacnut, Cnut's son and successor as king of Denmark, to be their king. They soon regretted that decision for Harthacnut increased the fleet from the sixteen ships that Cnut had normally maintained to sixty-two, and the English had to pay for them.

In 1042 the English chose as their next king Æthelred's son, Edward. He had spent his years of exile in Normandy and naturally favoured Normans rather than Danes, but the links with Scandinavia were not easily broken and for some years Edward even retained a small Scandinavian fleet. When, in January, 1066, he died childless, his successor, Harold son of Godwin, was challenged by both Harald, king of Norway, and William, duke of Normandy, both of whom invaded England. The Norwegians were beaten, and their king killed, at Stamford Bridge, east of York, on the 25th September. Three weeks later William won the Battle of Hastings. He was then accepted, after some hesitation, by most, but not all, of the English nobility. The most persistent opposition appeared in the Danelaw, where the resistance was reinforced from time to time by the arrival of a Danish fleet in the Humber. William, like Æthelred, had to pay them to leave, but he did more. Castles were built and manned by local garrisons, reinforcements were recruited across the Channel when necessary, and paid with England's wealth, and some rebellious areas, notably Yorkshire, were ruthlessly devastated.

The Danes, however, remained a serious threat for most of William's reign and in 1085 the Danish king, a second Cnut, himself planned to lead an invasion. In the words of a contemporary chronicler:

> When William, king of England, who was then in Normandy, found out about this, he went to England with a larger force of mounted men and infantry from France and Brittany than had ever come to this country, so that people wondered how this country could maintain all that army. And the king had the army dispersed all over the country ... and had the land near the sea laid waste, so that if his enemies landed, they should have nothing to seize on so quickly.

Cnut's fleet never sailed and he was assassinated in the following year. Scandinavian hopes of conquering England died with him. England's fortunes were henceforth to be linked with France, not Denmark.

PETER SAWYER

I 5

I 1 THE ANGLO-SAXON CHRONICLE
British Library [Cotton MS Tiberius B. iv]
Vellum; 218 folios, 28.5 × 19cm. Anglo-Saxon.
Written about 1050, with additions down to 1079.

A number of variant versions of the *Anglo-Saxon Chronicle* survive, providing one of the most important sources for the history of England in the period before and immediately after the Norman Conquest. This particular copy, known to scholars as manuscript D, belonged to Worcester and its later entries have a strong local flavour.

However, the examplar from which it was copied seems to have come from the north of England, perhaps from Ripon, and to have contained a particularly well-informed account of Anglo-Scandinavian relations in the time of Cnut. The left-hand exhibited page (folio 65b) carries the opening of the entry for 1015, including a description of Cnut's arrival in England, his suppression of Wessex and Ealdorman Eadric's decision to join him. On the right-hand page (folio 66) is the entry for 1016, recording how Cnut went with Eadric to harry the north and how Edmund gathered levies to oppose him.

I 2 The Battersea Sword
River Thames, Battersea P-RM [PR 1555-2580]

The two-edged iron sword has a curved guard inlaid on both sides with longitudinal brass wires. On the upper face of the guard is a basket-work pattern of inlaid wires. The semi-circular pommel is inlaid with brass and copper wires forming a conventionalised acanthus pattern. On the blade is an illegible inscription and on the reverse is a decorative pattern. L.88.0cm.

I 3 Incomplete iron two-edged sword
River Thames, Wallingford Bridge, Berks. RM
Thames Conservancy Collection [170.65]

This sword has a fullered blade inlaid with a maker's mark. The guard and upper guard curve away from the grip, and like the trilobate pommel are decorated with brass, copper and silver wires. L.58.5cm.

This is one of a group of late Anglo-Saxon swords, descended from the type represented by the Gilling and Fiskerton swords, nos. D3 and D2, dating to the tenth century.

I 4 Iron two-edged sword
River Thames, Tenfoot Bridge, Shifford, Oxon. RM.
Thames Conservancy Collection [287.47]

This has a fullered blade inlaid with an inscription. The guard curves away from the grip, and the upper guard is straight. There is a five-lobed pommel. The hilt is decorated with silver and copper-alloy inlay. L.82.0cm.

The inscription on the blade appears to read ULFBERH + T, a maker's name. Such blades were probably imported from the Rhineland, and are known also from Scandinavia.

I 5 Five stirrup irons
Kilverstone, Norfolk NCM [58.36]
River Cherwell AM [1886.443]
River Witham between Kirkstead and Washing-
borough, Lincs. Lin.M [9663.06]
No known provenance, UMAA, Cam. [1923.1157]
Great Somerford, Wilts. DM

Each has a rectangular suspension loop; also a narrow, sub-triangular loop, the side elements of which are separated from a sub-rectangular side plate by a knop. The wide foot-plate is slightly convex. The outer surface of all but one of the stirrups is decorated with inlaid copper-alloy scroll work. L.30.0 × W.14.0cm.

Some fourteen such stirrups are known from England, and it has been suggested that they were made in the Danelaw, a hypothesis supported by their distribution which is mainly in the Midlands and East Anglia. They are modelled on a Scandinavian form of stirrup iron.

I 6 Two iron axe heads
River Yare, Surlingham, Norfolk NCM [158.946]
River Witham between Kirkstead and Washing-
borough, Lincs. Lin.M [9661.06]

Each has an asymmetrically expanding blade, a convex cutting edge, and projecting spurs on either side of the socket. W.22.0cm.

The use of projecting spurs on the sockets is a feature of Scandinavian rather than Anglo-Saxon axe heads.

I 7 Iron axe
River Thames, Whitehall, London BM [56, 7-1, 1422]

The axe has a narrow neck and asymmetrically expanding blade, the lower end of which is squared. W.13.5cm.

I 8 Iron axe
River Thames, Hammersmith, London BM [1909, 6-26, 8]

It has an asymmetrically expanding blade with a convex cutting edge. There are spurs projecting from the lower edge of the socket. W.21.5cm.

I 9 Socketed iron spearhead
London BM [56, 7-1, 1452]

It has a lozenge-shaped blade of lozenge-shaped section. The socket is encrusted with silver and ornamented with incised Ringerike-style decoration. L.37.9cm.

Twenty-four spearheads with eleventh-century Ringerike-style decoration on the socket are known, mostly from Norway and Sweden.

I 6

115a

110   Socketed iron spearhead
River Thames, London BM [83, 1-12, 1]

It has a narrow blade of lozenge-shaped section
with an angular shoulder between the socket and
blade. The socket is split and decorated with groups
of incised lines around the circumference.
L.69.5cm.

111   Socketed iron spearhead and ferrule
Bracebrdge, Lincs. Lin.M [3-4.27]

The spearhead has a long, narrow blade of lozenge-
shaped section, with an angular shoulder between
the socket and blade. The socket is undecorated,
apart from an incised line around the circumference at the upper end, and two pairs of incised lines
around the lower end. The conical ferrule is also
undecorated apart from three incised lines around
the circumference at the open end. L.39.0 and
35.0cm.

The spearhead and ferrule were found together
and presumably belonged to the same weapon. In
form the spearhead closely resembles examples
from Scandinavia, but lacks their characteristic
encrusted decoration ond the socket.

112   Socketed iron spearhead
*River Witham near Bardney, Lincs. Lin.M
[345.14]*

It has a narrow, slender blade of lozenge-shaped
section with an angular shoulder between the
socket and blade. These are separated by a collar,
and there is a rivet through the socket at its open
end. L.46.0 × W.4.0cm.

113   Socketed iron spearhead
*River Witham near Bardney, Lincs. Lin.M
[9715.06]*

The spearhead has a leaf-shaped blade. The socket
is longitudinally facetted, and has a perforation for
a rivet at the open end. L.34.0 × W.4.0cm.

114   Socketed iron spearhead
River Witham, Lincs. Lin.M [9712.06]

It has a lozenge-shaped blade of lozenge-shaped
section. The socket is roughly broken.
L.24.0 × W.5.0cm.

In form the closest parallel is a spearhead from
the River Thames above Hampton Court, dated to
the tenth or early eleventh century.

115a   Iron axe head
London Bridge. Mus. of Lon. [A23346]

This axe has an asymmetrically expanding blade, a
convex cutting edge, and spurs projecting from the
socket. Into the socket fits a copper-alloy sleeve
decorated with incised Ringerike-style ornament,
and having a row of vandykes projecting from the
lower edge, now largely lost. 19.0 × 21.0cm.

Found with seven other axes of similar form
(including another with a copper-alloy sleeve), six
spear heads, a pair of tongs and a four-pronged
grappling hook. The weapons, all found within a
restricted area, have been interpreted as the
remains of a Viking attack on the bridge.

115b   Long, slender iron spear-head
*River Thames, Putney Bridge. Mus. of Lon.
[A25395]*

It has a closed socket separated from the blade by a
decorative moulding. L.53.0cm.

Several spear-heads of this form are known from
London, some having the socket encrusted with
silver and copper-alloy.

**116   *LIBER VITAE* OF THE NEW MINSTER,
WINCHESTER**
British Library [Stowe MS 944]
*Vellum; 69 folios, 25.5 × 13.5cm. Latin and Anglo-
Saxon. Written and decorated in or about 1031,
with additions down to the sixteenth century.*

A *Liber Vitae*, or Book of Life, contains a record of
the members, friends and benefactors of a religious
community to be remembered in their prayers. The
New Minster *Liber Vitae* was probably begun in
1031, the scribe, who was probably also the artist,
being a monk called Ælsine.

The book is prefaced by series of three tinted
drawings, the first showing Cnut the Great and his
Queen presenting a splendid altar cross to the
monastery. This drawing is the only contemporary
representation of Cnut. The names of the royal
couple are written over their heads. The Queen's
name is given as Ælfgifu, by which she was
generally known in England. She was in fact a
Norman by birth, and her original name was
Imme, often Latinised as Emma, which is what she
is called in the *Encomium* (see no. 117). Above the
cross is the figure of Christ, flanked by the New
Minister's patrons, the Virgin Mary and St Peter.
Below, in an arcade, Ælsine has included a group of
his fellow monks.

117   ENCOMIUM EMMAE REGINAE
British Library [Additional MS 33241]
*Vellum; 67 folios, 17.5 × 11.5cm. Latin. Written
and decorated in north-east France in the mid-
eleventh century.*

This account of the the times of Cnut the Great and
his wife, Emma of Normandy, was composed for
Emma by a monk of St Omer soon after the
accession of her son, Harthacnut, to the English
throne in 1040. The first two of its three books are
devoted to Cnut, beginning with Svein's invasion
of England in 1013. The third records the period
after Cnut's death, when Emma was in exile under
the protection of Count Baldwin of Flanders. It
ends with Harthacnut's invitation to his half-
brother Edward to join him in ruling England.
Although the author of the book was very biased in

favour of his royal patroness and her family, this is one of the most important narrative sources for the period which it covers.

The manuscript is the work of two scribes and is very probably the special copy made for presentation to Emma on the author's behalf. The introductory miniature shows him offering the book to the Queen, who is attended by two crowned figures representing her two surviving sons, Harthacnut and Edward. Although the monk of St Omer contrives to obscure the fact, Edward (afterwards "the Confessor") was actually Emma's son by her first husband, Æthelred II, who was defeated and replaced by Cnut. The manuscript later belonged to the monastery of St Augustine's at Canterbury, where it was entitled *Gesta Cnuti*.

I 18 GRANT BY CNUT THE GREAT TO CHRIST CHURCH, CANTERBURY
British Library [Stowe Charter 39]
Vellum; 20 × 38cm approx. Latin. Twelfth-century copy of a document dated 1023.

This charter records a grant by Cnut the Great to the monks of Christ Church of the crown from his head, placed with his own hands upon the altar, and all rights and privileges over the port of Sandwich and surroundings. This included an area of land defined by the distance to which a small axe could be thrown from a ship floating in the river. It is dated 1023 and its witnesses include an imposing array of contemporary dignitaries, amongst whom are the Archbishops of both Canterbury and York. The exhibited version, which was written in the twelfth century, is one of at least seventeen Latin copies known, some of them separate documents, others included in cartularies. There are also three in Anglo-Saxon.

Sandwich, on the Kent coast at the mouth of the river Stour, was one of the most important ports in England in the early Middle Ages. It received much of the cross-channel traffic (Cnut himself made his first landfall there in 1015) and also commanded the principal sea route to the port of London. There is no reason why Cnut himself, known to have been a substantial benefactor to Canterbury, should not have made such a grant. However, there is no copy of it in existence written earlier than the latter part of the eleventh century, and it is quite possible that the whole document is in fact a post-Conquest fabrication for the benefit of Christ Church Cathedral Priory.

I 19 End slab of a box-tomb or sarcophagus: the St Paul's stone
St Paul's Churchyard, Mus. of Lon. [4075]

The oolitic limestone slab was found in 1852 during building excavations on the south side of St Paul's churchyard. Decoration: Side A: backward-turning quadruped with spiral hips, bound in intertwining tendrils which, in front of the beast, terminate in a second animal's head; in the upper corners are pear-shaped lobes linked to a knot; Side B: two line Scandinavian runic inscription reading "k(i)na : let : lekia : st/in : pensi : auk : tuki :" (Ginna and Toki had this stone set up). Early eleventh century. L.57.5cm.

This fine example of English Ringerike ornament with its clusters of elongated tendrils still preserves fragments of an umber-coloured gesso base for blue-black and brown-yellow paint (best seen on the head); the entangling snake carried white spots on its body. The ultimate origin of the composition is Harold Bluetooth's stone at Jelling and a close parallel for the treatment here is provided by the Heggen vane, Norway. The inscription indicates that the stone was carved in a Scandinavian milieu in London, possibly by a Swedish craftsman.

I 20 Recumbent slab, in two pieces
City of London BM [83, 12-19, 1-2]

The non-adjacent pieces, in oolitic limestone, were found in the City before 1884. Decoration: floriate cross formed from clusters of elongated tendrils and pear-shaped lobes. On the edge are possible traces of a runic inscription '...ki:...'. Early eleventh century. H.53.3 and 38.1cm.

Like the St Paul's slab the Ringerike ornament on these stones closely resembles work in this style in Scandinavia.

I 21 Copper-alloy buckle
Thetford, Norfolk NCM [12.950 (1160)]

It has a straight bar and a flattened, sub-triangular loop decorated with conventionalised Ringerike-style foliage. The tongue develops from a stylised animal head. L.3.5cm.

Found above the burnt clay floor of a building, in an eleventh-century context. Ringerike-style objects in metal, bone, and stone are relatively

I 20

common in southern England (see nos. 119 and 122) and such items in Scandinavian taste presumably reflect the political supremacy of the Danish king Cnut and his immediate successors.

122 Cast copper-alloy buckle loop
River Thames, Barnes. BM [56, 7–1, 1474]

It has a straight bar and flattened semi-circular loop decorated with conventionalized Ringerike-style animal ornament. The tongue is lost. L.7.1cm.

The loop appears to be unfinished and was therefore probably made in England. The best parallel is the Thetford buckle (see no. 121).

123 Two-sided ivory comb
No known provenance. BM [1957, 10-2, 1]

It is made from a single piece of walrus ivory, the two sets of teeth being of different fineness. Between them is a rectangular field decorated on one side with a pair of confronted bipeds, separated by a plain frame, and on the other with an interlacing snake-like animal. L.5.4 × W.4.1cm.

The comb is interesting as it illustrates the overlap between Anglo-Saxon and Viking art, the bipeds being in the Anglo-Saxon tradition, and the ribbon-like animal in the Scandinavian Ringerike style. Walrus ivory was collected in northern Norway and traded into western Europe where it was used for the manufacture of luxury products.

124 Bone pin
River Thames, Hammersmith BM [93, 6-18, 72]

It has a prominent, flattened, sub-rectangular head decorated with incised Ringerike style foliate ornament. The head is perforated just above the junction with the short shank which is of circular section. L.17.0cm.

125 Bone disc
River Thames, City of London BM [66, 2-24, 1]

The front is convex and decorated with a human figure, the head of which is now lost but which originally projected beyond the edge of the disc. The legs are turned upwards, and like the arms and torso are filled with pelleting. Two ribbon-like animals interlace with the figure. The underside is hollowed to leave a perforated bar. D.6.0cm.

The disc may have been a toggle. It is decorated in the Scandinavian Mammen style. Objects decorated in this style are rare in England, probably since it was current c.950–1010, a period when the Anglo-Saxon kings were politically supreme.

126 Incomplete bone pin
Leadenhall Street, London. Mus. of Lon. [A13556]

It has an expanding, perforated head decorated with incised Ringerike-style ornament. L.8.5cm.

Although it is elaborately decorated the form of the pin can be compared with no. 124.

127 Cast copper-alloy mount
Mildenhall, Suffolk AM [1909.414]

One end is bent at right angles to the body of the mount, and there are two perforations for attachment near the bend. At the other end is a single rivet hole. The main field is of irregular shape and is decorated with a pair of three-element

plants, one developing towards the centre from each end. These are enmeshed with ribbon-like animals or plant tendrils. L.5.3cm.

The decoration is difficult to interpret as the piece is heavily rubbed, but it is decorated in the Ringerike style. It may be identified as a book mount since it is similar in form to the book mounts no. L2 and L8.

128 'Kunigunde's jewel-box': a copy in painted plaster of the Bamberg casket
The original from Bamberg Cathedral, West Germany. It is said to have been the jewel box of Queen Kunigunde, daughter of Cnut. It is now in the Bayerisches National Museum in Munich, from which the copy was purchased in 1873. NM1 [835]

The core of the original is of wood, on which are laid ivory plates clasped by gilt-bronze mounts. The casket is square and has a slightly pitched lid, in which are key-holes. Each side is divided into three rectangular fields and the lid has four triangular fields. Each field consists of an ivory panel and is separated from its neighbour by decorated strips of gilt bronze. There is a gilt-bronze mount in the centre of the lid; at the four corners of this mount, and at the corners of the lid, are gilt-bronze animal-heads cast in the round. In the middle of the top of each side a gilt-bronze mount with a human mask stands proud of the edge. The panels are carved with animals, birds and masks in the Mammen style. L. (side) 26.0cm. H.13.0cm.

Kunigunde married the son of the German Emperor Konrad, later to become Emperor Henry II. She died young. The casket is of Scandinavian workmanship, but its association with Kunigunde is uncertain; it can only be traced back as far as 1743. It was not uncommon in the eighteenth century to connect outstanding museum objects with important personages.

126

128

CAPITAL AT WINCHESTER

ON 18 OCTOBER 1016, FOLLOWING a year's hard campaigning, Cnut, the son of Svein Forkbeard and his Polish queen Gunhild, defeated King Edmund at Ashingdon in Essex. When Edmund died at the end of November, Cnut found himself at the age of twenty-one in undisputed possession of England. Three years later he was secure enough in England to lead the first of the four expeditions by which, between 1019 and 1028, he took control of his Scandinavian inheritance. By 1028 he was King of England, Denmark and Norway, Lord of the Orkneys and Shetlands, overlord of the King of Scots and perhaps of the Kingdom of Dublin, with claims over yet more distant parts.

As ruler of England for nearly twenty years, during which he was out of the country for perhaps less than five, Cnut was king of the largest, richest, and most unified state of its time in north-western Europe. At its heart lay the old royal and episcopal city of Winchester, beginning now to emerge in some senses as a capital, its skyline dominated by the towers of its three great minster churches.

The evidence we have for the residences and itineraries of English kings before the Norman conquest is all too thin, but there is just enough to show that Winchester was for Cnut a principal, possibly the principal seat, as it was certainly for his wife Emma, after his death. It was to the New Minster in Winchester that Cnut and Emma donated the great gold cross which they are shown in the *Liber Vitae* as placing on the altar (no. 116). It was in Winchester that Cnut kept his treasure, for it was there that on his death it fell first into the hands of Emma and was then seized by Harold, his son by another woman. And it was in Winchester at one Christmas in the years between 1020 and 1023 that Cnut promulgated with the advice of his councillors the code of laws, both ecclesiastical and secular, which is not only the longest but was also after the Conquest the most respected of the Old English codes. Here it was too that Cnut's body was laid to rest in the Old Minster, with Queen Emma eventually by his side; and here that Harthacnut their son was buried in 1042.

Cnut's marriage to Æthelred's widow Emma in 1017 had sound political and dynastic justification, and foreshadowed the union of the two kingdoms of Denmark and England within two years. This union may also have been celebrated in a great narrative frieze of carved stone, perhaps comparable in scale and character to the Bayeux Tapestry, which seems to have been erected in the cathedral church of the Old Minster during Cnut's reign. Apparently depicting mythological events common to the genealogies of the royal houses of Wessex and Denmark – the story of Sigmund and the wolf is the only identifiable surviving fragment – such a frieze in the principal royal church of the kingdom would have served to emphasize the appropriateness of a Danish ruler in the heart of Wessex (no. J 1).

When Cnut came to rule, Winchester was already a millenium old. Successively a pre-Roman Iron-Age settlement and the fifth largest city of Roman Britain, urban life had been brought back by Alfred in the 880s, after some four centuries of non-urban existence, as a royal residence and from the mid-seventh century onwards as the see of a bishop. As part of his organisation of the defences of Wessex against the Danish armies of the late ninth century, Alfred established a series of fortified towns, some on new sites, some using former Roman cities. Winchester was by far the largest of these fortified towns: its Roman walls were refurbished, its gates and ditches remodelled, and within the walls a rectilinear grid of streets was laid out not only to allow defensive movement on interior lines but also to divide and apportion the land within the walls for permanent settlement. As recreated by Alfred, Winchester was part of the first large-scale effort of town planning in early medieval Europe.

When Cnut came to Winchester, a hundred and thirty years later, the success of Alfred's refoundation was apparent on every side. Suburbs spread along the streets outside its gates; and from the walls, only a few years before, the citizens had watched Svein's marauding army march past with the loot of the surrounding countryside. Within the walls, the street frontages were by now almost, if not entirely, built up with rows of wooden houses, some set sideways, some gable-on to the streets. Different trades were already concentrated in separate parts of the town, and were reflected in the street names which were even then coming into use: Tanner Street, Fleshmonger Street, Street of the Shieldmakers, Shoemaker Street, and more. Along the great east-west axis of High Street lay the principal market areas, and here at the very centre were the workshops of the moneyers, more than forty of whom struck coins and exchanged bullion in the city during Cnut's reign.

In the south-eastern quarter, ringed by their own walls into one single religious enclosure, lay the three great monasteries, all of royal foundation: Old Minster, four centuries old, seat of the bishop, burial place of kings, centre of pilgrimage to the shrine of Swithun; New Minster, built by Alfred's son Edward as the church of the new city, the burial church of Alfred and his family, itself greatly favoured by Cnut and Emma; and Nunnaminster, founded by Alfred's wife Eahlswith. To either side of the minsters lay the two palaces, the bishop's palace to the east at Wolvesey, and the old royal palace, its origins perhaps stretching back to the days of the end of Roman Britain, to the west. Here in a literal quarter of Winchester, this grouping of royal and ecclesiastical buildings was without parallel in Western Europe of the time and formed in embryo the administrative, political, artistic and intellectual centre of the kingdom. In the reign of Cnut and even more in that of the Confessor, these structures were to be for the Old English State what Westminster was to become from the later twelfth century onwards.

This was the city which Cnut was to know so well and in which he was to lie in death, a man 'large of build and very strong, a most handsome man in every respect except that his nose was thin and slightly aquiline with a high ridge', the first Viking, as Sir Frank Stenton has written, 'to be admitted into the civilized fraternity of Christian kings'.

MARTIN BIDDLE

RIGHT *Winchester's Old Minster as it might have been seen in the time of Cnut. (See J14, p170.) Below right, an interior view looking down the church towards the king's throne high over the West door. And below, a plan of Winchester as it stood in the eleventh century.*

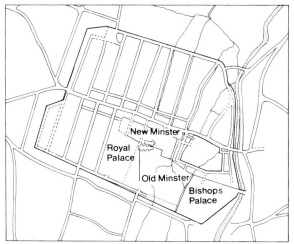

167

J 1 Fragment of frieze – the Sigmund stone
The Old Minster, Winchester WM [WRU. WS.98]

Made of Box Ground oolite, it was found during excavations in the eastern crypt of the Old Minster in 1965. Decoration: on the right, a man lies on the ground, bound by his neck and right hand, whilst a wolf or dog thrusts its tongue into his mouth; on the left is an armed man in a shirt of mail. Eleventh century. H.69.5cm.

The frieze was discarded when the Old Minster was demolished in 1093–4 and was probably part of its decoration. The right-hand scene appears to depict part of the story of Sigmund and the wolf, as later recorded in the *Volsung Saga*, where the hero escapes by pulling out a wolf's tongue. The frieze may have been carved during Cnut's reign (1016–1035) as a celebration of the common ancestory of the Wessex and Danish royal households, but stylistic links to the Bayeux tapestry suggest a slightely later date.

J 2 Decorated head-stone from Gunni's grave
The Old Minster, Winchester WM [WRU. WS.104.1/2]

The head-stone (of Bembridge stone) was found during excavations to the east of the Old Minster apse in 1965. It is ornamented with a hand holding a cross. The coped grave-cover which accompanied it bore the inscription (in capitals) +HER L(I)Ð G(UN)N(I) EORLES FEOLAGA "here lies Gunni, the earl's (Eorl's) companion". Late tenth or early eleventh century. H.71.2cm.

A memorial to a man bearing a Scandinavian name, perhaps attached to Cnut's court. The hand of God holding a cross is probably a Doomsday symbol and is paralleled on another stone excavated from the Cathedral Green, Winchester in 1970.

J 3 Incomplete walrus ivory (?) figure surviving from the waist to mid-shin level
Cathedral Green, Winchester WRU [SF.2412]

The figure wears a short skirt falling from the waist to the knees in a series of close vertical folds. The legs are bare below the knees. L.9.0 × W.3.4cm.

The figure can be identified as that of Christ from a crucifix. It is closely related to manuscripts decorated in the 'Winchester' style, and in particular to the crucified Christ in the Psalter BL. Harley 2904, probably made between 974 and 986 at Ramsey Abbey (a daughter house of the Old Minster, Winchester).

J 4 Incomplete ivory spoon, the stem being lost
Cathedral Green, Winchester WRU [SF.610]

The shallow expanding bowl has a rounded end and issues from the open mouth of an animal. L.6.0 × W.2.5cm.

J 1

J 4

J 5 One complete and three fragmentary bone spoons
Westgate Car Park, Winchester WCM [483.56]
St George's Street, Winchester WCM [1585.38]
Middle Brook Street, Winchester WCM [1381.525]
Lower Brook Street, Winchester WRU [SF6 202]

One has a stem of circular section separated from the bowl by a knop which is treated as an animal head. The second was originally double ended but one of the bowls is lost. Of the remaining spoons only parts of the bowls survive, roughly broken at the narrow end. Each bowl is decorated with incised acanthus ornament, which on one is surmounted by a bird. L.18.8cm.

These are examples of a group of six similar spoons known from Winchester, all of which are decorated with debased acanthus ornament, possibly related to the Ringerike style. All can be dated to the eleventh century.

J 6 Cast silver-gilt strap-end
Cathedral Green, Winchester WRU [SF.272]

This has a rivet in each corner at the upper end, and a single rivet hole in the rounded lower end. It

J 13

J 5

is decorated with a contorted Jellinge-style animal. L.4.0 × W.2.0cm.

This may have formed part of the same object – possibly a piece of horse harness – as the rectangular silver-gilt plaque no. J17. The strap-end would have been riveted onto a leather strap, part of which still survived when it was found.

J 7 Rectangular cast silver-gilt plaque
Cathedral Green, Winchester WRU [SF.179]

In the centre is a quatrefoil, containing a contorted quadruped, which is flanked by a pair of trefoil fields each containing a backward-looking quadruped. The gores between the fields are filled with plant ornament. There is a single rivet in each corner. L.4.5cm × W.1.9cm.

Found with part of the leather strap still attached (see J6).

J 8 Incomplete, single-sided bone comb
Lower Brook Street, Winchester WRU [SF.6977]

Similar to no. YAB4, the connecting plate is decorated with simple incised ornament, and there is a perforation for suspension in the end tooth plate. L.13.5 × W.3.1cm.

Single-sided composite combs are more characteristic of such Anglo-Scandinavian sites as York, than Anglo-Saxon centres like Winchester, where two-sided combs were more common.

J 9 Bone comb case
Lower Brook Street, Winchester WRU [SF.7289]

Similar in form to nos. YAB12 and 13, the connecting plates are decorated with simple incised ornament. L.11.9 × W.2.2cm.

J 10 Copper-alloy strap-end
Cathedral Car Park, Winchester WRU [SF.146]

The strap fitted into a split in the upper end and was held in place by two rivets. The body of the strap-end tapers towards the animal-head terminal and is decorated with conventionalised plant ornament. L.4.8 × W.0.7cm.

This is a typical Anglo-Saxon strap-end of the ninth century, the only unusual feature being the marked taper. Such strap-ends are the most commonly found items of late Anglo-Saxon metalwork, and over a hundred of them are known. Most, like this example, are in base metal, but some are of silver (see no. C15).

J 3

J 11 Copper-alloy strap-end
Lower Brook Street, Winchester WRU [SF.2857]

This is similar in form and decoration to no. J10, but the long sides are convex. L.44.0 × W.0.7cm.

J 12 Iron pan
Cathedral Car Park, Winchester WRU [SF.669]

The shallow bowl, with slightly sagging base, is made from a single sheet of metal. The handle is composed of two twisted iron rods welded to the bowl at one end, and forming a loop at the other. The bowl has been repaired three times with separate iron sheets welded on. L.62 × W.30cm.

The pan is probably of late ninth- or early tenth-century date.

J 13 Copper-alloy openwork strap-end
Cathedral Green, Winchester WRU [SF 1396]

The strap was held in place by four rivets against the undecorated upper end, from which develops a symmetrical acanthus plant inhabited by a pair of inward-facing quadrupeds above a pair of inward-facing birds. L.4.0 × W.2.8cm.

J 12

The high quality decoration is related to "Winchester" style manuscript art, and in particular to decoration in the Corpus Christi *Vita Cuthberti*, and the New Minster foundation charter. On these grounds it has been dated to the latter part of the tenth century. It is a fine example of late Anglo-Saxon art which flourished side by side with Viking art styles.

J14   Model of Winchester's Old Minster in the time of Cnut the Great
In its final form the Old Minster was 73 metres long with a greatest width of 30 metres. It was built of flint rubble and mortar, with dressings and details of Box Ground oolitic limestone.

By the reign of Cnut the Anglo-Saxon cathedral church of Winchester, known as the Old Minster (to distinguish it from the later New Minster) had reached its final form as a result of more than four centuries of architectural development. In Cnut's day, the Old Minster played a role of exceptional importance as the principal royal church in the Kingdom, as the see of the bishop, and as the focus of pilgrimage to the tomb and relics of St Swithun (Bishop of Winchester, 852–62).

The church later known as Old Minster was founded by King Cenwalh of Wessex in or about 648 and dedicated to St Peter and St Paul. It was probably intended to serve the adjacent royal residence, but became a cathedral when Wini, the first Bishop of Winchester, was consecrated about 660. Little is known of the early history of the church but it was the scene of royal ceremonial and of a long sequence of royal burials. On 15 July, 971, the body of St Swithun was translated from its original grave outside the west door of the early church. Between 971 and a dedication in 980 the original church was extended westward over the site of St Swithun's grave. The first design, which was actually achieved, was for an immense double-apsed martyrium or shrine centred on the saint's grave. For unknown reasons this was very soon remodelled as the great towered west-work, dedicated in 980. The Old Minster was then extended eastward to a new apse and the eastern part of the original structure was entirely remodelled to form the principal crossing, flanked by new apses to north and south – the setting for the high altar, surmounted by a staged tower. The completion of these works was marked by a second dedication in 993–94.

In its ultimate form, as revealed by escavations in 1962–69, the church's most remarkable feature was the west-work dedicated in 980, probably about 30m (98 feet) in height. West-works of this kind, similar to the surviving example at Corvey on the Weser, West Germany, were sometimes arranged to accommodate the throne of a ruler in a high position from which he could observe the greater part of the interior of the church. The royal palace lay immediately to the west and it seems probable that the proximity of palace and church was reflected on those occasions such as Easter when the king wore his crown in the cathedral, and perhaps appeared to the populace from a gallery in the west-work.

The palace, the Old Minster, and the New Minster just to the north, formed a group of monumental buildings on a grand scale apparently unequalled elsewhere in England until the emergence of Westminster in the mid-eleventh century.

It was in the Old Minster that the narrative stone frieze (no. J1) was erected which seems to have told the shared traditions of the Danish and English royal families. And it was here that Cnut was buried in 1035, his son Harthacnut in 1042 and his wife Emma in 1052.

MARTIN BIDDLE, BIRTHE KJØLBYE-BIDDLE

THE ENGLISH IN DENMARK

Scholars assessing the extent of Viking settlement in England have at their command a large and varied source-material on which to base their debate. But if we look towards Denmark, to see the effects of events in England on the home country, we are confronted by a profound darkness. The literary and linguistic evidence, so rich on the English side of the North Sea, is almost entirely missing on the other; and the archaeological evidence of the Viking expeditions is so scanty, that one seriously begins to doubt the ability of archaeology to reflect the historical course of events. Yet – when the eye accustoms itself to the gloom, we can begin to discern some misty contours of events, which, in their time, must have been of the greatest significance to the entire Danish community.

The raids are the most noticeable aspect of the Viking Age; the plunder and extortion in England are well documented in Anglo-Saxon sources. But what happened to the booty? Was it taken back to Scandinavia? Only for the last stage of the Viking era can we reply with a fairly unconditional affirmative. From around the year 1000, when the tormented English had to pay Danegeld almost annually, to buy themselves a short respite, until 1051, when Edward the Confessor levied the final *heregeld* in order to pay off the last Scandinavian mercenaries, a stream of silver left England with Viking warriors.

A particularly large number of Anglo-Saxon coins arrived in Scandinavia in 1018, when Cnut the Great levied the heaviest Danegeld of all, £72,000, most of which he used to pay off the majority of Vikings who had helped him conquer England. We meet these discharged warriors on Swedish rune-stones, whose inscriptions tell of men who "took geld" from Cnut and other leaders of Viking fleets. Trophies from the wars are found in various places – some choice English swords in Skåne, for example, and gilt stirrups at Velds in northern Jutland. But we chiefly know the veterans of the English expeditions through buried hoards containing Anglo-Saxon coins, which must derive from such payments. Sometimes they are the modest profits of the common warrior: thirty-four Æthelred coins lay beside a large stone in Vestermarie on Bornholm. Sometimes the sums are large: more than 600 coins were tucked away in a cowhorn on the beach at List on the island of Sylt. The hoards are so numerous that the Anglo-Saxon coins of this period are known far better from finds in Scandinavia than from England itself.

The picture is completely different, however, when we seek the booty from the fierce ninth-century Viking attacks on England. There are virtually no mementoes of these raids in the Danish soil. Not one buried hoard, with coins or other valuables from England, has been found anywhere in Denmark. This lack of demonstrable booty has been taken to indicate that the ninth-century Vikings generally remained "over there" and used their loot to establish themselves abroad.

No doubt, many at that time did leave Denmark forever. Some became farmers under distant skies, others kept to their warrior-occupation and roamed western Europe until death caught up with them. But we should not necessarily accept the lack of hoards as proof that, during the ninth century, great wealth did not flow from England into Denmark. Hoards are clearly related to war and unrest, and in England there was unrest in abundance. But in Denmark peaceful conditions seem to have prevailed during most of ninth century.

All the same, we may well benefit from looking at the contents of the hoards. There are hardly any coins. Solid silver predominates – arm-rings and neck-rings of native manufacture, and occasionally ingots. The silver is in itself remarkable, for during the preceding centuries there had been very little precious metal in Denmark. Even the best jewellery was made of bronze, gilding replaced gold, and silver was rare. In the ninth century silver reappeared, but where did it come from? We know that the Arab silver mines in Central Asia provided a great deal of Viking-Age silver. But the Arabian supply did not reach Denmark on a large scale until around 900, so it may be assumed that the country's silver wealth, which we see in the ninth-century hoards, was founded on the melting-down of silver obtained mainly in western Europe and perhaps predominantly in England.

This silver did not necessarily arrive in Denmark as a result of hostilities, however. The ruler of the seas also holds the key to international trade, and the Vikings quite clearly realised this. Many scholars consider, with good reason, that the expansion of trade was a more important aspect of the Viking Age than battle and bloodshed. We have a very informative source from about 1000 describing trade with England which relates that "York was enriched with the treasure of merchants who came from all quarters, particularly from the Danish people".

Obviously, these Danish merchants also enriched Denmark. A large number of hoards with a mixture of coins, mainly English and German, were probably obtained by trade. But it is by no means certain that the merchant returned home with English goods; most of these were probably sold elsewhere. It is possible, though, that beautiful English cloth, a highly prized commodity in western Europe, was popular in Denmark too. The solution to

RIGHT *The upper part of a silver-encrusted Anglo-Scandinavian sword (K2).* BELOW *Drinking horn mounts in the Ringerike style (K16) of the eleventh century.*

this problem has so far proved beyond the reach of archaeology. Nor is there much evidence of other English goods in archaeological finds. Modest jewellery and decorated mounts of Anglo-Saxon origin are occasionally found in excavations of Viking-Age towns and villages, which may have been brought to Denmark by merchants. But why did these merchants provide the country with so little of the excellent English pottery? That would have improved the kitchen shelves in a big way.

In addition to war and trade, emigration was an important factor in the Viking period. Scholars are greatly divided as to the extent of Danish settlement in England. I must confess I am of the number who consider the many place-names showing Danish influence, and numerous Danish loan-words in the English language, as firm evidence that there was a sizeable emigration from Denmark to the Danelaw in the wake of the Great Army at the end of the ninth century. One would like to know for how long these emigrants retained their contacts with Denmark, and to what extent they enriched Danish culture with new ideas from their adopted country.

The generally accepted view in the past was that Scandinavian art, from the eighth century onwards, received important impulses from the Anglo-Saxons. Today, matters are regarded rather differently. The early influence is now thought to have been chiefly indirect – a result of the impact of vigorous English missions in Frisia and Saxony on Continental art styles. The Jellinge style, it was believed, originated in England; but today it is generally agreed that the influence moved in the opposite direction. This is perhaps evidence of emigration to the Danelaw continuing into the tenth century? Sound arguments for English influence on Danish art cannot be upheld until the advent of the later Ringerike style. This influence was most likely transmitted via the ornaments in the indispensable liturgical books, brought to Scandinavia by the missionaries.

This leads us to the significance of the English Church in the conversion of Denmark to Christianity which took place during the tenth century. Denmark was part of the missionary field of the German Church, and it was a missionary from Germany who, in about 960, moved King Harald Bluetooth to accept Christianity. The conversion was, in the words of a Danish author, "a curiously silent event", which, unlike the conversion of Sweden and Norway, happened very swiftly and without any severe complications. The immigrants in the Danelaw may have contributed to this peaceful transition. They had already absorbed Christianity by the second generation, and it is possible that they transmitted their knowledge of the new faith to their relatives back home. On the quiet, a little back-door gospelling may have gone from England to Denmark. It is worth noting that a number of ecclesiastical terms in the Danish language appear to have come from England. This is even the case with the word *kristne* – to Christianize.

Other cultural influences came from England as well. There are strong indications that the metres of the Scandinavian scaldic poems were affected by Anglo-Saxon poetry. At all events, it is certain that a number of legends from Anglo-Saxon heroic poetry travelled across the North Sea during the Viking Age and were dressed in new Danish garb. Thus the Danish legendary hero *Uffe* has a past in England, as the mighty Offa, whose story contains elements from, among others, that of King Offa of Mercia.

During the reign of Cnut the Great over the joint kingdom the English impact on Denmark assumed new forms. Specialists were sent from the culturally and economically better developed England to raise Denmark to England's level. This may have occurred in many fields, but we can only safely point to two – coinage and the Church.

Before Cnut, minting in Denmark was of modest proportion, and compulsory use of Danish coin – when practicable at all – was no doubt limited to a few important trading towns. Now, within a short space of time, coinage became established throughout the entire country, with extensive production at numerous mints. The legends on the coins, as well as their general appearance, indicate that English moneyers were in charge of this.

The contribution of the Church to the development of Denmark was particularly apparent in the appointment of English clergy to Danish bishoprics. Svein Forkbeard established an English bishop in Denmark; his son Cnut sent at least three. The furthering of Christianity in Denmark was not perhaps the main purpose of these appointments; it would most likely have managed without them. Rather, the English bishops were intended to help the kings resist influence from the south, for the Danish Church was subject to the archiepiscopal see of Hamburg/Bremen, an instrument of the German Empire's foreign policy.

During the reign of Cnut the Great, about 1030, Denmark's first stone-built church was erected in Roskilde by Estrid, the king's sister, and specialists were summoned from England to execute the task. Estrid's church has long since gone, but within a few years a second stone church was built in Roskilde, St Clement's (now St Jørgensbjerg) Church. A portal is preserved from this building, executed in the characteristic style otherwise known only from contemporary stone churches in eastern England.

With the collapse of the North Sea Empire in 1042, the nature of the relationship between England and Denmark changed again. A last reminder of the period of greatness may be seen in the cathedral at Lund, built by Cnut the Holy about 1085. The director of the archaeological excavation there has reconstructed it as a major church, built on the model of older Anglo-Saxon churches. The evidence is slight, but if substantiated, he may be right in his assumption that the church was the work of Danes from England, expelled after the Norman conquest, who in this fashion, expressed their longing for the England which had become their home.

OLAF OLSEN

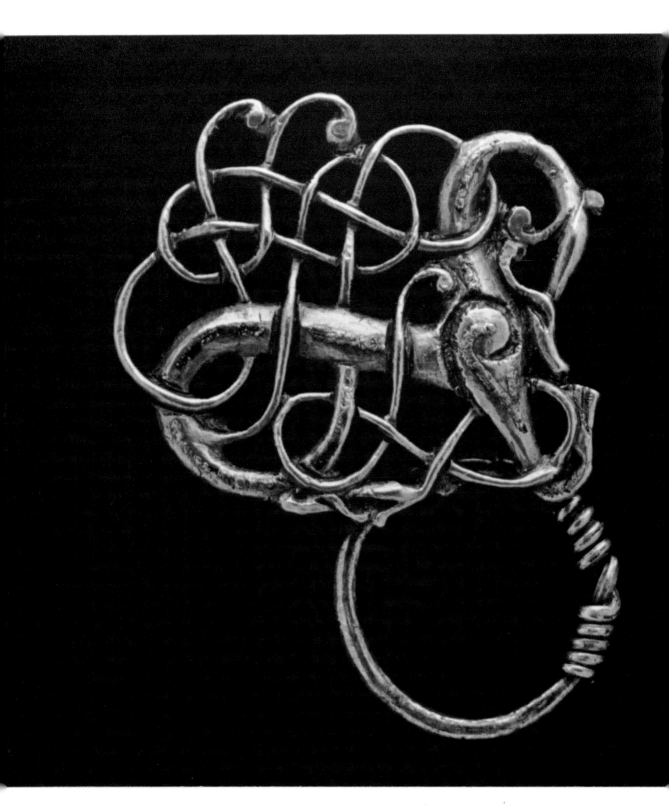

LEFT *The Lindholm Høje brooch is probably the most beautiful of its kind. It is silver and designed in the Urnes art-style showing a stylised animal entwined with a snake (L1).*

K1   Sword, probably English
Støvringgård, north Jutland; single-find. NMI [D2335]

The double-edged, pattern-welded and fullered blade is broken and repaired; it has a curved lower guard, probably with traces of silver and a separate curved ?upper guard. The pommel is missing. Date: probably about 900 or tenth century. L. (total) 67.5cm. L. (blade, probably incomplete) 57.5cm. L. (of tang above lower guard) 9.0cm.

K2   Upper part of a silver-encrusted Anglo-Scandinavian sword
No provenance. FHM [224]

The blade is incomplete both in length and width. Both guards are curved, the lower showing traces of silver. The pommel is approximately semi-circular in the upper outline and encrusted with silver; two large spirals are the most prominent features of the remaining ornament. Three silver mounts on the grip have designs which also include spirals. L. (now) 26.5cm. Grip 7.5cm.

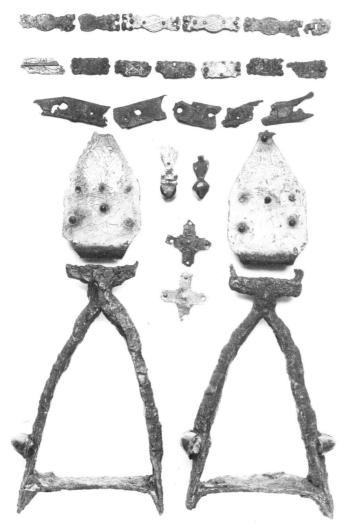

The sword is dated to about the year 1000 or a little later. The form of the guards is English, but the ornament is in the Scandinavian Mammen or Ringerike styles. It was either produced in Scandinavia under English influence or in England under Scandinavian influence.

K3   Sword with silver and gold hilt. English, or possibly made in Scandinavia under strong English influence
Dybäck, Skåne; single-find. SHM, Stockholm [4515]

Double-edged sword with fullered blade (part of which is missing). The lower and upper guards are curved, the pommel missing. Below the lower guard is the mount from the mouth of the scabbard; the rest of the scabbard has not survived. The guards and scabbard mount are of silver, decorated with birds, animals, ribbons and tendrils in high relief and with engraved and stamped details, further embellished with gilding and niello. The upper edge of the scabbard mount is finished with twisted gold wire. The grip is bound with fine gold wire. L. (now) 52.3cm.

The sword is dated to about 1000. This is probably the most magnificent sword from the Viking Age found in Scandinavia. The ornament is closely related to that of the pommel and upper guard from Vrångabäck, Skåne (no. K4), and in general to English metalwork of the contemporary Winchester style.

K4   Sword pommel and upper guard of silver. English, or possibly made in Scandinavia under strong English influence
Vrångabäck, Skåne; single-find. LUHM [22930]

Silver with gilding and niello. The guard is curved, the pommel tripartite. The ornament consists of birds, animals, snakes and ribbons in high relief with engraved and stamped details. L.5.8cm. W.7.7cm.

Date about 1000. This incomplete hilt is closely related to no. K3.

K5   Stirrups and strap-mounts from England
Velds, central Jutland; grave-find. NMI [11518-24, 11631]

1 Two iron stirrups with traces of copper encrustation on the sides, each with a large decorative plate of gilt bronze. The strap-mounts are all of gilt bronze, some are still attached to the original leather. The stirrups are triangular with straight foot-plates; on each long side is a small mount of semi-circular cross-section. The decorative plates were attached to the stirrup-leather and went through the suspension loop of the stirrup. They are decorated with birds (their long necks intertwined) and plant ornaments. H. (stirrup and plate) about 34.0cm.
2 Approximately thirteen identical decorated strap-mounts, fitted at one end with a bell (most of which are missing). L. (without bell) 5.5cm. W. (maximum) 1.7cm.
3 Approximately twelve identical mounts, together with about another seventeen attached to the leather strap. The strap is about 62cm long and at its widest 2.3cm. The size of the mounts varies slightly, but one is 3.9cm long and 1.6cm wide. Two identical strap-distributors are slightly damaged. Greatest surviving length 4.6cm.

This find is dated to the end of the tenth century. The ornament shows a close similarity to the English Winchester style. The leather strap and strap-mounts were probably part of the bridle, together with a bit (not exhibited) which was also found in the grave.

K6 English cruciform bronze mount
No provenance. NM II [D677/1979]

This somewhat fragmentary open-work mount is of bronze with traces of gilding. There are perforations for nails in the centre and on each of the arms. Two cross-arms and some details of the open-work have been repaired. H. and W.7.5cm.

The mount dates from the end of the eighth century or the beginning of the ninth. It was probably a book-mount. An almost identical mount, also without provenance, is now in the Rheinisches Landesmuseum, Bonn, West Germany. Closely related objects are known, for example, from Whitby Abbey in north England (C3).

K7 English seventh-century bronze mount, perhaps from a reliquary. Later re-used
Hedeby, from settlement. SHL

Bronze with traces of gilding and the remains of a border of silver and niello; in the centre an empty setting. A large portion of the edge is broken. The ornament consists of highly stylized faces, masks and perhaps animal figures. The original arrangements for fastening have apparently been cut away and replaced with four iron nails in new holes to form an irregular square. D.6cm.

The plaque was already ancient when it reached Hedeby. It may have been attached to an old box stolen by Vikings in England. The new holes show that it was subsequently adapted to serve another function.

K8 English decorated bronze mount adapted as a brooch
Vejleby, Lolland; grave find. L FSM [D12282]

Bronze with traces of gilding. The mount is circular with a ribbed conical centre and interlace ornament on the flange. There are three boss-headed rivets at the edge (the fourth is missing) and another at the centre. The rivets do not protrude on the back, which is plain except for traces of a secondary pin. D.5.8cm. H.0.8cm.

Date: eighth century. This is one of many Viking-Age examples of foreign objects being adapted as exotic pieces of jewellery.

K9 Silver hanging-bowl with gold mounts, from the north of England
Lejre, Zealand; grave-find or part of hoard. NM I [11374]

The bowl is fragmentary, much of the walls are missing; it is mounted on a stand. It has rounded sides, outward-curving rim and a flat base. Circular gold mounts, decorated with ring patterns in beaded wire of two thicknesses, are mounted one inside and one outside the base. Below the rim, patination, faint scratches and small rivets and rivet-holes indicate the original positions of four groups each with three triangular mounts – their apexes point downwards. D. (rim) 13.5cm. H.7.3cm.

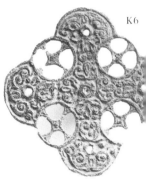

K6

Date: eighth- or early ninth-century. This is one of many hanging-bowls which were produced in the British Isles, but, apart from this example, only two other silver examples are known. The function of hanging-bowls is controversial: it has been suggested that they were associated with churches but there is increasing evidence that they may have been secular finger-bowls, suspended as decoration after use.

K10 Sherds of glazed pottery, probably from England
Lund, Sweden; from the settlement. KM [59126:218, 58220:45, 66166:778, 57135:218, 62892:1301]

A sherd with rim and handle; a spout sherd; a rim sherd; a wall sherd with horizontal grooves and another wall sherd. Reddish fabric and on the outside lead glaze in colours ranging from yellowish-brown to dark green. L.6.5cm.

The sherds, dating from the eleventh century, are a selection of glazed pottery from the earliest period at Lund, found in various excavations. Glazed pottery was not produced in Denmark until the thirteenth century. In the eleventh century, therefore, glazed pottery represents foreign, imported table-ware. The sherds have many features in common with contemporary English pottery (Stamford ware G44).

K11 Raw material, half-finished and finished objects of jet, probably from England
1 Hedeby; from the settlement. SHL
2 Aggersborg, north Jutland; from the settlement. NM I [A3-3373]
3 Ribe; from the settlement. ASR [j. no. 19M80C:BK]

1 Raw material: rounded lump; largest measurement 7.6cm. Half-finished objects: the blank for a ring; largest measurement 4.1cm. Finished objects: fragment of an arm-ring. A finger-ring; external diameter 3.1cm. A round domed gaming-piece; diameter 2.2cm. A quadrilateral pendant, length 3.2cm.
2 Half of a round bead, L.0.9cm.
3 Half a finger-ring. D. (external) 2.4cm.

Dated to the Viking-Age. The best jet comes from Whitby, Yorkshire, England, and it is probable that these objects were made from material derived from this source. Jet was worked into jewellery and other decorative pieces. As these objects demonstrate, this was sometimes done at Hedeby from imported raw material (see YJAG6–13).

K12 Anglo-Scandinavian bronze strap-end
Aggersborg, north Jutland; from the settlement. NM [A3-635]

Tongue-shaped strap-end terminating in an animal-head. The decorated area on the front, which follows the shape of the strap-end, contains two interlaced snakes, their heads highly stylized and joined by two free rings. The stepped reverse is contoured; the strap was secured by two rivets through the split butt-end. L.6.1cm. W.1.9cm.

Dated: tenth century. The shape of the strap-end is English, but the ornament is of Scandinavian origin. Similar strap-ends are known from York; the Aggersborg example was probably made in England.

K8

K13 English strap-end, probably walrus ivory
Lund, Sweden; from the settlement. KM
[53436:769]

The strap-end, dated to the first half of the eleventh century, is tongue-shaped; the upper end is missing. A symmetrical decoration produced from a highly stylized mask is carved on the front. On the smooth reverse, a basically symmetrical plant ornament is crudely engraved. L. (now) 4.4cm.

K14 Gilt bronze brooch with ornament inspired by English coin
Trelleborg, Zealand; from the fortress. NM I
[Q1378]

The brooch is circular and flat. Inside a border round the edge is a man's head modelled on an Æthelred II coin. On the back a pin. D.2.8cm.

This is dated about 1000 (not before 978). Brooches inspired by coins were fashionable at this time; it is therefore only natural that we can recognise on such brooches some of the many coins which arrived in Denmark as Danegeld.

K15 Two deer-antler combs with English male names incised in runes: Hikuin and Eadrinc
1 Århus; from the settlement. FHM [1393 EQN]
2 Lund, Sweden; from the settlement. KM [7798]

1 An almost complete comb. The name 'Hikuin' is incised on one plate. L.17.0cm.
2 Comb fragment. On the edge of the side-plate the name 'Eadrinc' is incised. L. (now) 20.3cm.

Comb (1) is dated to the tenth century and (2) to the eleventh century. The inscriptions presumably indicate the names of the owners. The combs themselves may well have been made in Denmark and the name demonstrates either that Englishmen were living in Denmark or that English names were given to Danes.

K16 Drinking-horn mounts decorated in the Ringerike style
Århus, Jutland; from the settlement. NM I [C9487]

Bronze with traces of gilding. 1. A slightly distorted rim-mount with the remains of rivets. Decorated with seven strutting birds, their extremities ending in attenuated tendrils, each with its neck interlaced with the tail of the bird in front. D. (internal) *c*.8cm. H. (maximum) 4cm. 2. Circular mount with a central boss, curved to fit the shape of the horn and decorated with ribbon interlace terminating in four projecting lobes flanked by tendrils. L. (maximum) 5.5cm.

The mounts are dated to about the year 1000 or the first half of the eleventh century. One source of inspiration which led to the creation of the Ringerike style was the contemporary English Winchester style with its characteristically abundant tendrils. The Ringerike style is known both from Scandinavia and England, but there is no doubt that these mounts are of Scandinavian workmanship.

K17 English coins struck by Æthelred II and copies of English coins struck in Denmark by Cnut
All coins are in NM VI.
1 KP 980, KP 1626
2 Devegge 1252, UP
3 BP p.160, UP
4 Enner, east Jutland, from a hoard, FP 69

1 Small-cross type
a Æthelred II, Lydford. Moneyer GODA. Weight 1.37g.
b Cnut, Lund. Moneyer ASCETEL. Weight 1.29g.
2 Hand type
a Æthelred II, Canterbury. Moneyer EADWOLD. Weight 1.50g.
b Cnut, Viborg. Blundered inscription. Weight 0.74g.
3 Long-cross type
a Æthelred II, Winchester. Moneyer BYRHTNOD. Weight 1.69g.
b Cnut, Lund. Moneyer BERHTNOD. Weight 1.44g. (Photo.)
4 Agnus Dei type
a Æthelred II, Nottingham. Moneyer OSWOLD. Weight 1.81g. (Photo.)
b Cnut, Lund. Blundered inscription. Weight 0.83g. (Photo.)

K18 Cnut coins: the same type struck in England and in Denmark
All coins are in NM VI.
1 UP, UP, KP 1156
2 Kongsø, east Jutland from a hoard, a and b,
FP 973:122 and 146 c, KP 1715
3 Kongsø, as above, a and c, FP 973:106 and 3; b,
KP 1326

1 Quatrefoil type
a-b England 1017–1023. c Denmark.
a Lincoln. Moneyer AELFNOD. Weight 0.83g.
b Stamford. Moneyer GODRIC. Weight 0.85g.
c Lund, Moneyer LEOFNOD. Weight 1.43g.
2 Pointed helmet type
a-b England 1023–1029. c Denmark.
a London. Moneyer BRVNINC. Weight 1.00g.
b Stamford. Moneyer DVRSTAN. Weight 1.06g.
c Roskilde. Blundered inscription. Weight 0.93g.
3 Short-cross type
a-b England 1029–1035. c Denmark.
a Lincoln. Moneyer GODRIC. Weight 0.76g.
b Stamford. Moneyer OSWARD. Weight 0.97g.
c Lund. Moneyer ODDENCAR. Weight 0.75g. (Photo.)

K19 English, Danish and German coins: silver hoard from the foundation trench of a church in Roskilde built in the English style
St Jørgensbjerg, originally St Clemens' Church in Roskilde, Zealand; discovered in the foundation trench of the earliest stone church on the site. NM VI [FP 2374a]

One hundred and ten coins: 2 of Æthelred II, thirty-two of Cnut from England, six of Cnut from Denmark, sixty-one of Harthacnut from Denmark and nine German coins.

The church was built when the hoard was deposited about 1040. Built of calcareous tufa, the church was one of the earliest stone churches in Denmark. Details from windows and doors, re-used in the present church of St Jørgensberg, demonstrate that the earlier church was built by an English master-builder, or by one trained in England. There was a strong English influence on all aspects of the Danish Church at this period.

K20 English wooden pen-case lid
Lund, Sweden; from the settlement. KM
[53436:1125]

Sycamore wood. Oblong sliding-lid for a pen-case

with a curved top decorated with a carved dense foliate pattern. It terminates in a large animal-head with open jaws and a mane of tendrils. On the flat underside are some Roman letters, including the word LEO (presumably referring to the nature of the animal-head) and a rectangular panel with cross-hatching. L.33.3cm.

The pen-case lid is dated to about 1000 or the first half of the eleventh century. It is a beautiful example of the English Winchester style and could well have arrived in Denmark with one of the many churchmen who were active in the country during the reign of Cnut and Harthacnut.

BELOW *A double capital from Norwich Cathedral seems to reflect in its sinuous dragons the Urnes phase of Scandinavian art. It dates from the twelfth century and somehow captures the departed spirit of the Vikings.*

THE END IN ENGLAND

THE VIKING ATTACKS THAT LED to the later conquest of England by Svein and Cnut cannot be traced from the few silver hoards of this period found in England nor from the few finds of precious ornaments or elaborately decorated weapons. This has suggested to some that Anglo-Saxon fashions had entered a period of deliberate austerity in which the vanity of public display of wealth had been abandoned. But given that the documentary sources tell of churches giving up ecclesiastical treasures, including the gold and silver figures that embellished shrines, in order to contribute to the payment of Danegeld, it seems probable that the deficiency of such finds may be attributed to the fact that many secular brooches and rings must also have gone into the melting-pot – in the payment of taxes destined to produce the many millions of coins that were drained from the country. This taxation did not prove crippling, but perhaps one consequence of this drain in capital can be detected in a decline in church building at this period.

The presence of Scandinavians in England in the eleventh century is more difficult to detect archaeologically than it is for the earlier settlements, apart from occasional finds of weapons and stirrups, generally from rivers, including a large group from the Thames in London. For in the ninth century they were pagan, but by this time they had become Christian and their burials were therefore no longer accompanied by grave-goods. There are, however, a number of funerary slabs – such as that from Otley in Yorkshire and one from London (perhaps from St Paul's churchyard) – with good quality foliate ornament in the Scandinavian Ringerike style of the first half of the eleventh century (no. I 20).

Undoubtedly from St Paul's churchyard, and unquestionably one of the most important monuments anywhere of the Ringerike style at its best, is a carved and painted slab with an inscription in Scandinavian runes down one side, stating that "Ginna and Toki had this stone set up" ... to whom we do not know, for the inscription will have continued on another stone. The surviving stone consists of a small slab ornamented only on one face and is one end of a sarcophagus, or similarly-shaped memorial placed over the grave, of a wealthy Scandinavian – presumably a follower of Cnut, to whose reign it is likely to date. Its lion-and-snake scene is derived from that to be seen first in Denmark on the tenth-century stone erected by King Harald at Jelling. A great beast charges across the face of the stone with its mane and tail, stylised into tendrils, flying out from its body; the lesser, snake-like animal is knotted around the lion's front legs, but then its body degenerates into a pattern of tendrils. Traces of paint have proved sufficient to allow its original appearance to be reconstructed, but are hardly visible to-day under normal conditions, except perhaps for the blue-black necks of the animals, speckled with carefully painted white spots (no. I 19).

There are a few other examples of the Ringerike style from England which are of similar quality and which may thus have actually been made by Scandinavian craftsmen. On a more humble level there is a bone pin from the Thames in London (no. I 24) with accurately designed and neatly incised Ringerike tendrils on its head. That metalworkers, trained in the style, were at work in London is demonstrated by the find of an unfinished buckle (no. I 22); it would have been from such craftsmen that the Anglo-Saxons learnt to produce Ringerike decoration.

In the tenth century some Anglo-Saxon metalworkers had already experimented with the motifs of Viking art, as witnessed by a pair of silver casket plates (no. E7), inlaid with niello, which combine reminiscences of the English Trewhiddle style with influences from Denmark's Jellinge. It is poorly executed, as also is a similar attempt at combining Anglo-Saxon and Scandinavian motifs on a disc-brooch from Canterbury. Another large disc-brooch of the same Anglo-Saxon type, found in a silver hoard with coins of William the Conqueror at Sutton, Isle of Ely (no. L4), has elements of the Ringerike style in its ornament, but is again of inferior quality. A minor piece displaying greater competence of workmanship is found in a small bone comb (no. I 23), of unknown provenance, with a Ringerike snake on one side and a pair of Anglo-Saxon animals of late tenth or early eleventh-century form on the other.

It has often been observed how the Ringerike style's foliate patterns chimed well with those based on acanthus leaves used in the Winchester art style of southern England in explanation of its appeal to Anglo-Saxon taste. But the late Viking art-styles never became dominant in England, although a slight degree of taste for them lingered on even into the early twelfth century. There exists a handful of metal objects, increased by a number of recent finds including a splendid open-work mount from Lincoln (no. L7), which are ornamented in a recognisable English version of the Scandinavian Urnes style – the last art-form of the Vikings. Most of these are of indifferent design and workmanship, but a brooch from Pitney in Somerset (no. L5) and a new mount from Hemel Hempstead, Hertfordshire, demonstrate the superb quality that could be achieved by English metalworkers in this style. Even more remarkable is the fact that a Norman bishop, buried in Durham Chapter House, should have chosen to possess a crozier which had a pair of

Urnes-type snakes looped and knotted around its socket.

Motifs from the English version of this Urnes style also occur in sculpture in various parts of the country, but most recognisably in an animal carved below the figure of Christ in Jevington Church in Sussex.

Historians point to the importance of institutional evidence for helping to gauge the density and impact of Scandinavian settlement in England. Although the Danelaw was an integral part of the English kingdom, it consisted of a third of the country when it was known as such in the twelfth century. The Danelaw was distinctive for its administrative and legal differences from the rest of England, for peculiarities in the methods of assessing fines and penalties, for differences in the social divisions – features to be explained by Scandinavian immigration.

In terms of communication at this period, Old Norse was still being spoken and understood in England until after the Norman conquest, but the differences between Old English and Old Norse had not been such as to inhibit communication between native and settler. The two languages become so mingled in the Danelaw that by the year 1100 one could well describe what was being spoken in the north and east of England as Anglo-Scandinavian. Amongst everyday words borrowed into the English vocabulary from Old Norse are 'husband', 'egg' and 'law'. It was to be the language of eastern England from which the main lines of standard modern English were to develop.

JAMES GRAHAM-CAMPBELL

BELOW *By now the Vikings have left England or have been absorbed. Their art, however, lives on. An eleventh-century tympanum over a door in Southwell Minster, Nottinghamshire, shows St Michael with sword repelling a very Scandinavian dragon.*

L1   Danish silver brooch in the Urnes style
Lindholm Høje, north Jutland; from the settlement.
AHM [129 × 1397]

Openwork silver brooch with details in niello, decorated with a stylised animal entwined with a snake. There are traces of a pin on the back and a loop from which a ring is suspended. W.32.0cm.

The Lindholm Høje brooch is perhaps the most beautiful of the many known brooches of this type. They occur over the whole of Scandinavia and were also used in England. A workshop where these brooches were manufactured has been discovered in Lund.

L2   Incomplete copper-alloy sub-triangular mount
Mile Cross Bridge, Norwich. A. Brooks, Esq.

It is decorated in openwork, with a sinuous biped in profile, having a spiral hip and long neck. The head is missing. The animal interlaces with a narrow strand. At the base there is a rectangular flange at right angles to the body of the mount, perforated for attachment. L.4.5cm.

This is one of a group of similar mounts decorated with an English variant of the Urnes style, which was current in the late eleventh century. They are all thought to be book mounts.

L3   Copper-alloy openwork mount taking the form of a coiled animal
Sedgeford, Norfolk KLM

The animal has a ribbon-like body with a protruding head. The rear limbs are extended to form loops around the body. There is a damaged lug at the animal's nose, and three other holes for attachment in the openwork. L.4.2cm.

Like the Norwich mount (no. L2), this is in the English Urnes style. It has been identified as a box or book mount.

L4   Silver disc-brooch
Sutton, Isle of Ely, Cambs. BM [1951, 10-1, 1]

The brooch has nine equally-spaced bosses of which one is lost. The decoration is lightly incised and based on four intersecting circles, which create four main fields separated by lentoids linking the bosses. In each field is a single animal. The minor fields are filled with incised decoration based on leaf ornament. On the reverse the remains of the attachment plate for the pin has incised on it rune-like characters. Near it are two incised triquetras. Around the edge is:
ÆDVPEN MEAG AGEHYODRIHTEN
DRIHTENHINEAPERIEÐEMEHIREÆFTERIE
BVTONHYOMESELLEHIREAGENESPILLES.
D. (max) 16.4cm.

The brooch was found in 1694 in a lead casket with five gold rings, a silver disc or dish and coins of William the Conqueror (1066–87). The brooch type is Anglo-Saxon, but the animal ornament incorporates Ringerike-style elements. The inscription can be translated "æduwen owns me, may the Lord own her. May the Lord curse the man who takes me from her, unless she gives me of her own free will".

L5   Gilt copper-alloy disc brooch
Pitney, Somerset BM [1979, 11-1, 1]

The brooch is decorated in openwork with a coiled animal having a ribbon-like body, interlacing with

a snake. The whole is contained within a scalloped border. D.3.9cm.

Like nos. L2 and L3 the brooch is decorated with an English variant of the Urnes style, but the use of the combined motif – an animal and a snake fighting – places the brooch much closer to the Scandinavian version of the style than is the case with the other examples.

L6   Sub-triangular copper-alloy mount
Lincoln BM [67, 3-20, 20]

There is a circular extension pierced for attachment at the apex, and at the base is a rectangular flange at right angles to the body of the mount, also pierced for attachment. The mount is decorated in openwork with a coiled animal. L.5.7cm.

Like no. L2, this is probably a book mount decorated in the English Urnes style.

L7   Cast copper-alloy openwork mount
Danes Terrace, Lincoln LAT [DT74.1 Ae108]

It is decorated in openwork with two pairs of animals, their bodies seen in profile and their heads from above, biting at each other. These flank an inverted U-shaped animal. L.6.1 × W.3.3cm.

The function of the mount is uncertain, although it has been suggested that it may have been a scabbard mount. It is decorated in an English variant of the Urnes style.

L8   Book mount; copper-alloy
Ixworth, Suffolk
UMAA, Cambridge, Z.14967

The mount is sub-triangular. At the base are two rivet holes, and at the apex is a lobed extension pierced by a rivet hole, and flanked by two out-turned leaves with tightly curled ends. The main field is decorated with a quadruped looking upwards, with the front leg raised. The tail passes between the legs and across the body to end in a tight scroll behind the animal's head. L.5.0cm.

Similar book mounts are known from Fordham (Cambs.); Rochester (Kent); and Wiltshire.

L9   The Norwich capital
Norwich Cathedral, Norfolk. The Dean and Chapter

This double capital, which probably came from the cloister arcades of the cathedral, dates from the twelfth century. It has dragon decoration on all four sides, surviving only in outline on side B. H.20.0cm.

Unique among the Norwich capitals, this piece seems to reflect, in its thin sinuous dragons with their occasional lip lappets and spiral joints, the Urnes phase of Scandinavian art.

L10   Cast of fragment of architectural decoration
Original in St Andrews Church, Jevington, E. Sussex

It shows a scene of Christ crushing the head of the serpent and lion from Psalm 91. The figure is clad in a loin cloth, holding a cross in His right hand, with which He thrusts down a beast. A second, serpentine creature coils to His left. Late eleventh or early twelfth century. W.44.0 × H.91.0cm.

Though the solid proportions of Christ are in the Romanesque tradition, the beasts below clearly reflect that interplay of broad and thin ornament-lines, set in fluent looping curves, which characterises Urnes art.

L2

L3

L5

L6

L8

L11 Danish runestone in memory of Vikings who were buried in England

Valleberga, Skåne (present-day Sweden). Now erected in Lund

The stone is of granite and broken in two pieces. There are runic inscriptions contained in ribbons on both faces. On one side (a) the ribbon forms part of an interlaced cross; on the other (b) the ribbon terminates in four small spirals. The inscriptions read:

a Svein and Thorgöt made this memorial to Manne and Svenne
b God help their souls well. And they lie in London

There are four known runestones from Viking-Age Denmark raised in memory of Vikings who had been in England or 'in the west'. Two are from the Hedeby area and two from Skåne. Long after such memorials went out of fashion in Denmark, they continued to be raised in Sweden where they are more numerous and sometimes mention the Danegeld and famous leaders like Cnut the Great. A stone from Väsby in Uppland has the inscription:

Alle had this stone raised to his own memory. He took Cnut's geld in England. God help his soul

These Swedish runestones, and many English Danegeld coins found in Sweden, demonstrate that the conquest and exploitation of England around the year 1000 and the early eleventh century was not a purely Danish enterprise.

runestone (right), was ...ed to the memory of two ...ings and brings our story ...n apt conclusion:

...d help their souls well. ...d they lie in London.'

We would like to thank the following for their help:
Helen Brown, the Ashmolean Museum, Oxford, on the Arab coin entry
Margrethe Flach de Neergaard, York Archaeological Trust, for her research on
   the catalogue
David Hill, Manchester University, for his as yet unpublished maps
Jenny Mann, Lincoln Archaelogical Trust, for work on the city's Viking objects
Caroline Raison, Winchester Research Unit, for coordinating Winchester research
Peter Snowball and Victor Shreeve, *The Sunday Times*, for their illustrations on
   pages 98 and 106
Penny Walton, York Archaeological Trust, for advice on textiles

Members of the Danish National Museum:
Maj Stief Aistrup, conservation 14th Dept.
Lars Haastrup, architect 10th Dept.
Kirsten Lindhard, assistant 1st Dept.
Lise Lomholt, assistant 10th Dept.
Marianne Lundbæk, conservation 14th Dept.
Gerd Elling Magnus, conservation 14th Dept.

And for additional photography:
R. Bartkowiak 119
Torkild Balslev 125
British Library 160
British Museum 47, 50, 74, 75, 184, 185
Cambridge 63, 75, 77
Danish National Museum 146, 152
Department of the Environment 14
Mike S. Duffy 123

And churches at Gosforth, Cumbria; Jevington, Sussex; and Sockburn, County
Durham, with the Misses Gatheral, for permission to make casts of their Anglo-
Scandinavian sculpture.